WHIPPET

THE COMPLETE

OWNERS GUIDE

Essential facts tips and information about keeping Whippet's including; Feeding, Health, Housing, Training, Canine Psychology, Grooming, Breeding and much more.

Jeff Fielding

D1420289

About the Author;

Jeff Fielding has been involved with animals his whole life. Dogs in particular have been a passion of his. He has been blessed over the years with many four legged friends. He considers it an absolute privilege and labour of love to be involved in this publication.

Acknowledgements

As for work put into the creation of this book I would like to thank my parents and family for their perpetual love and support. And with a special gratitude, my canine friends past and present, who have taught me the true meaning of friendship, devotion and loyalty, to name but a few of their fabulous traits. Their constant love, positivity and enthusiasm for life is truly inspiring.

TABLE OF CONTENTS

Author Note

If you are reading this information as an experienced dog owner, then parts such as the glossary will already be familiar to you. Having said that, the information is intended for everyone and I am sure that even the experienced dog person will find a lot of new facts and information.

It is not my intention to patronize the reader and to tell you how you should read a book. However, unless you are an experienced dog person and are confident enough to skip certain sections, I would highly recommend that you thoroughly read all of the contents before you begin to implement any of the instructions. You may wish to take notes as you go or re-read the book a second time noting important steps to give yourself an action plan.

Also, please note that the use of pronouns like 'his', 'him' or 'her' throughout the text, is simply for ease of reading. It is generally intended to refer to both sexes. It is not meant to indicate a preference by the author of one sex over the other.

CHAPTER ONE

UNDERSTANDING WHIPPET DOGS

The Whippet is seen by many as the ideal house dog. Some would say 'the lazy mans dog', because of their adaptability and low maintenance expectations. In 2013 and 2014, Whippets were the 17th most popular dog breed registered with the Kennel Club UK.

They are generally devoted, love-able, affectionate companions, known for being versatile, dignified, quiet and regal. Their short coat makes them easy to groom and therefore easy to keep clean. Their short coats also mean that they are not ideal to be kept outdoors, as some robust, double coated breeds can happily do.

The Whippet is by no means a delicate breed and despite their thin, fragile looking frames, they are a very hardy, disease resistant dog. This and the following chapters are intended to give you all the information you need to become the best Whippet owner you can be.

1.) What are Whippet Dogs

Again the Whippet is one of the most popular dog breeds today out of the eleven breed clubs in the United Kingdom.

The Whippet, a medium-sized member of the sighthound group, is undeniably like the Greyhound in appearance. Incidentally sighthounds are one of the most ancient families of canines. Sighthound refers to the Whippets visual inclination as opposed to dogs who rely on scent. If they see something that is interesting to chase, they will race after it with reckless abandon.

Whippets along with Greyhounds are among the fastest dog breeds when it comes to running/sprinting. Whippets can run at speeds of over 30 miles (48.3km) per hour. A Whippet race of whatever distance is generally over in seconds. Whippets excel at racing and coursing, yet unlike Greyhound racing there is no gambling involved. Whippet racing is generally considered to be an amateur sport for like minded enthusiasts. We will talk more about Whippet racing in a later chapter.

2.) Whippet Breed History

The word Whippet is used to describe a fast moving little dog. In fact they have always been considered a Greyhound in miniature. When dogs were legally used for coursing, it was considered that Greyhounds were used for catching hares, and Whippets more logically intended to catch rabbits.

Although the Whippet's origin is not certain, similar Greyhound-type dogs that resemble the Whippet have been depicted in art throughout the ages. The tombs of the ancient pharaohs depicted dogs that resemble the Greyhound family. Again, the Greeks adorned pottery and made statues of dogs resembling the Whippet. Even the British Museum hold a piece of Graeco-Roman art known as 'Group of Dogs', which includes dogs strongly resembling the Whippet. It would certainly be the case that in ancient times when hunting was vital for survival, a dog with the power and speed of the Whippet, would be a highly valuable asset. Of course a Whippet, would not be suitable for all types of hunting, but for small fast moving prey such as rabbits, they would be invaluable.

More recently however, it is thought that early development of the Whippet originated by crossing the Manchester Terrier, the Old English White Terrier, (although other terrier types have been used) and the Italian Greyhound. Breeders wanted to breed a dog that had the feistiness and gameness of a terrier, and combine that with the speed, grace and stamina of a Greyhound. The passion for and consequent development of the Whippet was largely credited by the coal miners of Yorkshire, Lancashire and Northumberland, in England. Whippet popularity increased with the British working class in general as a utility dog, and also as a companion dog. They raced in leisure time for sport, and provided rabbits during coursing, for the dinner table. The Whippet breed that we know today is over a hundred years old.

Whippet Clubs

The Whippet as a breed was granted official recognition by the UK Kennel Club in 1891. The Whippet Club, England, was formed in 1899. This was the first Whippet Breed Club in the world. The UK Kennel Club, officially recognized this as a breed club in 1902.

Whippets arrived in The United States, together with British immigrants during the 19th century. Whippets were recognized as a breed by the American Kennel Club (AKC) in 1888. In 1930 The American Whippet Club was founded, and sometime after established a set of breed standards that were consequently approved by the American Kennel Club

3) Facts About Whippet Dogs

Today, Whippets are one of the most popular show breeds competing in the Hound Group. They are versatile and enjoy competing in obedience, flyball, agility and Frisbee. Because of their gentle and sensitive temperament, they also make wonderful therapy dogs. As an intelligent and affectionate breed, most Whippet owners find the breed to be well-behaved, confident indoor companions that are easy to train.

Whippet temperament

As previously mentioned, Whippets are sight hounds, and this group is not for everyone. Sight hounds can be independent, sometimes aloof and arrogant. However, some

Whippets do have a tendency to be quite "clingy". Again because the Whippet is a sight hound with a racy confirmation, and quest for speed, they can, if the mood takes them, take off running and leave you in a panic shouting after them. In this respect, they need to be trained, with basic obedience training, early on to avoid this. Nonetheless, they are different from other sight hounds in that they do readily obey commands, once they realize this is what is required of them. The Whippet may not be the easiest dog to train at first, but rest assured they are very intelligent and quick to learn new commands.

Whippets are known for their playful nature, yet are not as relentlessly playful as some of the other dog breeds. This breed does get bored easily chasing a ball, and probably won't want to bring it back after the first try. They enjoy playing 'tag' and 'catch me if you can' games. For obvious reasons, they never lose at these games. Whippets have been known to be Frisbee fanatics, but you'll need to train your Whippet first to have him develop an interest in catching disks.

Whippets do not bark easily at other people or dogs, so are not the best guard dogs in the world. They will rarely bark without reason. Some won't bark even if there is a reason to do so. However, most will give a warning bark if there's a visitor or new dog around. I have known Whippets that can be quite territorial and hostile to strangers. But generally, Whippets will greet a visitor with a tail wag, or perhaps a look of annoyance if you have just woken them up.

Whippets do require regular exercise, at least three times per day is ideal, and preferably off leash runs. But please remember that off leash runs should only take place where it is safe, preferably in an enclosed field away from roads. Most Whippet owners will confirm that they cannot be trusted 100% off leash. If they spot and give chase to a rabbit, there will be very little you can do to stop them, except hope they do not give chase across a road. Again I repeat, please be mindful of where you allow your Whippet off leash runs. Most Whippet dog owners find that the best way to exercise a Whippet is to provide access and exercise in a large fenced yard or paddock that is secure.

They don't enjoy getting wet from the rain, and prefer to stay indoors in wet weather. As previously noted, Whippets do not tolerate extremely cold weather, and need to be kept indoors if it is very cold. You certainly should not consider keeping a Whippet outdoors in a Kennel. Double coated breeds can cope being outside in a Kennel, but certainly not a Whippet.

Breed Standard Overview

The Whippet Standard states what a Whippet should look like. Unless a potential owner understands what the breed standards are for a particular breed, there is no basis for judgment of one's own dogs or other people's dogs.

The 1945 Whippet standard opened with the following passage

"The Whippet should convey an impression of beautifully balanced muscular power and strength, combined with great elegance & grace of outline. Symmetry of outline, muscular development & powerful gait are the main considerations; the dog being built for speed & work, all forms of exaggeration should be avoided. The dog should possess great freedom of action; the forelegs should be thrown forward & low over the ground like a thoroughbred horse, not in a Hackney-like action. Hind legs should come well under the body giving great propelling power, general movement not to look stilted, high stepping or in a short mincing manner."

"This important description remained in our Standard until the most recent revision when, to fit into a format, it was considerably condensed. The USA Standard wisely retained it and it is quoted here because it is such a vivid description of what is wanted, that it can hardly be bettered."

South West Whippet Club

For more information, visit: *www.southwestwhippetclub.co.uk*

"The Kennel Club Standard for all pedigree breeds, by which a breed is judged in the United Kingdom, is written by the Breed Council in consultation with the Breed Clubs. It is put to the Kennel Club, and after being approved, is published and remains the guide by which a breed must be judged under the Kennel Club rules. This holds until it is amended."

www.kennelclub.org.uk

We will go into more detail about the breed standards in the chapter on showing. Please note however that although the breed standards are particularly important for show purposes, in certain aspects Whippet racing strictly adheres to breed standards also.

Summary of Whippet Facts

Whippet Facts!

» **Breed Size:** Small/ Medium

» **Height:** Bitch 17 to 21 inch (43 to 53cm). Dog 18.5 to 22 inch (47 to 56cm)

» **Weight:** 27.5 to 30 pound (12.5 to 13.5kg)

» **Coat** : Short, smooth, fine and dense

» **Activity level:** Moderate and certainly not as high as some despite an athletic breed capable of fast speeds. Excel at racing, agility, flyball etc.

» **AKC/UK.KC Group:** Hound (sighthound)

» **Colour:** Large variety; solid colours black, white, blue etc., brindle, shades of brown, colored patches etc.

» **Eyes and Nose:** Nose black or colour tone matching coat colour. Bright, lively oval eyes

» **Appearance:** Muscular and powerful, moves with grace and elegance. Tapered Muzzle, head long and lean. Fine rose shaped ears. Neck is long and well muscled. Body is fairly long, deep chest, arched, muscular, powerful loins. Long, fine but strong legs. Long, tapered tail

» **Grooming:** Relatively low shedding. At least brush once a week, some recommend every day. Usually have a main shed twice per year, usually spring and winter, although some dogs hardly shed throughout the year.

» **Lifespan**: Average 12 to 15 years

» **Health:** Relatively healthy breed with very few hereditary diseases, but a number of predispositions have been noted over the years. However, cases noted are generally of a low frequency.

» **Temperament:** Make excellent pets. Highly adaptable; happy as a sporting/race dog as well as trotting at heal or lounging at home. Love home comforts. . Well mannered, neat, clean and tidy. Gentle and affectionate companion/family dog. Easy to care for (often referred to as 'the lazy mans dog'). Not a fussy eater. Get along well with other dogs. Should be supervised initially when introduced to other pets as they do have a prey instinct. Usually get along with cats and other small animals

» **Training:** Not the easiest dogs to train at first, but they are intelligent and relatively quick to pick up new commands. They are sensitive, so positive, gentle training methods should be used.

» **Exercise Needs:** Average daily walk. Long periods of exercise unnecessary but must be every day, preferably 1 hour with some off lead. Cannot be trusted 100% off leash so must be in a safe enclosed area, away from busy roads. Protective coat recommended for outdoor walks in cold weather.

» **Breed History:** Original origin uncertain, but descendants thought to originate as far back as ancient Greece and Egypt. Most recently became popular in the 19th century as both a hunting/coursing dog for vermin and small game. Also became popular particularly in Northern English mining communities as a sport/racing dog

CHAPTER TWO

WHAT TO KNOW BEFORE YOU BUY

Buying or adopting a Whippet puppy on a whim may only cause heartbreak later, if you are not fully aware of all the implications. This chapter will detail many of the important aspects that you should consider before committing to becoming a Whippet guardian.

The most important thing to be aware of is that you are prepared to give the time necessary to care for a puppy. But a lot of prospective dog owners do not take into consideration the cost implications. It therefore makes good sense to put real thought into what it takes to bring up a puppy and factors such as regular walks, health implications and costs, initial and on-going costs etc.

Choosing any breed, whether a Whippet or Labrador should always be taken on a long term basis. Whippets can live for up to 15 years. Some Whippets with the right care, live even longer. Before embarking on your selection, take a moment to think about and make sure that a Whippet is the dog for you.

PLEASE NOTE: We will go into more detail in the next chapter about what to look for when buying a Whippet. If you do have your heart set on the Whippet as a breed, then your only criteria for buying is likely to be that the puppy is healthy and of a good pedigree. However, if you are intending to either show, race or even breed for either, your criteria will need to be different. As you know, puppies in general leave their litter at 8 weeks of age, at least. However, a dog intended for show purposes will carry no guarantees, despite an excellent pedigree, of future show potential. Similarly a dog intended as a potential race winner will not carry any guarantees at 8 weeks of age. It is for this reason therefore that many experts will advise you to wait until a puppy has reached five or six months of age. By that point that dog will

have developed to almost adulthood and will be showing obvious signs of an ideal physicality for show, or superior speed for racing. Although I am sure this is possible, you will probably find these options are few and far between. These types of high quality pedigree puppies are usually quickly snapped up. A lot of the time you have to go on a waiting list. But these options do occur and it is therefore worth inquiring just in case. I personally feel that you would be very unlucky if you buy a puppy from proven champion parents, that the puppy would not have similar potential.

1.) Do You Need a License

Becoming a pet owner is a big responsibility. When you bring your dog home, he immediately becomes your responsibility. You must therefore do your part to take care of him as best you can. Not only do you need to feed and walk your Whippet, but you also need to take care of some practical responsibilities including licensing your new pet. Before you buy a Whippet you should take the time to learn whether a license is required in your area. If so, to take the proper steps to obtain one. In this section you will learn about licensing requirements for Whippets in the United States and in the United Kingdom.

a.) Licensing Whippets in the U.S.

There are no federal requirements regarding the licensure of dogs in the United States. Rather, these requirements are made at the state level. Before you buy a Whippet puppy or an adult Whippet you need to apprise yourself of local dog licensing requirements. Most states require dog owners to license their dogs and, in order to obtain a license, your dog must also be up-to-date on rabies vaccinations. Obtaining a license for your dog is not difficult. Try asking your veterinarian for information or contact your local council instead.

Even if your state does not mandate that you license your Whippet dog, it is still a good idea to do it anyway. When you license your dog you will need to provide contact information for yourself. If your dog gets lost and is still carrying his license, whoever finds him will be able to use that information to contact you. Obtaining a dog license requires you to fill out a simple form and to pay a fee around $25 (£16.25). You must renew your license each year, although you may have the option to purchase a five-year license or a lifetime license in some states.

b.) Licensing Whippets in the U.K.

Licensing requirements for dogs in the U.K. are a little different than they are in the U.S. Dog licensing in the UK was abolished in 1987. However, licensing is still mandatory in Northern Ireland, and you can find further details from the website link at the end of the paragraph. Northern Ireland mandates that all dogs carry a license, and the only exception is for assistance dogs and police

dogs. Whippet puppies may be able to get away without a license until they are 6 months old as long as the owner of the puppies is the owner of the mother as well. Dog licenses are renewable annually, just like U.S. licenses. For further information regarding licenses please consult the following link:

http://www.nidirect.gov.uk/dog-licensing-and microchipping

2.) How Many Whippets Should You Keep

Do you get one or two Whippet puppies or dogs if you decide to opt for the rescue route. In a lot of cases this is not necessarily breed specific and can often be down to the personality of the dog. Some dogs are quite solitary whereas some require constant companionship. Please therefore consider the following section.

Whippets are very affectionate, friendly, gentle, sensitive, easily likeable, but also capable of great focus and intensity during a chase. Every Whippet is different in temperament, with some being whimsical and winsome. Although the Whippet is considered to be a very adaptable breed they do need attention, affection and mental stimulation. This breed is not one that can be left alone at home for long periods of time, as they can become depressed or destructive. However, the time and attention you do give will be rewarded many times over! This loving and intelligent breed will quickly endear himself to you.

People are often tempted to bring home more than one 'small' puppy from a litter. It is certainly true that dogs are social creatures and choose to be around each other. You only need to see the way that the dog seeks others out whilst on walks to see this. In the wild, dogs live in family groups, feral dogs choose the individuals that they want to spend time and mate with. A completely natural wolf pack is a family group consisting of parents and their young. A pair of dogs play, interact and bond. A pair of dogs is easier on the conscience because you are not leaving a dog completely alone whilst you are at work or socializing. They have the company of one another, which is a much better option for the dog. Some shelters are looking to re-home dogs in established pairs. These particular dogs are usually friends and highly bonded with each other. Only one of the pair may be a Whippet dog whilst some may be two of the same breed. This takes some pressure away from you as the dog owner to meet all of the needs of your dog.

This said, a pair can be difficult to handle if they form a pack like mentality and become reactive on walks and in the home. All dogs have individual personalities so the way that a pair of dogs react will really depend on the nature of each dog. Although Whippets are generally amiable, friendly dogs, again two dogs can develop the pack mentality and become a hustle of growling and barking excitement on walks. If you are looking at puppies though, taking two from the litter is not usually a good idea if you yourself want to be an integral part of your dog's emotional life.

Puppies that are taken from the same litter will be very bonded with each other and as they reach adolescence one of two things can happen. Firstly they may only focus on each other making them difficult to train and control. Secondly they may begin to compete, causing friction between them. That said, the pair could just as easily settle down and be happy together but it is important that you are aware of the risks. If you want two Whippet dogs because of all of the positive points of a bonded pair, then you can either look for a pair in rescue or bring one dog home, spend a few months getting to know the dog, socializing him or her perfectly, then look for another dog to join your family. This is an approach that will work well with dogs of all ages. You may find that one Whippet dog and a dog of a different breed get on really well together instead of a pair of Whippets. The Whippet has a friendly personality and an even temperament but they require a reasonable amount of attention and exercise. Raising one Whippet puppy can take a lot of time an energy so you should think carefully before bringing home two of them. The Whippet is a very social breed but he tends to prefer the company of people to that of other dogs. Your Whippet will form a very strong bond with you and he will want to follow you around the house, getting as much attention as you are willing to give. If you work a full-time job and are not home a lot during the day, the Whippet might not be the right breed for you. Having a second dog to keep your Whippet company might help but it will not be a substitute for the level of human interaction this breed craves.

3.) Do Whippets Get Along with Other Pets and children

If raised from puppies, with smaller pets such as cats and rabbits, they tend to bond and become good friends. Keep in mind though that if you bring an adult Whippet to your home, you'll need to keep pets such as rabbits, guinea pigs and cats far away initially. They may well chase, attack and kill anything unusual to them. Hopefully your Whippet will soon get used to other pets as a part of the family. But certainly in the early stages, they should never be left unsupervised with other animals.

They are great with children, and kind with one another, other pets (please refer to the above) and large animals. Nonetheless, this could lead them to becoming vulnerable to attacks from other dogs or being mishandled by young children. They are generally known to growl or snap, very rarely and only if relentlessly provoked. It is therefore important that you socialize your Whippet puppy with children as soon as he comes into your home. Children should be taught to respect and care for the puppy and told to never tease or hurt them. They are not a toy and should never be treated as such. In these early stages, please do supervise children handling and playing with the new puppy. Everything will be strange to the puppy including excitable, energetic children, but they will soon get used to each other and accept each other as part of the family.

4) A Boy or a Girl

A lot of prospective dog owners choose a female as they wish to breed from them at some point. However, if this is something you are considering, please don't be tempted to breed with her on a continuous basis. It is always good to have one litter to keep the generation of your beloved pet going. However the only potential draw back with never breeding from her is the potential for developing pyometra later in life. This is a uterine infection, that requires the removal of the female reproductive system.

As far as temperament, although this is stating the obvious, female Whippets can be quite dainty and feminine. What I mean by this is some bitches have a tendency to be aloof and reluctant to participate in games of fetch or ball and stick chasing. The male on the other hand are generally more boisterous outgoing and less aloof. They are also generally considered to be more inclined to come back to you when called. This obedience trait is sometimes lost on the female. There are also misconceptions that the male will be typically male, outgoing, boisterous or aggressive and the female quiet and dainty. But in many cases a dog can be really well behaved and hardly ever bark and the female is as above outgoing, boisterous or aggressive. The point is, it sometimes comes down to personality. Two dogs of the same breed and the same litter can have completely different personalities. But sometimes, dog owners who have always had dogs for years simply prefer either a dog or a bitch.

5.) Ease and Cost of Care

In addition to thinking about whether your Whippet will get along with other dogs or pets etc., you also need to think about the costs associated with keeping a Whippet. Not only do you need to provide your Whippet with shelter and exercise, but necessary costs also include food, veterinary care, grooming, accessories etc. Before you decide to buy a Whippet dog you should seriously consider the costs associated with keeping a dog, and make sure that you can cover them. In this section you will find a list of initial costs and monthly costs associated with Whippet ownership.

a.) Initial Costs

PLEASE NOTE: The following is offered as a guideline only, as costs can vary depending on where you are located, where you buy from, the time you are looking etc.

The initial costs for owning Whippets include those costs you must cover to purchase your dog and to prepare your home for his/her arrival which include purchase price, a crate or kennel, spay/neuter surgery, vaccinations, micro-chipping, and other accessories.

On the opposite page is a summary table of each expense.

With the following you will find an overview of each expense as well as an estimate:

Purchase Price – Whippet puppies from good litters can be purchased for around £400 ($675) to £1,000 ($1,450) and possibly several thousand for a Show Whippet. Prices will vary from breeder to breeder and location to location. Whippet adoptions for an adult dog, from rescue centres etc., are much lower, and if your budget is an issue, it is definitely worth considering.

A more popular and recognized Whippet breeder will have more expensive puppies, especially if high-quality, and good representatives of the sire and dam are used. You are also likely to find that this type of breeder will not advertise and therefore only come via word of mouth or through organizations such as AKC or KC UK.

Where ever you purchase, always try and ensure that your Whip-

Initial Costs for Whippet Dogs *

Cost	One Dog	Two Dogs
Purchase Price	$675 to $1,450 (£400 to £1,000	$1,350 to $2,900 (£800 to £2,000)
Crate or Kennel	$35 (£22.75)	$70 (£45.50)
Spay/Neuter	$50 to $200 (£32.50 to £130)	$100 to $400 (£65 to £260)
Vaccinations	$50 (£32.50)	$100 (£65)
Micro-chipping	$15 to $50 (£9.75 to £32.50)	$30 to $100 (£19.50 to £65)
Accessories	$100 (£65)	$200 (£130)
Total	$925 to $1,885 (£600 to £1,225)	$1,850 to $3,770 (£1,200 to £2,450)

*These rates are based on a conversion rate of $1 U.S. to £0.65 U.K. Rates are subject to change.

pet has a written health guarantee against hereditary and congenital defects.

Crate or Kennel – Having a crate or kennel for your Whippet puppy is very important. Not only will it be instrumental in house-training, but it will give your puppy a place of his own in the house where he can retreat if he wants a nap or just needs a break from people. You will need to upgrade your puppy's crate as he grows, but to start with, a small crate should only cost you about $35 (£22.75) or so.

Spay/Neuter Surgery – Having your Whippet puppy spayed or neutered is incredibly important, especially if you do not plan to breed your dog. There are a number of opinions as to when is the best time to spay a female dog. Some vets recommend that you spay or neuter your puppy around 6 months of age to reduce the risk for certain types of cancer. The ASPCA points out that the traditional age to spay is 6 to 9 months. The Blue Cross further asserts that there is no benefit in delaying spay surgery until after their first season. They also suggest that certain health benefits are reduced if you wait until after the first season. Others will assert that the dog should be fully mature and developed, consequently carrying out spay surgery in between the first and second season. Always discuss this with your veterinary surgeon. Spay/neuter surgery can be very expensive if you go to a regular veterinarian. But there are plenty of low-cost clinics out there that offer affordable spay/neuter surgery options. If you go to a clinic or shelter, neuter surgery will very likely only cost you $50 to $100 (£32.50 to £65) and spay surgery with a private vet will generally cost $100 to $200 (£65 to £130).

Vaccinations – Before your Whippet puppy turns one year old, he/she will need to get certain vaccinations. If you buy your puppy from a reputable breeder the pup may already have a few of these vaccinations taken care of by the time you take him home. Speak to your veterinarian about a vaccination schedule for your puppy and plan to spend up to $50 (£32.50) for your puppy's initial vaccinations.

Micro-chipping – Not only may you need to have your puppy licensed, but you should also consider micro-chipping as well. A dog license is worn on a collar around your dog's neck but a microchip is implanted underneath the skin so that it cannot be lost. The procedure does not hurt your dog and it only takes a few minutes to complete. You should be able to have it done at your local animal shelter for as little as $15 (£9.75) at a shelter or up to $50 (£32.50) for a veterinarian to do it.

Other Accessories – In addition to your dog's crate, you will also need certain accessories. These accessories will include a food dish, water dish, collar, leash, grooming tools, and toys. What you spend on each of these items is up to you and the cost will vary depending on quality. You should expect to pay about $100 (£65) for these accessories, though you could easily spend $200 (£130) or more if you purchased high-quality or designer items.

b.) Monthly Costs

The monthly costs for owning a Whippet include those recurring costs you must cover on a monthly on-going basis. Monthly costs include the food and treats, veterinary care, grooming, license renewal, and other costs.

Opposite you will find a summary table of each monthly expense.

The following is a detailed overview of each expense and an estimate:

Food and Treats –Costs may vary depending on what kind of food you buy; but it is not recommended that you shop by price. The quality of the food you give your dog has a direct impact on his health and wellbeing, so do not skimp. Because the Whippet is a medium-energy breed you may want to consider an active breed formula, especially if you train your dog for dog sports. You should plan to spend about $30 (£19.50) on a large bag of dog food that will last you about one month. In addition to food, you should budget an extra $10 (£6.50) per month for treats, especially when you are training your dog.

Monthly Costs for Whippet Dogs

Cost	One Dog	Two Dogs
Food and Treats	$40 (£26)	$80 (£52)
Veterinary Care	$7 (£4.55)	$14 (£9.10)
Grooming	$8.30 (£5.40)	$16.60 (£10.80)
License Renewal	$2 (£1.30)	$4 (£2.60)
Other Costs	$15 (£9.75)	$30 (£19.50)
Total	$72 (£47)	$144 (£94)

*These rates are based on a conversion rate of $1 U.S. to £0.65 U.K. Rates are subject to change.

Veterinary Care – In order to keep your Whippet in good health, you should plan to visit the veterinarian about every 6 months. Your Whippet puppy may need more frequent visits during the first year for vaccinations, but after that, two visits per year will be adequate. You should expect to spend about $40 (£26) per visit which, with two visits per year, averages to about $7 (£4.55) per month.

Grooming – In all fairness, Whippets are so easy to groom and keep clean that a lot of owners will brush their dogs once per week and perhaps bath them every 2 or 3 months. Grooming costs are mentioned here as some people like the occasional professional groom for their dogs.

Because the Whippet has a very short coat you will not need to take him to the groomer's very often. You will be able to do most of the brushing and bathing yourself at home but you still might want to take your Whippet to the groomer every 4 to 6 months to ensure that his coat and skin remains in good health. You should expect to spend about $ 50 (£ 32.50) per visit so, with two visits per year, the average monthly cost for grooming evens out to about $ 8.30 (£ 5.40) per month.

License Renewal – (Again, this does not apply to every country or even U.S. state)Licensed renewal is not a major expense. You only need to have your dog's license renewed once a year and it generally costs about $25 (£16.25) which averages to just $2 (£1.30) per month.

Other Costs – In addition to veterinary care and grooming costs, there are other costs which you may need to cover once in a while. These costs may include new toys, replacement collars as your Whippet grows, new grooming tools, cleaning products, and more. To be safe, you should budget about $15 (£9.75) per month for these additional costs.

IMPORTANT: Part of being a responsible dog owner is meeting the needs of your dog. If you cannot comfortably cover the initial costs and monthly costs described in this section you should not purchase a Whippet dog.

6.) Pros and Cons for Whippet Dogs

Pros for Whippet Dogs

Pros!

» Usually well mannered, quiet and elegant disposition.

» Clean house pets and minimum hair shedding

» Easy to train

» Very adaptable to a variety of circumstances.

» Female Whippets make excellent brood mothers

» Friendly and reliable; good with children, and other pets when socialized.

» Although they look fragile and delicate, they are remarkably strong and agile. Fractures are rare.

» Considered by the Kennel Club as 'an ideal companion'

Cons for Whippet Dogs

Cons!

» Can be highly strung and flighty

» Some can be clingy and have problems associated with separation anxiety

» As they are sighthounds, they are not predictable off lead and will chase small mammals which can be hazardous near busy roads

CHAPTER THREE

PURCHASING WHIPPET DOGS

By now you should have more or less decided whether looking after a Whippet is something you still feel you can commit to. If it is, you are ready to move on to learning about buying a Whippet. In this chapter you will find tips for finding Whippets for sale, information about choosing a Whippet breeder, and suggestions for picking out a healthy Whippet puppy.

THE most important thing to consider when buying any dog not just a Whippet, is the health of the puppy. The following will give you a lot to think about in terms of choosing a reputable, preferably highly recommended breeder, and consequent health testing etc. The other thing that is important when choosing a Whippet as opposed to other dog breeds is the racing aspect. Many owners are happy with an ordinary happy healthy dog, which is great. But some have the desire for a high pedigree show dog, which can be true of all breeds. The important exception to this is if you have the desire to race your dog. We will go into much more detail later regarding this unique aspect of owning a Whippet. But for now, please do think about whether you have aspirations for a champion race dog. Some are more than happy to pursue the sport as a hobby at club level for yours and your dogs pleasure. But please at this stage be aware that in the same respect that a pedigree show dog is the result of years of genetics, the same is true of champion race dogs. It is also interesting to note that the two characteristics do not always go hand in hand. A champion race dog from historical champion blood lines will not necessarily be a show dog champion and vice versa. It also follows that there is no guarantee that the pup of a champion will also be a champion. But the potential is there. In this respect, many prospective owners, particularly where race dogs are concerned prefer to wait until the puppy is several months old and is showing obvious potential Again,

much more will be talked about later, but at this stage it is worth bearing these considerations in mind early on.

Also be aware that in the same respect that AKC and KC (UK)breed standards need to be adhered to for show dogs, there are also certain restrictions for race dogs. For potential show dogs you can safely assume that the puppies will have similar conformations, shape, height etc. to the parents. But please bear in mind that historically, certain race organizations have also placed certain restrictions to race dogs such as height limits etc. According to the WCRA this has limited bitches having to be under a 20 inches (50 cm) limit and dogs under 21 inches (53 cm). When you visit the WCRA site and others, you will see that there are many acceptable weight categories, but height has to be adhered to. The good news is that most dogs will be around that height anyway. Very few are greater than 22 inches.

So if you are choosing from a litter of puppies where the parents are suitable heights, it may be wise to not choose the largest pup which may grow taller than the parents.

Another problem affecting racing is the restrictions placed on bitches when they come into season. It has in the past been considered unhealthy for a bitch to race shortly after she has come into season. When this happens it is recommended to restrict racing for at least 12 weeks after she comes into season. I would personally recommend 12 weeks after she finishes her season. So the point here is, perhaps choosing a bitch puppy would not be ideal for you if racing is very important.

So again, if you do intend to race Whippets in any capacity, please read the various race club websites for specific information, in particular the WCRA and its various affiliated clubs.

Also please be reassured that even the most enlightened experienced Whippet people will offer the following advice. There is a good possibility, not probability, that buying a pup from proven champions is likely to produce champions also. At the very least a high class pedigree blood line will probably produce an excellent Whippet type. But if you are looking for a guarantee, even the experts with all their knowledge and experience admit to sometimes getting this choice wrong.

PLEASE NOTE: The following offers as much information as I am aware about pitfalls and potential problems you may encounter with certain breeders. However, I need to add at this point that a Kennel Club certificate does not necessarily guarantee that the dog you have bought is the same as the pedigree suggests. As unbelievable as this may sound, some unscrupulous breeders have been exposed and prosecuted for selling puppies with false KC registered papers. In some cases the puppies have not even been the breed they were supposed to be and at worse, had major health problems or potential physical defects.

Unfortunately in this day and age of scammers and fraudsters, some un-reputable breeders have been known to pass on puppies with falsified papers. You can also do all the checks you like on a breeder that is registered with the KC and has council approval, but your research and investigations should not stop there. The Kennel Club does have their 'assured breeder scheme', which was set up to protect dog purchases. Effectively they list breeders who have been checked and verified by the Kennel Club. You can search this at the link at the end of the paragraph. When you click on a breed, it gives you the following message, that if there is a green tick beside the breeder that 'This Symbol indicates that a breeder has had a successful inspection carried out to standards assessed by the United Kingdom Accreditation Service (UKAS). These standards were formally introduced in January 2013 and only Kennel Club Assured Breeders that have completed a successful visit since that date are issued with a UKAS Certificate'

http://www.thekennelclub.org. uk/services/public/acbr/Default.aspx

In addition, you may also find the following link useful:

http://pedigreedogsexposed. blogspot.co.uk/2013/12/the-discredited-breeder-scheme-kennel.html

If you haven't already also please visit the Whippet Breed Club website thewhippetclub.com, for their advice before purchasing: *http://www.thewhippetclub.com/the-whippet-breed/whippet-puppies/*

A breed club secretary from the National Kennel Club will similarly be able to advise.

http://nationalkennelclub.com/contact_us.htm

EMAIL: contactus@nationalkennelclub.com

Please do research as much as you can. It is a good idea to visit many Whippet kennels, and to speak to as many breeders as possible

1) Ethical Whippet Breeders

Choosing which breeder to deal with, is just as important as deciding which breed to get. Buying from poor sources such as puppy mills and backyard breeders is a bad choice, and contributes to the continuing overpopulation of pets, and even to large numbers of dogs surrendered at shelters today.

A well-respected Whippet breeder will usually be able to give you a list of references. This list should contain the names of people that have bought puppies from that breeder over the past few years. The Whippet breeder should also have his veterinarian available to answer any questions you may have about the health history of the puppies, and the breeder's adult dogs. If your Whippet breeder is reluctant to give you any information related to veterinary care or previous buyers, this should raise a red flag, and you are probably best to look elsewhere!

Ask whether or not a written health guarantee will be made available. In many instances, the Whippet breeder that provides all this information is a good breeder.

PLEASE NOTE: I am bound to be repeating myself here, but if at all

possible, purchase a puppy whereby the parents have been health tested.

You will find the following website useful:

http://whippet-health.co.uk/#/health-testing/4531648512

A good U.S equivalent is as follows: http://www.whippethealth.org/

The only exception I would ever make to only purchasing a puppy from health tested parents is adopting a rescue dog. I have rescued a number of dogs that I had no idea about their historical pedigree or health test history. These dogs were exceptionally healthy and only ever had minor ailments. Perhaps I was lucky, but in a lot of cases these rescue dogs are desperate for loving forever homes. I would certainly take a rescue dog any day, regardless of possible health issues. However, the choice ultimately has to be yours.

A useful site which lists breeders in the UK who health test parent dogs is as follows:

http://www.champdogs.co.uk/breeds/whippet/breeders

You should find breeders that health test the parent dogs, highlighted in red.

Health tests are not a Kennel Club requirement for the Whippet, or any other breed. However, many breeders do believe in using the tests available because they have a strong ethical belief in the care and welfare of the breed. If at all possible, deal with these breeders only. If a breeder does not routinely supply a puppy that has been health checked, they may suggest that you can have this done by your own veterinarian.

There are a few other things to consider when buying a Whippet puppy and if you carry out careful research right at the start then you can be sure that you bring home the right dog for you.

There are many good reasons for choosing a puppy carefully, most of which people are generally unaware. It's easy for us to be trusting of breeders and those that sell puppies but in actual fact dog breeders need to be chosen extra carefully for the following reasons;

> » Puppy genetic background.
>
> » Puppy health.
>
> » Puppy social skills.
>
> » Welfare of the puppy parents.

Irresponsible breeding is the main reason for unwanted and sick dogs in the Western world today. When genetic testing is not carried out; the temperament of the parent dogs is not considered. If the puppy is not socialized from as early as birth then as the pup matures to adulthood, the dog may well have problems. If you buy a puppy from an irresponsible breeder, the dog is at risk of health or behavioural problems, or maybe even both, at any time in his life.

The only dog breeder to consider is the one that has a conscience.

This is the type that loves the breed and only breeds one or two litters. They will also carry out all of the testing required before making a decision to breed a litter. This type of breeder knows about puppy socialization. They also know about genetic health, and dog welfare is at the forefront of their minds.

The good dog breeder has a list of people wanting the puppies before they even allow the parent dogs to mate. They are extremely interested in finding the correct puppy home, and are not afraid to turn people away. The good breeder does not have to use classified sites, Facebook or newspapers to advertise their puppies. They are not cagey about the parent dogs and they will always, without fail, allow you to see the puppies with their Mother in the home environment.

You may even feel interviewed, on your initial phone call, by a dog breeder if you are looking for a puppy. If this happens then you can be pretty much certain that you are enquiring about much loved and well-bred Whippet puppies. In addition to asking you a lot of questions the good dog breeder will state that they must always be given the option to take the dog back, at any point during its life, if you can no longer care for it. There may even be a contract.

The puppies will be wormed, health checked, vaccinated and at least eight weeks old before they leave their Mother.

2) Beware of the Puppy Farmer!

The opposite side to the ethical breeder is the 'puppy farmer'. Not everyone with Whippet puppies for sale is a good and ethical dog breeder. In actual fact some care very little about the dogs in their charge.

This is a trap that most people fall into when looking for a puppy. It's actually hard to believe that people would farm dogs in this way, but it happens and if you are looking for a puppy, you can be sure that at least some of your options are puppy farmed dogs.

The pet store puppy is usually from a puppy mill as are those sold in big sized litters through classifieds. This is not to say that buying puppies from classified ads is a bad thing. Some excellent puppies are available this way, and often this is the most convenient way a reputable 'hobby' breeder can find potential puppy parents. Although all puppies look the same, usually healthy, clean, fluffy and with that addictive puppy scent, the farmed puppy is very different indeed.

Soon we will talk in detail about puppy development and how vital it is towards a puppy's overall mental health. This knowledge is equally important to the act of sourcing a puppy. For now, in case you are tempted by the pet store Whippet puppy it is vital that you know how he got to be 'That Doggy in the Window'.

The puppy mill is a harrowing place. It is much the same as a factory farm for pigs, cows and chickens. Dogs are kept in small pens and bred from, each time the dog comes into season. The Mother dog is stressed throughout her life and often puppy farmed dogs never go for a walk. They rarely, if at all, receive veterinary attention.

The dogs are kept in small pens and rarely cleaned up after. They are also rarely handled and are fed on cheap food. As you can probably imagine, bacteria thrives in this type of environment and stress levels are high. With the ever increasing link between low quality commercial food and illness, a puppy born and whelped in this type of environment will have a very poor start in life.

Studies are increasingly showing that the presence of stress in a pregnant mother dog can lead to flighty and fearful puppies with the behaviour only showing up in the dog's adolescent and adult life. So how do you recognize a puppy farmer or a puppy that has been bred for money alone?

The signs of a puppy farmer are quite easy to spot when you know what to look for. The important thing to remember with this type of dog breeder is that the most important thing to them is money, and the way that they act will betray this.

Warning signs when deciding on a dog breeder are as follows:

Beware!

» The breeder will have a lot of dogs available and often of different breeds.

» The puppy may be quite cheap.

» There will be no proof of worming, vaccination or veterinary checks.

» Meeting the mother of the puppy will not be possible.

» The breeder will not allow you to see the puppy in the whelping environment.

» The puppy will be younger than eight weeks old when it is sold.

» The breeder will ask very few questions about the home you are offering.

» The breeder will offer to deliver or meet you somewhere with the puppy.

It may be tempting to buy a puppy from this type of breeder anyway and see it as a sort of rescue attempt. This is highly inadvisable because the puppy farmer only exists as a result of people buying their puppies. Therefore to buy a dog in this way is funding the cruel practice of puppy farming. In addition to this, any dog that comes from this type of environment is at high risk of stress based behaviour problems developing later. The risk of genetic and environmental health problems caused by bad care of the parent dogs and their offspring from pregnancy onwards, is greatly increased when buying any puppy from a puppy farmer.

3.) Where to Buy Whippet Dogs

If you have decided that the Whippet is the right breed for you, your next step is to find a Whippet for sale. Finding a Whippet puppy may not be as simple as just stopping in to your local pet store. Even if it were that easy, buying a puppy from a pet store may not be your best option. In this section you will find tips for buying a Whippet in the U.S. and in the U.K. You will also find information about Whippet rescue dogs.

Apologies if you are based elsewhere. But please be aware that you simply need to make contact with similar organizations listed here for your location. Additionally, Google searched for [Health Tested Whippets for sale, [your area/country]], will doubtless provide appropriate results.

a.) Buying in the U.S.

When it comes to buying puppies in the United States you have two main options; a pet store or an independent breeder. As mentioned previously, unfortunately, many pet stores receive their stock from puppy mills. Again, a puppy mill is a breeding facility where dogs are kept in squalid conditions and forced to breed until they are no longer able; they are then disposed of. The puppies that come from puppy mills may be inbred or bred from unhealthy stock which means that they too are likely to be unhealthy. Buying from a pet store is generally not a good option unless you know exactly where the puppy came from and you can confirm that it is from a reputable breeder.

When you buy a puppy from a reputable breeder you are assured that the breeding stock is in good health. Most reputable breeders put their breeding stock through genetic testing before breeding to ensure that they are not going to pass on congenital conditions such as hip dysplasia or progressive retinal atrophy. Responsible breeders also know a lot about the breed and can help you to decide whether it is a good choice for you.

In the next section you will find more detailed information about choosing a reputable breeder. For now, however, you will find a list of U.S. Whippet breeders next, which may have Whippet puppies for sale:

The following are breeders which at the time of press, where actively health testing the parent dogs.

PLEASE NOTE: The following, to the best of my knowledge are all good, reputable breeders. However, I am in no way connected/affiliated to them, nor am I endorsing/recommending anyone in particular. I urge you as always to do a thorough research of all possibilities, consider all options and make your own mind up.

Meisterhaus Basenjis and Whippets, Louisville, Kentucky

http://www.meisterhaus.com/index.htm

Cherche' Whippets Atlanta, GA.

http://www.cherchewhippets.com/

Summerwind Kennel; Sparta, Tennessee

http://www.thewhippet.net/whippet-dog-breeders-in-usa.html

Nautilus Whippets; Florida

http://www.nautiluswhippets. com/about-whippets/whippet-health/ genetic-conditions-in-whippets#. VqyVGfmLTIU

Aperture Whippets; Knoxville, TN

http://www.aperturewhippets. com/

Surrey Hill Whippets; Pennsylvania

http://surreyhillwhippets.com/ litter-news/

Cali Whippets; North Carolina

http://www.caliwhippets.com/ about-us

The American Kennel Club has a useful link to breeders and available Whippet puppies as follows:
http://marketplace.akc.org/se arch?for=dog&breed=254&locat ion=&filters%5Bgender%5D=&_ t=1454152675970

Also please take a look at the following:
https://www.apps.akc.org/apps/ classified/search/landing_breed.cfm

You can also find Whippet breeders using the Breeders Club directory:
http://breedersclub.net/html/ breeds/Whippet.htm

b.) Buying in the U.K.

Purchasing Whippet puppies in the U.K. is very similar to buying them in the U.S. Always do your research before buying Whippet puppies in the U.K. to ensure that the Whippet puppies for sale have been bred properly. The last thing you want is to pay for a puppy from a breeder just to find that it is unhealthy. On the next page you will find a list of breeders with Whippet puppies for sale in the U.K.

AGAIN PLEASE NOTE: The following, to the best of my knowledge are all good, reputable breeders. However, I am in no way connected/affiliated to them, nor am I endorsing/recommending anyone in particular. I urge you as always to do a thorough research of all possibilities, consider all options and make your own mind up.

Blue Streak Whippets
http://bluestreakwhippets.com/

Ashville Bur German Shepherd and Whippets
http://www.ashvillebur.co.uk/

Kennel Club list of breeders
http://www.thekennelclub.org.uk/ services/public/findapuppy/display. aspx?breed=1030&area=0

Champdogs
(Again this link will provide many possibilities)
http://www.champdogs.co.uk/ breeds/whippet/breeders

There are others that you could locate by doing a Google search along the lines of [Whippet Puppies For Sale UK]. Again my emphasis is always 'Health Tested'. However, that is not to say that a certain breeder you may find, does not have excellent healthy puppies for sale.

You can also research sites such as http://www.pets4homes. co.uk/. This is probably what you might term a classified site. I have seen reputable breeders with adverts on this site. But please do not assume that all breeders advertising on here will not be 'puppy farm' agents also. Again, please bear in mind the advice given in this book. Above all, do your research and do not rush into anything without thoroughly checking things out first.

c. Adopting a Rescue Dog

Unless you specifically have your heart set on a Whippet puppy, you may be able to find an adult Whippet at a local animal shelter or Whippet rescue. There are many benefits to adopting an adult dog versus buying a puppy. For one thing, adoption prices are much lower than the cost of purchasing a puppy from a breeder. Adoption rates typically range from $100 to $200 (£65 to £130). Furthermore, when you adopt an adult dog it may already be house-trained and have some obedience training.

While raising a puppy is great, it can take a lot of time and commitment and it can be a challenge. If you do not want to deal with a puppy having accidents in your house or if you want to avoid the whole teething stage, adopting an adult dog may be the right choice. Furthermore, when you buy a puppy from a Whippet breeder you do not know what its temperament and personality will be when it grows up. If you adopt an adult dog, what you see is what you get.

If you are thinking of adopting a Whippet rescue dog, consider one of the following rescues or shelters:

U.S.A Whippet Rescue Centres

Whippet Rescue and Placement;

Located throughout continental United States, Alaska and Hawaii

http://www.whippet-rescue.com/

All Breed Rescue: Donmar Kennels, Yucaipa, CA 92399.

As the name suggests they rescue all breeds and you can find out more at the following link. However, please do not overlook this rescue centre as they have rescued and successfully re-homed many Whippets, as the second link shows.

http://www.allbreed-rescue.org/ adoptions/index.html

http://www.allbreed-rescue.org/ special_breeds/adopted/adopted. html

Texas Italian Greyhound & Whippet Rescue: Dallas, Texas

http://txigrescue.org/

Other useful links are as follows:

http://www.thewhippet.net/usa-whippet-rescue.html

http://whippet.rescueme.org/

http://americanwhippetclub.net/
about-whippets/how-find-whippet

http://whippetcanada.com/whip-
pet-rescue/

http://www.whippetrescuesouth-
east.com/

http://www.adoptapet.com/s/
adopt-a-whippet

http://www.ncwfa.com/whippet-
rescue.html

http://www.dogsblog.com/cat-
egory/whippet-cross/

U.K. Whippet Rescue Centres

JR Whippet Rescue
http://www.whippetrescue.org.
uk/

Hounds First Sighthound Rescue
http://houndsfirst.co.uk/dogs-
for-adoption/

Just Whippets Rescue
http://www.justwhippetsrescue.
co.uk/?gclid=CjwKEAiA27G1BRCE-
opST9M39gykSJADQyqAljDODkiY
X5eNe3gpdtnEgurEiRl69POBG487
LXMjy3hoC1Unw_wcB

Greyhound and Lurcher Rescue
(They do occasionally have Whippets available)
http://www.greyhoundan-
dlurcherrescue.co.uk/dogs.aspx

Greyhound Gap
(Again they do occasionally have Whippets available)
http://www.greyhoundgap.org.
uk/homing-and-adoption/homeless-
hounds?gclid=CjwKEAiA27G1BRC
EopST9M39gykSJADQyqAlZlz95dK-
tffku6RoXdxqPWQNK_u8tlXZzHy-
WQXiIUWRoC85zw_wcB

Other useful links:

http://www.dogrescuefederation.
org/uk-dog-rescues/

http://www.thewhippetclub.com/

http://www.allsortsdogrescue.
org.uk/
http://www.thewhippet.net/whip-
pet-rescue.html

Oldies Club
occasionally have Senior Whippets available.
http://www.oldies.org.uk/?cat=1,
2,3,8&tag=sighthound&gclid=CjwK
EAiA_ra1BRDV-byb_aDqpQoSJAA-
ofB92Q6XJo0XSpkdkKnIYAS9JG-
cYACKgugjYFLaT2e_iPBoC0CPw_
wcB

In addition to the above, please check your local RSPCA / ASPCA and any local dog rescue centres, by doing a Google search such as the following: 'Rescue dogs [home town]

4) Fostering

Fostering is an excellent option if you are unsure about whether you can commit to looking after a dog on a permanent basis.

The purpose of fostering dogs and other animals is to prevent euthanasia. Fostering can also provide better alternatives for all animals, by providing a safe and nurturing temporary home. Fostering also increases the live-release rate of all pets, and reduces the number of dogs and cats that die from homelessness. Many rescue groups rely on foster homes to do their great work. These rescue groups will also at times end up paying for dogs to board at kennels when they do not have enough foster homes to turn to.

Fostering entails a temporary arrangement of a limited time where a person takes care of a dog, until a permanent home can be found for that dog. It is not adopting. However, quite often, many foster parents will end up adopting the dog that they foster.

a) Whippet Fostering

This is an arrangement between a shelter or a Whippet rescue group and the person agreeing to foster. In this case there will be a contract between you and the Whippet rescue group, detailing the responsibilities between both parties such as whom is responsible for veterinary bills, training, transport and food.

b) Questions To Ask Before Fostering a Whippet

It is very likely that the rescue centre organizing the fostering would answer the following questions and more anyway. But it is good for you to be aware of the type of issues you will face, such as the examples below.

» How long will I be fostering this Whippet?

» What happens should I change my mind, or if I'm not a good fit?

» Do I get to keep him permanently?

» Does the Whippet have any behavioral issues that require training, and can you provide this? Can I choose my own trainer?

» Who pays for dog food, veterinary supplies and dog training supplies? This is likely to be you but is worth asking as some may be available via the center.

» If my foster Whippet has any behavioral problems, whom can I contact?

» What should I do if my foster Whippet does not get along with my other pets?

» What should I do if there's a veterinary emergency?

» Who pays the veterinary bills? Would that include all veterinary treatments?

» Is my foster Whippet currently on any medication, or in need of ongoing treatment?

» Do I speak with potential adopters, screening them and possibly introducing my Whippet to them?

» Will I be required to bring my foster Whippet to certain adoption events and if so, how many times a month?

5.) Choosing a Reputable Breeder

BE AWARE: It should take you a couple of months to find a Whippet, possibly a lot longer to find a high-quality Whippet for showing.

As well as breeders, it is a good thing to visit a few Whippet dog shows, where you will be able to meet and talk with other enthusiasts. Many reputable Whippet breeders frequently attend dog shows.

You may wish to visit a championship show were you will have the chance to see hundred's of Whippets. You will obviously see the best pedigree dogs available. After frequenting these shows and reading more about this breed, you will have a better idea of the standard of dogs and a better perspective of the prices you will be expected to pay particularly for show dogs.

Ideally at this point, you will have done a considerable amount of research. Hopefully you will have compiled a list of breeders that you can contact and eventually visit.

Important Questions You Should Ask Before Buying a Whippet Puppy

» How long has the Whippet breeder bred Whippets

» How does this breeder socialize their pups with other dogs, children, people and normal everyday noises

» How do they socialize their older dogs

» What is their exercise routine

» What are they feeding their puppies, adolescents and grown dogs

The appearance of the parent dog and bitch need to also be taken into consideration when choosing a Whippet puppy. Good and professional Whippet breeders usually have both parents either with them for you to view or the option to view the stud dog used to father the litter. They will sometimes have photos of their entire Whippet family. As a potential buyer, you should examine the pedigree lines for conformation champions. You will then also get a fair idea on where your puppy comes from, and how well your Whippet will do in the show ring or in racing. Genetics play an important role in the future potential of your Whippet.

Nonetheless, if you are adopting a Whippet, chances are that you won't be able to examine breeding papers. In this case a good temperament with a dog that appears sound with good health are the most important considerations.

PLEASE REMEMBER:

You should not necessarily buy the first Whippet puppy for sale that you come across. You need to do your research and make sure that you are purchasing from a responsible breeder. A responsible Whippet breeder will be careful about selecting healthy breeding stock and they will keep detailed records of their breeding practices. If the breeder does not appear to be experienced with the Whippet breed, or with breeding dogs in general, you should look elsewhere.

As well as researching the websites listed earlier, try asking around at your local animal shelter or a veterinarian's office for recommendations. Although the Whippet is a popular breed, there may be a breeder in your area that you do not know about. If neither of these options turns up any breeders, try looking in the phone book or perform an online search. You may also wish to contact one of the breeders listed earlier. Once you have compiled a list of several breeders you can then go through the list to determine which one is the best option.

Follow the steps below to choose a reputable breeder:

» Visit the website for each breeder, if they have one, and look for important information such as photos of the facilities, the breeder's experience.

» Narrow your list down to two or three breeders that seem to be a good fit and visit the facilities before you make a commitment to buy a puppy.

» Make sure you see the breeding stock for the puppies that are available to make sure that they are in good health and good specimens of the Whippet breed.

» A reputable breeder will offer some kind of health guarantee on the puppy as well as information about the parents to certify its breeding.

» Ask to see the puppies that are available and make sure that they are kept in clean conditions. Remember, if they are under 6 weeks of age, the puppies should be kept with the mother until at least 8 weeks old.

» Choose the breeder that you feel is most knowledgeable and experienced, and no just the one that has puppies available. You will also probably get a gut feeling as to whether they are a reputable breeder or not.

» Contact each breeder by phone and ask them questions about their experience with breeding and with Whippets. If the breeder is hesitant to answer your questions, or if they do not seem knowledgeable and experienced, move on to the next option

» Evaluate the breeder's interest in learning more about you. A reputable breeder will not just sell his puppies to anyone, they should be eager to ask you questions to see if you are a good fit for one of their puppies.

» Ask for a tour of the facilities and look to make sure that the dogs are kept in clean conditions and that they appear to be in good health.

» Ask about the process for reserving a puppy. You will probably have to leave a deposit by way of a down payment. In addition, ask what the price includes (vaccinations, worming etc).

6.) Selecting a Healthy Whippet Puppy

After you have gone through the process of selecting a reputable breeder, your next step is to choose a healthy puppy. While it may be tempting to buy the first puppy that comes up to you with a wagging tail, you need to be a little more cautious about the process. Taking the time to ensure that the puppy is in good health could save you a lot of veterinary bills (not to mention heartache) in the future.

How To View a Litter of Whippet Puppies

You'll need to prepare a checklist of questions similar to the one below:

» Inquire about your Whippet's pedigree. Again a reputable breeder will be only too pleased to go into detail about the pup's history. Be wary of anyone who is vague or evasive about giving you answers.

» Ask about your Whippet's hereditary pedigree health problems. In most cases Whippets are a naturally healthy breed anyway, but sometimes genetic defects occur, and you need to know.

» Always visit a Whippet puppy with his mother and littermates at the address where they were bred.

» Never purchase or adopt a Whippet on a whim.

» Never buy a Whippet from a third party who is acting on behalf of a breeder.

» Never support puppy mills, puppy pet stores.

» Make sure that you know the pup's breeding, history and veterinary contact.

Follow the steps below to pick a healthy puppy:

1. Ask to see all of the puppies at once and spend a few minutes watching how they interact with each other before you approach them.

2. Healthy puppies should be playful and energetic. They should not be lolling around or acting lethargic.

3. Make yourself available to the puppies but do not immediately try to interact. Wait and see which ones are curious enough to approach you.

4. Whippet puppies are very sociable and playful, so they should be eager to interact with you.

5. Spend a few minutes engaging with each puppy. Play with a toy to gauge

6. the puppy's activity and try petting him to make sure he doesn't respond with fear or aggression.

7. If you can, watch the puppies being fed as well to make sure that they have a healthy appetite. A puppy that does not eat is likely to be sick.

8. Examine the puppies more closely for signs of good health. Do not just look for obvious signs of illness

Below is a list of what you should look for in different categories:

» *Eyes:* bright and clear; no discharge or crust

» *Breathing:* quiet and steady; no snorting, coughing, or sneezing

» *Energy:* alert and energetic; eager to play

» *Body:* The puppy should look well-fed, not too skinny

» *Coat:* the coat should be clean and healthy without bare patches, flaking skin, or other problems; the color should be uniform

» *Hearing:* the puppy should react if you clap your hands behind his head

> » **Vision:** the puppy should be able to see clearly if you toss a toy or roll a ball across his line of sight
>
> » **Gait:** the puppy should move easily without limping or evidence of soreness/stiffness
>
> » **Genitals:** the genitals should be clean

Whippet puppies can look like Labrador pups when a few weeks old. Nonetheless, by six weeks they will resemble Whippet pups and become finer in looks.

If the puppies appear to be physically healthy and do not show any behavioural warning signs like aggression, excessive fear, or lethargy, then they are probably a good buy. Once you've assessed the condition of the puppies you can spend some more time playing with them to find out which puppy is a good personality match for you. Keep in mind that the personality and temperament of your puppy might change a little as he grows, but you have some control over that depending on how you train and socialize him over the coming weeks.

7) Naming your puppy

If you have finally chosen the dog or puppy you want then perhaps now is as good a time as any to decide on his name. If you have hopefully bought from a reputable breeder, and are leaving a deposit to then collect him in a few weeks time, then you can get the breeder to start calling him by that name. Choosing your dog's name is exciting. Even an adult dog can learn a new name and some have no choice, arriving into rescue nameless. It is pretty easy to teach your dog his new name and considering how clever this breed is, the process should only take a few days. The idea is simply to show the dog that the sound of a certain word (his name or training command), means that he will need to pay attention, because you are speaking to him.

Eventually your dog will know when he is being talked about just by the sound of his name. For now though, you can offer him treats and say his name, plus call him between two people then use his name as he approaches. I simply say the name, give the dog a small treat and repeat this five or six times each session.

You can also prefix every positive interaction with your dog with his name. This way he will learn it even quicker. Never use his name for anything negative or your dog will try his hardest not to respond when he hears it. Always make it positive and fun and soon your dog will know exactly who he is. You probably already have ideas yourself, but if not, please make the name short and sweet. Something like, Daisy, Tess, Max or a name that relates to his appearance such as Patch.

8.) Puppy-Proofing Your Home

Depending on when you visit the breeder, the puppies may not be ready to take home just yet. Again, a responsible breeder will not sell a puppy under 8 weeks old or until the puppies are fully weaned. Even if the puppies are available when you visit you should wait until you have prepared your home before buying the puppy. Below you will find some important steps to take in puppy-proofing your home:

Your Whippet will want to explore every nook and cranny of his new home. Part of that process involves his teeth. Keep all items that are valuable or dangerous away from him. This particularly includes electrical cables that may be live and therefore the puppy is risking an electric shock and at worse a fatality. Replace them with non-toxic chew-able puppy toys in bright colours. Any chewed items are your responsibility, and you should be aware of this when the puppy sees an interesting thing to chew. They do not see the value or the danger, so please be aware that it is not your Whippet's fault if something gets chewed. Never use harsh corrections. Not even a tap on the nose. Instead use a firm "No" and replace the item with a chew-able dog toy for teething pups.

Anywhere within your home that your Whippet puppy is allowed to wander needs to be puppy proofed. This is similar to baby proofing your home, and requires you to go down on hands and knees and see what dangers lurk at puppy eye level.

Puppies enjoy chewing the solid rubberized covering of electrical cords and outlets . Remember, these can result in a fatality. Pups can also pull down electrical appliances by yanking on the cords.

Be Aware!

» Prevent your Whippet from jumping up on any unstable objects like bookcases.

» Keep your doors securely shut and again prevent a potential accident.

» Never slam doors with a Whippet puppy in the house. Use doorstops to make sure that the wind does not slam a door in your Whippet's face.

» Clear glass doors also pose a danger since your Whippet may not see them and run right into one. Use a screen door. Your Whippet puppy could run right into something at break neck speed.

» Check for toxic plants, medicines, sharp objects, and even dead branches.

> » Do not allow your Whippet access to high decks or ledges, balconies, open windows, or staircases. Instead use baby gates, baby plastic fencing and therefore prevent accidents from happening.

The whole point of the preceding is to get you to think about any potential hazards for your Whippet. Remember, they are relying on you as their guardian, in much the same way as a child.

a) Toxins To Be Aware of in Your Home

> » Garden and pool products
>
> » Bathroom products
>
> » Coins, small batteries and other small objects that may easily be ingested
>
> » Insecticides
>
> » Human medications
>
> » Household cleaning products
>
> » Foods that we consume that have a toxic effect on dogs such as grapes and chocolates
>
> » Rodenticides
>
> » Plants

You'll need to watch your Whippet puppy very carefully for the first few months to make sure that he does not get into harm's way. Usually the kitchen is made into the puppy's room. In this instance, it's best to make sure that all cleaning supplies are removed and placed elsewhere. Whippet pups are curious, and it can take as little as a few minutes for your puppy to get into a poisonous cleaning product.

b) Checking For Toxins in Puppy Toys

Before purchasing toys for your Whippet to play with, you'll need to check that they are lead free and cadmium free.

Vulnerable puppies are at risk of been given chew toys that may contain lead and cadmium. Studies from the University of Wisconsin-Madison demonstrate that all toxic responses to environmental pollutants begin to appear in stressed animals. It's important to remove all environmental stressors from your Whippet's life, and to do all you can to prevent him from being isolated and succumbing to depression and anxiety.

Therefore select chew toys that are free from lead and cadmium. Dog toys that contain DEHP- bis (2-ethylhexl) phthalate have been found to have a huge effect on the reproductive system of rats, even at very low doses. Toy products from Cordura like the Frisbee contain no detectable amounts of lead, cadmium, or phthalates. Use nontoxic tennis balls from Planet Dog or other reputable sources. These balls are not only indestructible; they are entirely free of phthalates and heavy metals.

http://www.planetdog.com/ home/

Non-toxic play toys are very important for all Whippet puppies that experience stress when left alone. These toys serve as anxiety busters, and give your Whippet puppy something to do when left alone.

Puppy-hood does not last for very long, and is a very special time in everyone's lives. It is during the Puppy-hood stage that training, playing, socializing and all the preparation that you do with your Whippet puppy needs to be taken seriously. Puppy-hood is not all about play.

Puppies need so much more than love. They also need you to keep them safe and out of trouble. Whippet pups can get themselves into plenty of trouble. Every single interaction that you will have with your Whippet puppy will be firmly imprinted. Meet your puppy's emotional needs first, then learn how to live successfully with your Whippet by training and protecting him.

c.) Summary for Puppy-Proofing Your Home

» If your yard does not already have a fence, consider having one installed so that your puppy can play outside safely.

» If you own a cat, make sure the litter box is stored somewhere your puppy can't get at it.

» Try not to use tobacco products in the house where your puppy might breathe the smoke. You should also dispose of ash and cigarette butts properly so your puppy doesn't get into them.

» Keep all bodies of water (including sinks, bathtubs, toilets, etc.) covered. Even a small amount of water could pose a drowning risk for a small puppy.

» Keep a lid on all of your trash-cans and, if possible, keep them in a cabinet for an added level of security. You don't want your puppy to chew on something that he could choke on or that may be poisonous to him.

» Check to make sure that none of the plants in your house or on your property are toxic to dogs. If they are, make sure they are well out of your puppy's reach or put a fence around them.

» Make sure you don't leave any small objects on the floor for your puppy to find. This includes things like childrens toys, small articles of clothing, jewelry, and more.

» Keep all of your cleaning products and dangerous chemicals stored securely in a cabinet where your puppy will not be able to access it.

» Store all food in the refrigerator or pantry where your puppy can't get it. Any food that you leave out needs to be in a tight-lidded container.

» Make sure that all of your medications and toiletries are stored in drawers or in your medicine cabinet.

» Keep all doors closed to areas of the house that might be dangerous for your puppy (such as the garage or laundry room). You may even want to use baby gates to confine your puppy to whatever room you are in.

» Keep all electrical cords and loose blinds tied up so your puppy doesn't chew on or trip on the strings. Cover your outlets with outlet covers.

In addition to following these steps to puppy-proof your home you also need to carefully supervise your puppy when he is not in his crate. Your puppy doesn't know what is dangerous, so it is your job to keep him safe.

9) Where Will your Puppy Sleep

Deciding where your puppy will sleep is important. Many people choose to allow a little dog on their bed, which is fine. However, it's important to understand separation anxiety if you sleep with your dog, and are allowing him to be with you at all times.

Separation anxiety is caused by over-attachment, and sleeping in your bed can be part of the reason for that. That's not to say that your puppy can't be allowed to sleep with you, just that you need to look carefully at the separation anxiety area of this book (Chapter 15), and decide how you will be safeguarding your own dog against it.

On the first night when you bring your puppy home I suggest that you don't leave him alone. Imagine how he would feel after being in the warmth of his nesting area with his mother and siblings to be then completely alone. So make a conscious decision to stay in the room where your puppy will be sleeping for a couple of nights. You can also invest in a very specific puppy comforter meant for the first few nights in a new home, they can be warmed in the microwave and some even have heartbeats.

If your puppy is going to eventually be sleeping alone, then it's not a good idea to allow him to sleep on you. It would be much better to lie on the couch and have him on the ground beside you. That way you can offer a comforting hand when needed but he will be learning to leave behind the warmth of bodies at bedtime. You can introduce the crate right at the beginning if you prefer, or wait until that first couple of nights are over. Eventually you will be able to leave a happily secure puppy in his sleeping place with ease.

An older dog that will be sleeping in another room in the beginning will probably howl and bark for the first few nights. Do not panic though because this is often due to unsettled feelings rather than severe separation anxiety. It usually wears off when the dog begins to feel secure.

10) Setting Up Your Whippet's Crate

The important thing about introducing your dog, whatever his age, to the crate is to make it a nice place that he finds welcoming. Put a cosy bed, toys and maybe even a stuffed Kong or other activity toy in the crate and allow your dog to sit in there with the door open to begin with.

If you need to have the crate close to you, in order to make your puppy feel secure, then this is fine

too. But remember to then move it away later. The idea is to show your puppy that his crate is a most comfortable bedroom to the point that he chooses it as his resting place, all on his own.

When you do start to close the door, only do it for a short time. The idea is that your dog never thinks that he is going to be trapped against his will. Never just push the dog in and close the door as this can easily cause a phobia.

To make your Whippet feel at home, place his crate somewhere permanent and place his food and water dishes nearby. You should also place a box with his toys in the area as well. Ideally, your Whippet's crate should be kept in a location that is not in the middle of household activity but that is not too isolated either. You will be keeping your Whippet in the crate overnight and when you are away from home during the house-training period, so place the crate somewhere that will not be in the way. If you do not like the idea of confining your Whippet to the crate while you are away, you should set up a puppy play yard around the crate so your Whippet has a little more space. He will still be confined but will be safe from potential hazards. He will be able to move around a little more to play with his toys.

11) Bringing your puppy/ adult dog home

When you pick your puppy up from the breeder they are bound to provide some sort of puppy pack.

This should include at the very least all of the relevant paper work, including the pedigree and perhaps your new Kennel Club documents. You will also probably receive a health certificate. Always remember to ensure you also receive the following:

1. 1) A diet sheet giving you precise details of when the puppy has been getting his meals, along with the particular food. (Please continue to feed according to this plan, as any sudden changes will affect his digestive system with a possible upset stomach and diarrhoea). Do not worry too much if your puppy does not seem to be eating the recommended amount as he may have lost some of his appetite with the upheaval of leaving his mother and siblings.

2. Once he has settled in after a few days he should start to finish his meals. If he is finishing his meals every time then by all means give him more, and again if he leaves some, then cut back slightly.

3. Please also remember that each breeder will have different ideas about how they feed their puppy. Again, do not worry if it is different to what you may have read or been told. The important thing is that he is fed a high quality nutritious diet.

4. We will talk more about feed and feeding next, but just to give you a rough idea of a typical feeding schedule, it may include 4 or 5 separate meals spread out over the day from 7 or 8 am to 10 or 11pm. The food the puppy may have been fed could well consist of a quality commercial diet consisting of tinned puppy food with puppy mixer. It could also include cooked fish, scrambled egg, milk and rusk, cooked chicken, vegetables, rice, puppy milk, minced beef/lamb/pork etc. Again, in this day and age of BARF diets, do not be too alarmed to find your puppy has just started a predominantly raw diet of some sort. Whatever the diet, stick to it and if you have a particular diet you would prefer to give him, give this gradually while substituting odd meals until the diet has been changed to your preferred one.

5. Remember to check his worming schedule, that is, when he was last wormed, when he is next due and which worming medication was used.

The First Day Home

If at all possible do not bring home a Whippet puppy during the holidays when your home is likely to be busy with guests and unusual noises.

Plan to take a few days off from work when you bring your Whippet puppy home. The next few days will be time consuming, and will need direct supervision from you. This will involve using management tools such as baby gates, crates, exercise pens and puppy pads. Bare in mind that baby gates, will be fine whilst your puppy is relatively young. But do not be surprised once he starts getting stronger he will have no difficulty hurdling over.

Bringing a new dog home is an exciting and sometimes even a terribly scary time. If you follow the right stages of introduction for the dog though, both into your home and your family, everything should go smoothly.

During this area of the book I will talk about the first few days of a new dog being in your home. I will explain how he may be feeling, how you can communicate properly with your new dog and how to make life easy for all of you within this crucial settling in period. One of the most tempting things to do when you bring a new dog home is celebrate their arrival. Everyone comes to meet the new family member and everyone wants a touch, particularly if the new arrival is a gorgeous Whippet puppy.

When you bring a new puppy home it is important to remember that he will be confused and learning all of the time. That said, if the young dog has a lot of positive, gentle interaction even from day one it will be good for him and build his confidence. For this reason the new and young puppy may benefit from some careful visitors. A new adult Whippet is a different matter. An older dog will need a quiet time in the home for the first few days. The adult dog will not welcome a stream of visitors on day one. The new dog will likely be scared and nervous. Remember that he will have little understanding about what is happening in his life and the best way you can approach this is keep quiet and allow him to get used to the new environment in his own time.

Similarly the dog should be left well alone by family members whilst he is settling in. He can get some positive attention and fuss if he asks for it, but should certainly not be cornered or forced to accept attention. Many canine rescuers have to take dogs back into their care because a problem has occurred on day one or two that could easily have been avoided if the dog was given space and respect to settle into the new home before excited new owners forced their attentions on him.

A dog learns how to react to things, in his life, based upon past experiences. In addition, canine communication is very different to the communication that occurs between people. In actual fact the average new dog owner trying to make friends with a scared Whippet by trying to touch him is having the exact opposite effect on their recently arrived dog.

I always ignore a new dog into the home. I barely look at them but offer attention if they ask for it. A very scared dog is allowed to hide where he is happy until he is ready to come out and learn to join in with everyday life in his own time.

Later on I will talk about body language and I think it is really important that you read through that, and the area on canine communication, before you bring your new dog home or at least as early as possible. By knowing how your dog acts when he feels a certain way you will be able to understand him better and start your new relationship off perfectly.

There is something that very few people tell you when they present you with a new dog, whatever age he may be. You may think that you have made a mistake. This is an absolutely normal reaction to such a big change in your life. Whether you have brought home a scared teenage dog, a confident adult Whippet or a needy puppy, you may panic before things settle down. With a puppy, you will worry about why he is crying, whether you are feeding him properly, and how you can be sure that he stays happy and healthy. When you bring home an adult dog, he may show separation anxiety, he may bark in the night for a few days and either be very clingy or completely aloof. An adult dog may be so worried that he shows his teeth in the beginning. It's important not to crowd a new dog and everything will settle down quickly. The dog that is left to settle on his own will have no reason to feel threatened.

So all I can say to you is expect accidents, expect upheaval and expect things to change for a short time; then if the dog settles perfectly, far better than you expected, at least you were prepared

12) First introductions

When you introduce your new Whippet to everyone else in the household it's important to be careful and respectful of how everyone feels and may react. If you are bringing home a young puppy this will be easier because the puppy, when carefully handled, will generally be accepting of anyone and everyone. In the case of bringing a puppy home, the other animals in the family must be considered. Some older dogs that you may already have, are completely overwhelmed by the new squeaking, face licking, and over keen puppy.

In the beginning they may want to be nowhere near the baby dog. If you live with an older dog, ensure that a puppy does not get walked on and harassed in those early days, particularly if he is worried. Similarly take extra care with the cat and any other pets you may have.

If you are bringing home an older dog, to a home with an existing dog, it is important to take all resources away that may cause friction. So pick up toys, treats and anything that either dog may guard. In particular, I have witnessed more dog fights than anything, where food is concerned. Remember that a new dog may feel insecure, therefore guard things for that reason alone.

45

It's a good idea to let two older dogs meet on neutral ground. At the park or somewhere similar, rather than just bring the new dog directly home. Walking them together first will allow them to get used to the scent of each other and do the 'meet and greet' without the tension of perceived territory.

13.) Introducing Your Puppy to Children

Whippets are a very social and people-oriented breed and as previously mentioned, they tend to get along well with children. This doesn't mean, however, that you can just put your puppy in a room with your kids and expect everything to be fine. Just as you need to ensure that your puppy is safe in your home, you also need to teach your children how to properly handle the puppy for their own safety.

Introducing your children to the new dog is important. The kids must learn that the dog is not a toy and a young puppy is very fragile. Never leave your children alone with a new Whippet of any age as this could be risky for all of them. Carefully explain to your children as much information as you can from this book and you will find that the dog and children become friends for life.

Just as you do between two dogs, watch out for resource guarding between dogs and children. Kids tend to grab at toys and food bowls, particularly the little ones. A dog could easily see this behaviour as a threat and snap in return. Similarly remember that any dog will not ap-

preciate uncomfortable poking and prodding before he tells the child to go away, in the only way that he can.

Do not allow your child to follow a dog that has tried to move away for the attentions. This is a recipe for disaster because the dog can feel cornered and think he has to resort to aggression simply to be left alone. If you manage your family well and teach an all-round respect, you will be able to integrate the new dog in perfectly. Before you know it, everyone will be great friends.

Follow the tips below to safely introduce your puppy to children:

1. Before you bring the puppy home, explain to your children how to properly handle the puppy. Tell them that the puppy is fragile and should be handled with care.

2. Tell your children to avoid over-stimulating the puppy. They need to be calm and quiet when handling him so he does not become frightened.

3. When it is time to make introductions, have your children sit on the floor in your home and bring the puppy to them.

4. Place the puppy on the floor near your children and let the puppy wander up to them when he is ready. Do

not let your children grab the puppy.

5. Allow your children to calmly pet the puppy on his head and back when he approaches them. You may even give them a few small treats to offer the puppy.

6. Let your children pick up the puppy if they are old enough to handle him properly. If the puppy becomes fearful, have them put him carefully back down.

If at any point during your introductions the puppy becomes afraid, you should take him out of the situation and place him in his crate where he can feel safe. Do not let your children scream or act too excited around the puppy until he gets used to them. It will take time for both your children and your puppy to get used to each other and you should supervise all interactions.

Please do remember, that where children are concerned or you already have a few pets, be extra careful of where your attentions go. After all, you want all of your pets to get along with each other, as well as your children. So do not create jealousy by fussing over your new Whippet puppy and ignoring your other pets. Share your attention equally between all your pets, so that the relationship starts off well. Much of the future relationship between all of your pets, will depend on what happens during the first few days.

With children in the picture, it's important that this new relationship starts off well and gently. If your Whippet puppy is your first puppy, as stated above, it's best to prepare young children with a firm explanation that all puppies need plenty of rest, quiet and gentleness. Prepare them ahead of time by showing them how to touch a small puppy, and what tone of voice to use i.e. low and comforting.

Children should never scream or run around a small, vulnerable puppy. They also should not pull his ears, tail or any other part of the puppy. It's best to be very firm with your children about all the puppy rules ahead of time.

CHAPTER FOUR:

Caring for Whippet Dogs

When you become a Whippet owner, you become responsible for meeting your dog's needs. This means more than just feeding your dog and taking him on a daily walk. You also have to provide him with a safe home environment and all the love and attention he needs. In this chapter you will learn the basics about habitat requirements and generally caring for and providing the nutritional needs of your Whippet.

Please be aware that the sections on feeding and nutrition are broad ranging and go into quite a bit of detail. Please do not be tempted to skim read or skip this part. Of all the chapters covered I would say that this is probably the most important and sadly over looked aspect of caring for your dog.

1) Habitat Requirements for Whippets

The Whippet is a small to medium-sized breed so it does not require a great deal of space, but this breed will appreciate having room to run and play outdoors, if possible. One important thing to remember with this breed is that the Whippet does not have a double-coat. He does not have an undercoat to protect him against harsh weather. This being the case, you should never keep your Whippet outside for extended periods of time during the winter, and certainly never consider kennelling them outdoors. As with many other short coated dogs, a lot of Whippet owners make use of coats for their dogs during cold weather. On the opposite end of the spectrum, high temperatures can be dangerous for your dog as well. If you let your dog spend a lot of time in the yard during the winter, make sure that he has a shaded area to retreat to and plenty of fresh water at all times.

2.) Necessary Supplies and Equipment

Whippet dogs do not need many accessories, but there are a few necessities you will want to have on hand.

Some of the necessary supplies and equipment for keeping Whippets include the following:

» Food and water bowls

» Collar and leash

» Crate or kennel

» Blanket or dog bed

» Grooming supplies

» Assortment of toys

Food and Water Bowls – Your dog's food and water bowls do not necessarily need to be fancy, they just need to be sturdy and sanitary. As the Whippet can be susceptible to bloat, many owners recommend elevated food and water bowls. The best material for food and water dishes is stainless steel because it is easy to clean and does not harbour bacteria. If you prefer, ceramic dishes are a good alternative and they come in a variety of colours to suit your preferences.

Collar and Leash – Whippets and Greyhounds have always traditionally worn wider collars and there is much debate as to the reasons for this (if you are not familiar with type of collar, please do a Google search for [Whippet collars]). Many suggest that the reason for wider collars is to lessen the impact as the Whippet may have a tendency to lunge and take off after a rabbit, and cause possible damage to their neck. Others suggest this is also because they have sensitive skin likely to become easily damaged. It is further suggested that traditionally Whippets as part of their training were encouraged to pull on the lead to build hindquarter and back muscle. The wide collar in turn would prevent choking. Whatever the reason or your choice, having a high-quality collar and leash for your Whippet is very important. It is also important that these items match your Whippet's size. When your dog is a puppy you will need a small puppy collar that you can adjust as your puppy grows. Once your dog reaches his adult size you can get a slightly larger collar. The size of your dog's leash may change as he grows as well. When your puppy is young you will want a short leash to use for training and walks. Once your Whippet grows up and gets some training you can upgrade to a longer leash.

Crate – One of the most important accessories you need for your Whippet is a crate. If you use it correctly your dog will not view time spent in the crate as punishment and there is no reason to believe that keeping your dog in a crate for short periods of time is cruel. If you use the crate properly while training your Whippet he will come to view it as a place to call his own. It will become his place where he can go to take a nap or to get some time to himself if he wants it. When selecting a crate for your Whippet, size is very important. For the purpose of house training, you want to make sure that the crate is not too big. It should be just large enough for your puppy to stand, sit, lie down, and turn around comfortably. The key to crate training is to get your dog to think of the crate as his home, or his den. Dogs have a natural aversion to soiling their den, and if your puppy's crate is only large enough for him to sleep in, it will be more effective as a house-training tool. When your puppy grows up you can upgrade to a larger crate. Admittedly this may seem like money wasted having to buy two crates. But as crates are relatively inexpensive, I would say this is money well spent and you may as well have the correct tool for the job.

Blanket or Dog Bed – To make your dog's crate more comfortable, you should line it with a soft blanket or a plush dog bed. When you are house-training your Whippet puppy, it is best to use an old blanket or a towel, just in case your puppy has an accident. Once your puppy is fully trained however, you can upgrade to a plush dog bed or a thicker blanket that will be more comfortable.

Grooming Supplies – Because the Whippet has a very short coat you will not need to worry too much about shedding. You should still brush your dog's coat on at least a weekly basis in order to keep it in good health. Some owners brush their dogs everyday as some Whippets lose more hair than others. You may also want to professionally groom your dog once or twice a year.

The grooming tools you may need to brush and bathe your Whippet at home include:

> » Soft bristle brush
>
> » Dog nail clippers
>
> » Gentle dog-friendly shampoo (a purifying shampoo and conditioner is often recommended)
>
> » Rubber grooming or hound glove.

Never use use grooming brushes/rakes more suitable for thick double coated dogs.

You will find more detailed instructions for grooming your Whippet in Chapter Eight.

Assortment of Toys – Offering your Whippet an assortment of toys is very important. Having toys to play with will keep your dog occupied when you are unable to pay attention to him and it will also provide him with something to chew on instead of your furniture and other household items. Different dogs, like different toys, so your best bet is to buy several different kinds and let your dog choose which ones he likes best.

3.) Feeding Your Whippet

In addition to providing your Whippet with a safe habitat, you also need to give him a healthy diet. The food you choose for your Whippet will have a direct impact on his health and wellbeing, so do not skimp! It may be tempting to save money by purchasing an inexpensive 'budget' food but you will be robbing your dog of vital nutrients. Skimping on cheap dog food might save you money in the present but it could lead to health problems down the line that might be expensive to treat. In this chapter you will learn the basics about dog nutrition and receive tips for feeding your dog.

a) Nutritional Requirements for Dogs

Just like all living things, dogs require a balance of nutrients in their diet to remain in good health. These nutrients include protein, carbohydrate, fats, vitamins, minerals, and water. Dogs are a carnivorous species by nature so meat plays an important role in their diet, but they do require some carbohydrates as well. Later you will read about the BARF diet. Part of that diet recommends that you feed carbohydrates such as raw fruit and vegetables. This is best served finely chopped, using a food processor or similar. Below you will find an overview of the nutritional needs for dogs in regard to each of the main nutrients. Keep these nutritional requirements in mind when selecting a dog food formula for your Whippet.

Protein – This nutrient is composed of amino acids and it is essential as a source of energy as well as the growth and development of tissues, cells, organs, and enzymes in your dog's body. It is particularly important for puppy growth, but when the dog reaches maturity, protein is only necessary for maintenance. When the bitch is pregnant and whilst she is feeding pups, she will also need extra protein. Protein can be obtained from both animal and plant-based sources, but animal-based proteins are the most biologically valuable for your dog. There are two categories of amino acids; essential and non-essential. Non-essential amino acids are those that your dog's body is capable of producing. Essential amino acids are those that cannot be produced by the dogs body and therefore he must get this from his diet. The most important essential amino acids for a dog include lysine, arginine, phenylalanine, histamine, methionine, valine, tryptophan, leucine, threonine, and isoleucine.

The quality of the protein can therefore be determined by what extent it contains these essential amino acids. The quality can also be indicated by how well the dog digests the protein. Commercially processed dog foods that contain high levels of cereals are generally considered to contain poor quality protein. The problem is that these products can indicate relatively high levels of protein, but the type of protein contains low if non-existent sources of essential amino acids. Good quality protein would be found in dairy produce such as milk and cheese also eggs and obviously meat.

Protein deficiency would cause all sorts of problems and generally have a serious debilitating effect on the body. Examples of diseases would include, immune deficiency, poor bone growth and muscle development etc. Adult dogs would be greatly affected, but imagine the devastating effects to growing pups. Again, this is a common problem with poor commercially processed or homemade diets that are either badly designed or contain poor quality cereals.

In the same way that a protein deficiency will cause problems so will an over consumption. The main problems with over feeding protein involve kidney disease. Growing pups and lactating mothers require almost twice as much as an adult dog. The actual percentage of good quality protein for an adult dog would be approximately 8 to 10%, and a lactating bitch and growing pups about 18 to 20%.

Feral dogs, or wolves in the wild, would unlikely be eating high levels of protein on a daily basis. A raw meaty bones diet for example, would make up approximately 60% of their diet

Carbohydrate – The main role of carbohydrates in your dog's diet is to provide energy and dietary fibre. Dogs do not have a minimum carbohydrate requirement but they do need a certain amount of glucose to fuel essential organs like the brain. Carbohydrates are derived from plant sources and are either soluble or insoluble. Soluble consist of simple sugars mostly found in fruit, as well as sugar cane etc. Insoluble carbohydrates, complex or starches as they are otherwise known, originate from vegetables and grains for example leafy veg, potatoes, corn, pumpkin, beans, peas etc. Vegetables as carbohydrates that we feed to our dogs should be raw and fresh. I hasten to add 'vegetables' and not produce such as corn, rice, wheat etc., or products such as pasta. The vegetables should also be processed, finely chopped or crushed, for greater digestion and therefore absorption. Carbohydrates have featured as a significant ingredient in processed dog food. But in a natural sense, carbohydrates are not as important to dogs as it is for humans as

a source of energy. Dogs should not be given large amounts of carbohydrate over a prolonged period. Their internal workings are not designed to handle significant amount of this type of food source.

Fibre - Fibre is also an important component of carbohydrates, which isn't ingested but aids greatly with the internal workings. Fibre is also either soluble or insoluble. Soluble basically means that it absorbs water; swells and bulks up to a gelatinous matter. Examples include; oatmeal, apples, beans etc. Insoluble fibres do not absorb water, but act as a bulking agent. Although stating the obvious, insoluble fibre is pretty much parts of vegetable matter that do not absorb water, such as the skins. They act to slow down digestion, aid greater absorption and make the stools easier to pass.

A dog's body is only capable of digesting certain kinds of carbohydrate and too much fibre in the diet is not good for them. It is usually recommended that a mixture of fast and slow fermenting fibres are best. The reason being that too much slow fermenting fibre such as cellulose is likely to cause a sluggish digestion. Bran is considered a good source of fast fermenting fibre but too much could cause diarrhoea. Somewhere in the middle is a moderately fermentable fibre such as beet pulp which is a common ingredient in dog foods.

Fats – This is the most highly concentrated form of energy so it is an important part of your dog's diet. Fats provide your dog with twice the energy of protein and carbohydrates.

Fats are also important for providing structure for cells and for producing certain types of hormones. They are also necessary to ensure that your dog's body can absorb fat-soluble vitamins. Your dog needs a balance of omega-3 and omega-6 fatty acids in his body and it is best if these fats come from animal-based sources instead of plant-based sources.

Again fat is the best energy food source, but the consumption of fat depends on the lifestyle of the dog. All dogs need some fat. But a sedentary, housedog will obviously need far less than a working dog or feral dog or wolf, which are dependent on food for survival. Too much fat, in the case of a house dog, would lead to obesity, high cholesterol and other diseases, possibly leading to death.

On a more positive note, fat is essential for providing insulation for the body as well as protecting the nerves. It facilitates absorption of vitamins A, K, D and E. In essence, fat is a vital component of every cell in the dogs body. It is important to note that like other food elements, fat has to be provided in the diet.

Essential fatty acids are especially vital for the correct functioning of the dogs body. Without this, the dog will develop a whole host of diseases. It is important to note that not all fats are recommended. There is a big difference between 'Essential fatty acids' and 'Non-essential fatty acids'.

There is a hormone called 'prostaglandins', which plays an essential role in regulating all bodily functions. Prostaglandins are formulated using essential fatty acids. If essential fatty acids are absent, then non essential fatty acids are utilized, and this results in an imbalance, malfunction and disease.

Essential fatty acids are the types of healthy fats we are told to eat such as omega rich 3, 6 and 9 fish oils. Chicken and pork fat, or lard, are surprisingly excellent sources of essential fatty acid, that may not be healthy for human consumption, but are excellent for dogs.

Non essential acids consist of fats such as beef or mutton suet.

On the next page is a table giving the saturated, mono-unsaturated and polyun-saturated values for 100g of beef, pork and chicken.

Chicken and pork fat are considered excellent sources of 'essential fatty acids'. Animal fat is generally saturated fat that is considered bad for human consumption. The table above indicates that beef, chicken and pork fat have similar levels of saturated fat. But look at the monounsaturated amount for beef. Chicken and Pork are the same and relatively low, but beef is over twice as much. Also notice the very low polyunsaturated amount for beef at only 4 g. Pork fat is almost 3 times as much and chicken fat is over 11 times as much.

Fats that are considered very healthy for human consumption include Olive oil and Canola or rapeseed oil. However, these are very rich in Monounsaturated fats, which if fed to dogs to any great extent would cause an essential fatty acid deficiency. Other oils high in mono-

(Values for 100g of beef, chicken and pork fat)

Beef Fat	Chicken Fat	Pork Fat
100 g	100 g	100 g
Saturated 42 g	Saturated 30 g	Saturated 32g
Monounsaturated 50 g	Monounsaturated 21 g	Monounsaturated 21 g
Polyunsaturated 4 g	Polyunsaturated 45 g	Polyunsaturated 11 g

unsaturated fats include: Peanut oil, sunflower oil, hydrogenated soybean oil, palm oil etc.

Other than pork and chicken fat, other excellent sources of 'essential fatty acids' include polyunsaturated rich oils such as corn oil, flaxseed/ linseed oil, soybean oil (however, be careful that the soybean oil is not hydrogenated. Hydrogenation is a process that effectively changes soybean and other oils from poly-unsaturated to monounsaturated.)

Safflower oil is also recommended as an excellent source of polyunsaturated fatty acid. However, be careful with Safflower oil, as there are two types, one is high in monounsaturated fatty acid and low in polyunsaturated, this is known as (oleic acid). The other high in polyunsaturated fatty acid and low in monounsaturated, known as (linoleic acid).

So to summarise, excellent sources of essential fatty acids include chicken and pork fat, and polyunsaturated rich vegetable oils. Fats to avoid include beef fat (tallow), mutton fat etc. , and vegetable oils rich in monounsaturated fatty acids.

Omega 6 Fatty Acid

These are essential fatty acids that are found in pig and poultry fat, as well as many sources of vegetable oil. Many of the commercially processed dog foods as well as home cooked foods based on beef and cooked grain, are likely to be lacking in these fatty acids. As you know, a lack of these essential fatty acids. results in a number of diseases for our dogs such as skin disease, reproduction and growth problems. High levels of Omega 6 fatty acid are found in the following list in descending order of potency; corn oil, cotton seed oil, un-hydrogenated soybean oil, linoleic sunflower oil, peanut oil. Also present, but to a lesser level of Omega 6 are flaxseed oil, olive oil, palm oil, rapeseed (canola) oil.

Omega 3

These important fatty acids are mainly found in fish oils and fish. They largely benefit the brain and nerve functions, so can affect vision, brain activity and fertility in males etc. Flaxseed/linseed oil, is particularly high in Omega 3 and to a significant but lesser extent, canola (rapeseed)oil and soybean. All other oils have omega 3, but to a smaller degree. As linseed/flaxseed is particularly potent, it will be tempting to use this. However, be very careful to only use linseed/flaxseed intended for animal or human consumption. The type available from DIY stores, intended to treat timber and make putty soft etc., is poisonous to dogs and should never be given to them. Also be very careful about giving your dogs fish oils as there is a risk of over dosing their supply of vitamins A and D. If in doubt avoid feeding fish oils.

Have a look at the following source link which gives a vast array of sources, flaxseed and fish oils being the highest:

http://nutritiondata.self.com/ foods-0001400000000000000000. html

Rich mammalian sources of omega 3 include; eyes and brains etc. Most meats are quite low, but rabbit and lambs liver are considered the best sources.

When supplementing your dogs diet with omega 3 and 6 fatty acids, always ensure to supplement with vitamin E also. Without the presence of vitamin E, these essential fatty acids have a tendency to go off and become rancid in the dogs body.

If you were looking for an oil with a good balance, corn oil and soybean oil are generally considered the best to combine both omega 6 and 3.

Vitamins – Your dog's body is incapable of producing most vitamins, so it is essential that he get them through his diet. Some of the most important vitamins for dogs include vitamin A, vitamin D, vitamin E and vitamin C.

Sufficient dietary minerals can be obtained from natural sources such as raw meaty bones and the veg, eggs, dairy products mentioned previously. There does seem to be a problem in this regard with processed foods, in that dogs can potentially receive far more minerals than they need. However, vitamins do have a tendency to be lacking in certain processed formulas, and therefore supplementation should be considered. Vitamins are vital for the correct functioning of the body and its many organs. A lack of certain vitamins will lead to diseases.

We typically know vitamins by their letters of the alphabet, A, B, C, D etc. If certain vitamins are absent, then deficiency diseases are bound to manifest. If the dog is getting just enough vitamins, then they will not necessarily show signs of obvious disease, but they are not really at an optimum healthy level. When vitamins are in abundance, then they not only prevent deficiency diseases, but act as a defence against disease.

So an abundance promotes health, resists disease, greatly aids reproduction and basically allows the dog to have long-term fitness and stamina against stress. In essence, an abundance of vitamins helps all the bodily functions to work efficiently to their optimum level. However, this does not mean that vitamins should be administered at higher unlimited levels. It is possible for an overdose or toxic level to be reached with certain vitamins such as A or D. For severe illness such as with cancer, quite often high doses of vitamin C are administered to combat the disease. Vitamin C and B for example are relatively safe to administer in this way.

Commercially produced dog food is at risk of lacking essential vitamins for a variety of reasons. Dog food is often made up of cheap fillers such as grain and animal by-products and then cooked at high temperatures. What little vitamin value that was present in its raw state is likely to be destroyed or greatly diminished during the cooking process. Vitamins can also be destroyed when mixed with minerals, we will talk more about this later. Also, vitamins that are exposed to air have a limited shelf life. So if dry dog food is not kept in an air tight container it will quickly deteriorate.

The exact same problem can occur if you home cook food for your dog. With the best will in the world, you can use a variety of top quality ingredients but during the cooking process many vitamins can be destroyed. In these cases, vitamins would need to be added back or supplemented. This would be more important during old age, puppy growth or stages of reproduction or lactation.

What are vitamins?

Vitamins comprise of water soluble and fat soluble. Examples of water soluble are vitamin C and B complex. Vitamins A, D, E and K are classified as fat soluble.

To a certain extent, water soluble vitamins are stored by the body, despite the contrary opinion that they must be supplied on a daily basis. As mentioned previously they can also be given at much higher doses than are recommended. There would be little point in giving high doses that are likely to be excreted, but a dose similar to a human dose would probably be adequate. Again, any that is not immediately used or stored is simply urinated out of the body. It is perfectly safe for the dog and no harm is done.

B Complex

They are extremely important for processing fats, proteins and carbohydrates and turning them into energy. This energy is vital for all bodily functions, for the general purpose of daily activity and for growth. A dog given sufficient Vitamin B would be full of life, bright and energetic, would generally be fit and look fit and healthy. The dog deficient would be totally the opposite, so lacking energy, dull, and overweight. They also play a vital role with the nervous system. Again a deficiency would indicate a nervous dog, whereas sufficient levels would indicate a calm, happy dog.

Similar to humans, a lack of the B complex vitamins can seriously affect the nervous system. It can also have a serious effect on the body during stressful periods. It can also have a significant effect on the energy levels of the dog. The B vitamins are usually administered all together as a complex rather than given separately, unless there is an obvious singular B Vitamin deficiency.

Other problems include:

» Under development

» Deficient immune system

» Production of antibodies is diminished

» Lack of antioxidants

» Thymus gland problems

» Lack of anti aging

» Tissue degeneration

» Free radicals are not eliminated from the body

» More prone to stress

» Problems with blood production, reproduction, tissue repair, growth.

» Skin and fur problems occur

In essence they are vital for all bodily functions. They are vital for the health and wellbeing of our dogs at all stages of life.

Rich food sources of B complex include:

The best sources of B complex as a whole are liver and brewers yeast. Brewers yeast is often recommended as an excellent source of B complex vitamins. It is also a good source of protein. But other B vitamins, not the full B complex, are present in foods such as brown rice, wholemeal bread, meat, eggs, offal, dairy produce, green leafy veg etc.

Vitamin C

The same rules apply to vitamin C as the above information on the B complex. They are stored by the body to an extent. Can be administered safely at high doses, albeit any not taken up by the body or immediately used, would be eliminated through the urine. Dogs do produce their own vitamin C to an extent, which leads some people to assert they do not need any additional. However, although opinions differ, it is best to give extra in order to ensure your dog is at optimum health. Dogs in the wild would still be eating a lot of vitamin C rich food, and probably to a greater extent than a lot of domestically fed dogs, who are reliant on receiving all their nutrients from commercial food.

Unlike humans who cannot make or store Vitamin C, dogs actually produce this in their liver. However, during times of stress or ill health they would require probably more than the body can naturally produce. Apart from stress and perhaps over work problems can occur relative to reproduction or for the growth of pups.

Vitamin C promotes the following:

» Helps eliminate toxins

» Fights infection and generally boosts the immune system

» Heavily involved in the healing of wounds etc.

» Greatly alleviates the stresses of reproduction, lactation, weaning

» Essential for collagen production and other growth factors

» Generally boosts the body in relation to wear and tear associated with exercise and body rejuvenation. Also greatly helps with the aging process

Again as with the B complex, this vitamin is not necessarily dangerous in high doses. However, excess vitamin C, can cause diarrhoea. Again this is not dangerous and a reduction in dosage clears the problem.

Although vitamin C is widely available in a lot of fruit and veg etc., some people also like to add a supplement also. This can be in line with what you may supplement yourself, and a general guideline is to add up to 100 milligrams per kilo. So if your dog weighs 10kg then a 1 gram or 1000 mg tablet could be given. That isn't to say that you should administer that dose regardless. Also please take into account fluctuations in stress levels. A relatively stress free dog would be fine on up to 100mg per kg. if your dog was under heavy stress such as over work, or lactation and weaning then this could be increased to about 300mg per kg. It is also advisable to split the daily dose given. So give 100mg in two separate doses of 50mg. if it were 300mg administered, then split this into 6 separate doses and so on.

'Bowel Tolerance' is a gauge as to whether your dog is receiving too much vitamin C, which is indicated by diarrhoea

If a dog is predominantly feeding on a raw diet, i.e. raw meaty bones along with vegetables and other ingredients, then only a minimum supplement of up to 100mg per kg, would be needed.

Under normal healthy conditions it will not matter a great deal what type of vitamin C your dog receives. Vitamin C is known as ascorbic acid, but be aware that there are different forms such as calcium ascorbate, ester C and sodium ascorbate. It is important to know this because if for example your dog suffers with hip dysplasia calcium ascorbate should not be given, because of the extra calcium. A dog with heart disease should not be given sodium ascorbate, due to the sodium.

Fat Soluble Vitamins

Vitamins A, E and K have anti ageing/antioxidant properties. Vitamin D and A, in particular should never be given at high doses as they are extremely toxic at high levels. The other problem is that unlike B and C vitamins, these are stored to a greater extent in the body. The effect of topping up, again can potentially build up to toxic levels. Having said that, despite the dangers of toxic overload, all of these vitamins should never be allowed to become non-existent as diseases will arise as a result of the deficiency.

Vitamin A, is vital for most if not all of the bodily processes. It is particularly important for sight, immune system functioning, mucous membranes, skin, adrenal glands, reproduction, growth etc. To supplement with Vitamin A an amount of between 100 to 200 iu per kg, would be safe. So a 20 kg dog would not need more than 200 x 20 = 4000iu per day. If however, you were feeding your dog liver once or twice per week it is unlikely you would need any extra supplementation.

Do check any commercial food levels of vitamin A. The likely hood is that there will be just enough, but not necessarily enough to keep the dog at optimum health. Usually commercial feed will be about 50 to 100iu per kg per day.

I would never recommend attempting to give the maximum non toxic level until you are sure what you are doing. Give smaller doses initially and if you see significant general improvement then gradually increase this per month. It is also a good idea initially to supplement for one month and then don't give anything the following month, then restart again.

Once again, feeding liver once or twice per week may be safer until you get experience and always monitor how your dog is doing.

When should you never supplement vitamin A?

Never supplement a dog with vitamin A if they have liver or kidney disease. Once again, if the diet is already rich in vitamin A, for instance if liver is regularly given, then again do not add any vitamin A supplement.

It is useful to know that where cases of toxicity and overdose occur, this has been when up to 100 times the recommended limits have been administered and usually for prolonged periods. The general opinion is that up to 10 times the recommended dose would be safe. Again, if this level of up to 10 times was exceeded for a short period of time, it is unlikely to cause any serious effects.

Signs of toxicity

The following list will give you some idea of abnormalities that can occur from overdosing Vitamin A

» Cartilage degeneration

» Internal bleeding

» Blood that doesn't clot easily

» Weight loss

» Appetite loss

» Enteritis

» Hereditary abnormalities

» Fractures

» Malformed bones

» Thickened skin

» conjunctivitis

» Red blood cell count reduction

» Liver and kidney malfunction

» suppressed keratinisation

What do the µg and iu symbols mean?

If you are not familiar with the µg symbol, it means micro-gram and can also be written as mcg. To give you some comparative values, 1 milligram = 1,000 µg, 1 gram = 1,000,000 µg,

Again, you may see food sources measured as IU, which stands for International Unit.

Whilst µg is obviously a quantifiable unit of weight, it is not as easy to quantify and therefore compare µg with its equivalent IU. So it is not simply a matter of saying 1 IU = X amount of µg.

Whereas µg, is simply the mass or weight, a substances IU is measured in terms of concentration of potency. So in other words, 2 exact

same substances for example may have concentrations of 100 mg and 300 mg respectively. It's the same thing but one is obviously more potent than the other. This occurs very often with herbal supplements. There are many products available for Echinacea for example. You will see several products with 30 tablets for example, sold for the different prices. It is only when you delve deeper and look at the % or mg of potency that you realise why.

So taking some examples from the following link;

https://en.wikipedia.org/wiki/ Vitamin_A.

If you scroll down the page of that site, you will see a large list of food sources in µg. But if you search for similar food sources on the following site, you will see similar food sources in IU;

http://www.healthaliciousness. com/articles/food-sources-of-vitamin-A.php

I think it is fair to say that cod liver oil is one of the richest sources of vitamin A, as the Wikipedia list confirms this at 30000 µg. But if you take sweet potato for example, on the Wikipedia site it is measured as 961 µg per 100 grams. On the Healthaliciousness site however, sweet potato, which is incidentally rated as one of, if not the most potent vegetable source of vitamin A, is stated as 19218IU per 100 grams, but also states its 'retinol' amount as 961 µg.

But please do not make the mistake of doing a simple calculation of dividing 19218 by 961 =

19.99792. Therefore concluding that 1 IU = 19.99792 µg as this would be incorrect. You will be able to calculate this way and get some surprisingly accurate figures. Take carrot for example, with 835 µg. If we multiply that by 19.99792 we get 16,698 and the actual IU is 17,033, so quite close. You could also take cantaloupe melon whose actual IU is 3382, and if you take its µg of 169 and multiply that by 19.99792 you get 3380, which is very accurate. But if you take mango whose µg is 38 and multiply that by 19.99792 you get 760, when its actual IU is 1082, so quite a bit of a difference there. All I would say is that it is possible to use this as a way to calculate some food sources, but I personally wouldn't want to rely on it as a definite way to convert in all cases.

The following list are examples of Vitamin A sources, in this case from Wikipedia: These are in order of potency.

» cod liver oil (30000 µg)

» liver (turkey) (8058 µg)

» liver (beef, pork, fish) (6500 µg)

» liver (chicken) (3296 µg)

» sweet potato (961 µg)

» carrot (835 µg)

» broccoli leaf (800 µg) please note there is a big difference between leaf and florets with broccoli florets only being (31 µg)

» kale (681 µg)

obviously there are many more examples but these are the most common with high potency of vitamin A.

All of the above are highly recommended sources for dogs, but for obvious reasons be very careful with cod liver oil as they are far more potent than the others and therefore a greater risk of toxicity. Other recommended sources are all other green leaf veg, corn, pumpkin and squash etc.

Vitamin A Deficiency – Vitamin A as you know, is a type of fat-soluble vitamin that comes from liver, dairy, and certain yellow vegetables. This vitamin is essential for the healthy formation of bones and teeth. It also plays a role in healthy skin, coat, and eyesight. A deficiency in Vitamin A may cause poor growth and development, skin problems, poor coat quality, eye problems, and immune problems. These deficiencies would be more problematic with dry food as apposed to canned.

Vitamin E

Vitamin E is a fat-soluble vitamin that plays a role in metabolizing fats and supporting healthy cell function; it is also a type of antioxidant. Sources of vitamin E include liver, vegetable oil, wheat germ, and leafy green vegetables. A deficiency of vitamin E can lead to reproductive disorders as well as disorders of the liver, heart, muscle, nerves, and eyes. It can also have a negative impact on your dog's bowels.

Free radicals that are present throughout your dogs body, pose a real problem in terms of cancer, premature ageing, arthritis, strokes etc. Free radicals are actually formed in the dogs fat tissues, and if left to sit there, can go rancid. Vitamin E, otherwise known as an antioxidant, is the best antidote for these free radicals.

Vitamin E combats so many problems that can affect your dog. Examples of this are; arresting premature ageing. Helping to prevent heart disease, blood clots that cause strokes. Acting as a barrier to disease, toxic heavy metals. Greatly aiding reproduction and energy production as well as producing vitamin C. Vitamin E is also necessary to help fight infection.

Vitamin E is also greatly needed if oils such as linseed oil, corn oil, sunflower oil, cod liver oil among others, are a significant part of your dogs diet. The major reason revolves around vitamin E preventing fat rancidity. When dogs ingest these types of polyunsaturated oils there is a risk they will go rancid, and vitamin E is the answer to make sure this doesn't happen. It is important to know that whilst vitamin E combats the effects of fat rancidity, the process of combating actually kills the vitamin E. So although it does the job your dog needs, it obviously needs replenishing. So feeding lots of polyunsaturated oil, without sufficient vitamin E in the system, will eventually lead to a deficiency and resulting disease.

It is recommended a 25kg dog for example, receives between 1 mg and 5 mg of Vitamin E per day

As we know 1 mg = 1000 µg (mcg), so if we want to find out the equivalent for 1 kg use the following;

A 25kg dog needs 1 to 5 mg, so that is 1000 µg to 5000 µg. So if we divide 1000 µg by 25kg we get 40 µg. So 1 kg = 40 µg. Do the same calculation for 5000 µg to get 200 µg.

So work out your dogs daily requirement by multiplying its weight in kg by between 40 µg and 200 µg. So again 25 x 40 is 1000 and 25 x 200 is 5000. If your dog weighs 10 kg then 10 x 40 is 400 µg and 10 x 200 is 2000 µg. So it is recommended that your dog receives between 40 and 200 µg per kilo of your dogs weight. Please note that these amounts would give your dog an adequate supply, not necessarily an optimum level, or even a toxic level. Once again, if your dog was receiving Vitamin E within those bounds recommended, please remember that they would need more if fish oils or polyunsaturated vegetable oils were regularly given.

Usually in this case it is recommended to supplement between 10 and 20 mg per day per kg of your dogs weight. So for a 10 kg dog, a safe dosage would be, 100 to 200 mg per day.

Sources for Vitamin E

High levels of vitamin E are found in dark leafy greens. They are also found in the polyunsaturated fats mentioned as causing a problem with rancidity. These are wheat germ oil, cottonseed, safflower, soybean etc. It may sound paradoxical, but although they have reasonably high levels of vitamin E, it only becomes a problem when the fat starts to go rancid. When this happens, as previously mentioned the vitamin E, counteracts this but in the process, dies off and so causing a deficiency.

Liver, eggs, certain grains as well as dairy produce are other good sources

Toxic side effects

Immediate large doses can cause temporary high blood pressure, but vitamin E is not known to cause any significant problems or side effects. Of course this does not mean you should administer large doses for the sake of it.

Vitamin D

You probably already know this as the sunshine vitamin, sunbathing or just spending short periods of time in direct sunlight, provides our bodies with vitamin D. However, if it is a cloudy day or the area is affected with airborne pollutants, mist, smoke etc., then the effects are greatly diminished and supplementation would be needed. The same goes for our dogs. It is thought that 10 to 15 minutes of 'direct' sunlight would provide our dogs with their 'recommended' daily dose.

Vitamin D plays an important function by aiding absorption of phosphorus and calcium. It also regulates the depositing and if need be, the withdrawing of calcium and phosphorus from the bones.

The main issue as to whether the dog is receiving enough vitamin D revolves around how much direct sunlight they are exposed to per day. If the dog is fed a meaty bones, BARF diet, and is exposed to even a small amount of sun per day, they will not need any supplementation. If that isn't the case, then they will probably need some form of supplementing.

Cod liver oil has always been seen as one of, if not the best source for vitamin D, but all the fish liver oils contain good amounts of vitamin D. Fish such as herring, catfish, salmon, trout, mackerel, sardine etc. are also great sources.

Toxic effects

Vitamin D is similar to vitamin A in that much care is needed to ensure your dog does not receive too much. One of the main problems involves calcium and the possibility that too much calcium is deposited in the body. This in turn can cause abnormal bodily functioning.

Recommended amounts

Vitamin D is particularly important for growing puppies as a deficiency can result in bone diseases such as rickets. If you notice a poor appetite and therefore poor growth and weight loss, then a deficiency of vitamin D could be the problem. Bone problems will be evident such as fractures, malformed or misshaped bones, enlarged joints etc.

The recommended daily dose for growing puppies per kilo body weight is 22 iu. It is suggested however, that that up to 100 iu per kg is a safe level. So a 4 kg puppy at this level can safely take 400 iu per day. As an example, the 450ml bottle of 'Seven Seas' cod liver oil that I have, suggests that 10ml (2 tea spoons) of oil contains 400 iu of vitamin D. However it also states that the same 10ml (2 tea spoons) would provide 4000 iu of vitamin A, which for a puppy would be a toxic level. So please be very careful with supplementing a puppies intake of fish oil such as cod liver oil. In this case, you could still give the puppy cod liver oil, but taking into consideration their recommended vitamin A limits. Also, be aware that potencies of cod liver oil supplies vary. Again check the 'iu' equivalent on the bottle as some may be stronger than others.

Deficiencies of vitamin D may well arise in dogs on a bad diet of poor quality commercially processed food, dogs predominantly fed meat, older dogs that have difficulty manufacturing vitamin D or even lack of sunlight.

Vitamin K

Vitamin K has a variety of health promoting uses. It is particularly important as a blood clotting agent, as well as growth, reproduction, healthy skin, anti ageing properties and as an antioxidant. There is an interesting connection with vitamin K and faeces, as vitamin K is produced in the large intestine, by bacteria which is then passed into the faeces of most animals. So if you see your dog eating another animals faeces, it could well be an indication of a vitamin K deficiency. It may not be,

but at least you know that they are actually getting nutritional benefits such as an intake of vitamin K. Incidentally faeces can provide high levels of protein, fatty acids, vitamins including B, K, antioxidants, minerals and fibre. Dogs that eat faeces may be indicating a lack of nutrients in their diet. But again, please do not automatically assume this is the case. I have known two dogs that were fed exactly the same diet and were both in excellent condition and yet one would regularly eat horse faeces whilst out on walks. This was never a significant amount. The dog in question would also stop at every puddle she passed and drink out of water containers left for horses. She could well be getting some mineral benefit but rightly or wrongly it was assumed she was one of those dogs that likes to pick at and taste anything.

Other sources of vitamin K are dark green leafy vegetables such as kale, chard, spinach etc. and other vegetables such as salad veg, brassica veg etc. Liver and fish are also good sources.

Vitamin K Toxicity

Natural vitamin K is actually non toxic, and it is unlikely your dog will eat enough natural foods in a day to cause an over load. However synthetically manufactured vitamin K can be toxic in high doses. Very high doses of over 100 times the recommended daily dose are likely to have a toxic effect. The recommended amount is up to 1 mg per kg of body weight.

Once again, providing your dog is receiving a BARF type diet with plenty of raw meaty bones, vegetables and other food sources, supplementation is unlikely.

Minerals – Minerals are a type of inorganic compound that cannot by synthesized and thus must come from your dog's diet. The most important minerals for dogs include calcium, phosphorus, Magnesium, Selenium, potassium, sodium, copper, zinc, and iron. Minerals are particularly important for developing and maintaining strong bones and teeth. Other ,

The two most important minerals for a dogs health, particularly the growing pup, and generally breeding and reproduction, are phosphorus and calcium. The main natural source of these in terms of a dogs diet are found in raw (not cooked) bones. As well as calcium and phosphorus, bones are also likely to store copper, chromium, iodine, iron, magnesium, manganese, potassium, selenium, strontium, zinc etc.

Dr. Ian Billinghurst, states in Give Your Dog a Bone

"Do realise your dog will not, cannot, suffer mineral deficiencies, imbalances or excesses, when raw meaty bones make up the bulk of its diet. This applies to dogs of all ages, including puppies. And I don't just mean puppies of the smaller breeds: I mean all breeds of puppies, including most definitely the giant breeds."

An imbalance of any essential vitamin, mineral or other element can obviously have major health consequences. But a major problem associated with mineral imbalance isn't necessarily a deficiency, but an over dose. Too much calcium can result in the calcium combining with other essential minerals such as zinc, iron, copper etc., and preventing the absorption of the zinc, iron, copper etc. This in turn would set up a deficiency of the zinc, iron, copper etc.

Too much sodium or salt can result in cardiovascular disease and hypertension. An excess of phosphorus can lead to diseases such as kidney failure. All of these problems can be the result of feeding dogs either poor quality commercial dog food, or over supplementation.

Problems with supplementation

Be very careful about supplementing in isolation. Calcium seems to be a big culprit of diseases and disorders for both growing pups as well as adult dogs. But because it is well known that calcium can negate other minerals, there is a temptation to supplement these other minerals such as zinc, copper and iron. There can be all manner of skin, skeletal growth and arthritic conditions associated with this kind of mineral imbalance. In fact any mineral that is supplemented in isolation can cause an overdose, imbalance and resulting disorder or disease.

Problems with blood tests etc. to establish deficiencies

Establishing a nutritional deficiency via a blood test should not be relied on as conclusive. The following link to an article highlighting this, indicates that certain blood tests have revealed no deficiency in particular diets. But after further investigation a serious deficiency has been diagnosed and successfully treated:

http://www.petmd.com/blogs/ thedailyvet/ktudor/2013/nov/why- blood-tests-are-not-good-for-testing- nutritional-status-in-pets-31029

Of course blood tests and other testing can in certain cases, be the most efficient way of diagnosing a problem. But again, where diet is concerned it is usually a question of elimination of symptoms and possible causes.

Water – Water is the most important nutrient for all animals. Your dog would be able to survive for a while without food if he had to, but he would only last a few days without water. Water accounts for as much as 70% of your dog's bodyweight and even a 10% decrease in your dog's body water levels can be very dangerous. Provide your Whippet with plenty of fresh water at all times.

It is common knowledge that tap water is processed using a number of chemicals and there is much debate as to possible links to cancer. Obviously the reasons for this chemical processing are to kill bacteria present in its raw state at sewage plants etc. Many people are now filtering tap water as a way to purify this tap water as much as possible. This is also a good idea for dogs. As you will regularly see dogs drinking out of puddles, another good idea is to try and recycle rain water. Admittedly in areas of pollution, there is a risk of acid rain etc., but there is a good chance that rain water will contain fewer potentially harmful chemicals than tap water.

b) The Importance of Diet – Nutritional Deficiencies

Although we cover diet in the feeding section, it is included here from a health, disease and deficiency point of view. As well as vitamin deficiencies mentioned above we will touch on mineral deficiencies here.

If you do not provide your dog with a healthy diet, his body will not be able to function as it should, and he may be more likely to develop illnesses and infections. In addition to providing your dog with high-quality dog food, you also need to make sure that his diet provides certain nutrients. Dogs are prone to developing certain nutritional deficiencies which can produce some very real and dangerous symptoms.

Some of the nutritional deficiencies to which your Whippet is most likely to be prone may include:

> » General malnutrition
>
> » Vitamin A deficiency
>
> » Magnesium deficiency
>
> » Iron deficiency anemia
>
> » Vitamin E deficiency
>
> » Calcium deficiency

General Malnutrition – Malnutrition is defined as the imbalanced, excessive, or insufficient consumption of nutrients. Some of the signs of malnutrition include an emaciated appearance, poor skin and coat quality, bad breath, swollen gums, abnormal stools, growth problems, poor immunity, lack of energy, and behavioural problems.

Magnesium Deficiency – Magnesium and potassium are the most abundant substances in cells, so a magnesium deficiency can be very serious. Magnesium is required for most metabolic functions and in the development of healthy bones and tissue. Symptoms of magnesium deficiency include weakness, trembling, depression, behavioural changes, and loss of coordination. Careful treatment for this deficiency is essential because too much magnesium can be fatal for your dog.

Iron Deficiency "Anaemia" – Iron is required to produce and develop red blood cells and those blood cells help to carry oxygen throughout your dog's body. A deficiency of iron can lead to anaemia, a condition in which your dog doesn't have enough healthy red blood cells to carry oxygen to organs and muscles. Symptoms of iron deficiency anaemia include loss of appetite, decreased growth, lethargy/weakness, depression, rapid breathing, and dark-colored stools.

Calcium Deficiency – Your dog requires a delicate balance of calcium and phosphorus to maintain healthy bones and teeth. Calcium is also important for nerve, heart and muscle function as well as blood clotting. A calcium deficiency can lead to spasms, lameness, heart palpitations, anxiety, bone fractures, arthritis, high blood pressure, and more. This type of deficiency is often caused by a high-meat diet because meat is very high in phosphorus. This can lead to an imbalance of phosphorus and calcium.

Additional Problems with calcium excess

Dried food has been more of a problem of calcium excess, with some cases showing up to a dozen times the amount actually needed. Obviously from a growth point of view calcium is a vital nutrient. However, in excess the calcium not absorbed by the body is eventually excreted in the faeces. The problem, as you have already learned, is that calcium combines with other essential minerals such as zinc and results in the zinc not being absorbed by the body. However, as well as zinc, copper and iron are affected in the same way which can result in anaemia. Where zinc deficiency occurs, the aforementioned problems associated with skin diseases, stunted growth in pups, reproductive and immunity problems are likely to manifest. In addition wounds take longer to heal, the nervous system is affected, bone abnormalities occur, testicular growth is affected, the thyroid gland doesn't function properly, the body loses protein, etc. To say the least, the results of a zinc deficiency are pretty grim.

An excess of calcium is also known to be a contributory factor in dogs suffering with bloat. When the body detects a calcium excess is produces 'gastrin', which is a hormone that thickens the ends of the stomach and makes the expulsion of gases difficult to pass.

So again, in addition to deficiencies in certain vitamins or minerals, dogs can also suffer from an excess of certain nutrients. For example, too much vitamin A can cause your Whippet's bones to become brittle and his skin to become dry. An excess of vitamin D could cause your dog's bones to become too dense and for his tissue and joints to calcify. Too much vitamin C can lead to kidney stones, excess calcium can lead to phosphorus imbalances, and too much polyunsaturated fat (such as from fish oil) may lead to a vitamin E imbalance.

c) Calorie Requirements for Dogs

Your dog requires a certain number of calories each day in order for his body to maintain proper function. Calorie needs for dogs vary from one breed to another and they also depend on the dog's age, size, sex, and activity level.

On the next page you will find a chart outlining the basic calorie needs for dogs at different ages:

The calorie information in the chart above is a basic guideline. Your dog's individual needs may be different. The best way to determine how many calories your Whippet actually needs is to calculate his Resting Energy Requirement (RER), and to then modify it according to his age and activity level. The formula for calculating your dog's RER is as follows:

$$RER = 30 \text{ x (weight in kg)} + 70$$

For example, if your dog weighed 45 pounds, you would use the following formula: RER = 30 x (45/2.205) +70. So (45/2.205) = 20.40816327, then multiply that by 30 = 612.244898, then add 70 = 682 rounded down to the nearest whole number. You will note that in order to determine your dog's weight in kilograms you need to divide it by 2.205 first. So using our formula and the example given as shown above, a 45-pound dog has an estimated RER of about 682 calories. To determine your dog's daily energy requirements you will need to multiply his RER by a factor that varies by age and activity level. Use the

Calorie Needs For Dogs (Per Day)

Type of Dog	10 Lbs	15 Lbs	20 Lbs
Puppy (Under 4 Months)	618 Calories	-	-
Puppy (Over 4 Months)	412 Calories	-	-
Normal Adult Dog	329 Calories	438 Calories	547 Calories
Active Adult Dog	412 Calories	548 Calories	684 Calories
Pregnant Female	618 Calories	822 Calories	1,026 Calories
Lactating Female	824+ Calories	1,096+ Calories	1,368+ Calories

chart on the next page to determine what number to multiply your dog's RER by:

So following on, if we use another example, in this case our 20 Lb dog in the chart, to get to 684 we calculate as follows:

20 divided by 2.205 = 9.070295. 9.070295 x 30 = 272.1088. 272.1088 + 70 = 342.1088

Now taking into consideration the activity level of the dog as light so multiply the RER by 2; we multiply 342.1088 by 2 = 684 rounded to the nearest whole number

Based on the information in the RER chart on the next page, you can see that puppies and pregnant dogs have much higher calorie needs than adult dogs. When your Whippet puppy is growing he will need to eat a lot more than he will when he is fully grown. Puppy foods are typically higher in both protein and calories than adult dog foods. This accounts for the needs of growing puppies. In pregnant females you typically do not need to start increasing rations until the last three weeks of gestation. Once the dog gives birth, her calorie needs will increase again so that she can produce enough milk for her puppies. The more puppies in the litter, the higher her calorie needs will be.

When your dog gets older, his calorie needs will drop. Senior dogs typically require 20% fewer calories than younger dogs because their metabolisms slow down and they

Resting Energy Requirements (RER)

Type of Dog	Daily Calorie needs
Weight Loss	1.0 x RER
Normal Adult (Neutered)	1.6 x RER
Normal Adult (Intact)	1.8 x RER
Lightly Active Adult	2.0 x RER
Moderately Active Adult	3.0 x RER
Pregnant (First 42 Days)	1.8 x RER
Pregnant (Last 21 Days)	3.0 x RER
Lactating Female	4.8 x RER
Puppy (2 to 4 Months)	3.0 x RER
Puppy (4 to 12 Months)	2.0 x RER

become less active. Many dogs become overweight as they age because their owners do not reduce their feeding portions to account for changes in metabolism and energy. Once a dog becomes obese it can be difficult for him to lose weight, so be especially careful with your dog's diet once he reaches "senior" level around 7 years of age.

So what is a good diet choice for your Whippet dog? Well you have many options and some dog owners like to mix and match, to keep things interesting for your dog.

d) How to Choose a Healthy Dog Food

Now that you have a basic understanding of your dog's nutritional needs you are ready to learn how to choose a healthy dog food. If you walk down the aisles at your local pet store you could easily be overwhelmed by the sheer number of options you have. Not only are there many different brands to choose from but most brands offer several different flavours or formulas. In this section you will learn the basics about how to determine whether a commercial dog food is

healthy or not.

Commercial Dog Food

The history of commercial dog food goes back to the 1850s when it was first manufactured in England. This product largely consisted of processed bone meal and cereals. Some 30 odd years later U.S. mill owners realised the huge profit potential of taking their by-products and turning it into dog food. In 1922 the first type of canned dog food was produced using horse meat. This basic idea is still used today with a few modifications. In an age where millions are spent on advertising, it is no surprise that commercially produced dog food is the most well known and unfortunately, popular method of feeding our pets.

Do not rule out a great quality dried food mixed with wet food of some type. When you are choosing a commercial food though, keep in mind that less is more. Don't look at the promises on the packaging, but turn it around and look at the ingredients on the back, this will tell you so much more.

If there is anything that you don't recognize don't buy the food until you have found out what the ingredient is. If the main ingredient is some kind of meat followed by the words 'meal' or 'derivatives' don't buy the food.

In our fast paced world were fast food chains flourish and ready meals fill supermarket shelves, it is unsurprising that dogs are fed in the same way. It has to be said, opening a tin of dog food or feeding a few scoops of kibble takes a few minutes of our time. Tinned stuff can be stored anywhere for years and an opened bag of kibble will remain relatively fresh for a month or so. All we need are the food manufacturers to feed us with words such as 'healthy', 'nutritious', 'premium', 'complete', 'balanced diet' and we are sold. I personally have mixed feelings about commercial foods. Again some brands are better than others and if you are pushed for time initially then it can offer an OK temporary alternative. I would not however, recommend this in the long term. I would at the very least incorporate raw natural foods, preferably a permanent BARF diet.

Get Cooking

Your second option is to cook your dog's food at home.

This is actually quite easy and there is no reason why you can't alternate between home prepared dog food and a good quality commercial food. Variety is the spice of life after all, and this applies to dogs too.

A careful mix of sweet potatoes, green leafy veggies, beans and legumes with added white fish or other protein source is a perfect homemade dog's dinner. Adding some type of oil is also good for the coat and the joints. Again, please do read the section on essential fatty acids and the various suitable oils.

If you make a big pot of food at a time and vary the types of carbohydrate and protein, then you should easily meet all of your dog's vitamin and mineral needs over a few weeks recurring.

However, be careful with home cooked food and realise that even though you know what has gone into this food, it may be deficient in certain nutrients. What some people tend to do to be extra sure that they are meeting their dog's nutritional needs is usually along the following lines. They alternate between commercial food and home-made then add a digestive enzyme with vitamin supplement prepared for your dog. Surely the fact that they are having to add a digestive enzyme and vitamin and mineral supplement indicates that the food is deficient in some way.

Why food is cooked

Wild feral dogs and wolves will eat rotten 'contaminated', flesh and bones, other animal faeces, animal guts etc. In other words, food that we would consider infected, laden with germs likely to make us ill. But for the dog, these are a rich source of nutrients the dog needs such as enzymes, vitamins, proteins, antioxidants, fatty acids etc. The digestive system of the feral dog is actually no different to the domesticated dog.

We view cooking as necessary as it breaks food down, making it more digestible for humans. Again the digestion of dogs is somewhat different to us, and the digestive system of domestic dogs is actually not dissimilar to its ancestor the wolf.

Many dog owners will assert that they feed their dogs cooked food and the dogs thrive and show no obvious immediate signs of ill health. The point is, the dogs are unlikely to die immediately, but there is a likelihood for them to gradually show signs of ill health and premature aging, resulting in an early death.

The main reason commercially produced dog food is cooked is to kill germs and parasites. Cooking also destroys much of the vitamin content and food therefore loses much of its nutritious value. Furthermore, cooking destroys antioxidants which again combat the effects of aging. Lysine and methionine, two essential amino acids are also thought to be destroyed by the cooking process. Without them, the dogs health in general and resistance to disease is affected. Problems associated with general growth, skin, bones as well as problems associated with pregnancy can also manifest.

The cooking process actually changes the molecular structure of food and affects the digestibility of proteins for dogs. This change results in the food becoming foreign to the body which can cause allergic reactions, indigestion and at worse, be carcinogenic.

Unfortunately, cooking additionally destroys enzymes. Living enzymes naturally break food down until it decays. Cooking kills the enzymes and therefore slows this process down, which means the food can be stored for longer. This is great news for the commercial dog food industry and us the buyer to an extent, but a lot less so for the dogs.

Enzymes present in raw food are proteins which not only aid the digestive system, but actually slow down the aging process. As well as aiding digestion, food enzymes are known to have major health benefits for dogs. These include: as well as anti aging, pancreas functioning, alleviating joint disease and arthritis. Lack of enzymes also contributes to a process known as 'cross linking'. Cross linking is a devastating aging process that contributes to inelastic wrinkled skin, hardened arteries, damaged genes resulting

in reproductive problems, birth defects and at worst cancer. Other diseases associated with premature aging include heart disease, kidney disease and arthritis.

It is generally the pancreas which produces enzymes. If sufficient enzymes are present in food, then the pancreas does not have to produce any extra. If the required enzymes are not present, then the pancreas has to work to produce them. If the pancreas is overworked, then certain conditions and diseases can appear such as Pancreatitis and diabetes.

Problems with home cooked dog food

» Lack of essential fatty acids

» A soft mush and therefore nothing to chew on to promote dental health

» Generally contains rice, pasta or other grain/ cereal based ingredients and therefore not dissimilar to commercially processed foods

» Problems associated with cooking i.e. killing of enzymes, vitamin and mineral degeneration, lack of antioxidants.

Again because of the combined stew/cooking, the same problems associated with mineral combination will occur, such as zinc and calcium.

Problems with feeding table scraps

In all probability, table scraps are unlikely to represent a complete diet. They are bound to be lacking in essential nutrients such as protein, calcium and other essential vitamins and minerals. They are also likely to be high in meat trimming such as fat or from gravy, and carbohydrates such as vegetables. Of course this sort of diet is likely to be very palatable for the dog, but particularly if high fat sources were given, would quickly lead to obesity. Many vets advocate that whilst perfectly acceptable in moderation and on occasion, table scraps should certainly not represent the bulk of a dogs diet.

Raw Feeding

Over the last few years raw feeding has become increasingly popular and most that try it never go back to cooked food for their pets. Raw feeding is so popular that manufacturers are preparing raw food in the same way as they have been preparing cooked food for years.

The idea behind this feeding type is that the dog's diet is as natural as possible. It is based upon the diet a wild carnivore would eat. Some meat and offal, some bones and green vegetables; all raw are fed to the dog in order to mirror the wild diet. The wild diet would usually have been small prey animals, grass, greens and bones.

Advocates of this feeding type usually state that it is the best decision that they have ever made on behalf of their dog whilst there are very few that turn away from raw feeding after trial-ing it.

There are some precautions to be aware of if you are considering raw feeding though. There have been some links between infection of arthritic joints and raw meat. Similarly too many raw bones can cause digestive blockages. Some experts also believe that our dogs were more scavengers as they developed and ate less meat than we think.

I suggest that if this feeding type is something you may consider, then do a lot of research first. The commercial raw foods are varying in quality much like the commercial cooked dog foods. If you are putting your dog's diet together at home then it's vital to consider varied and balanced nutrition.

If you are changing your dog's food at all then remember to wean gradually from one to the other as a quick change can easily be the cause of stomach upsets.

Barf Diet

The BARF diet (Biologically Appropriate Raw Food Diet) was first developed by veterinarian, Dr.Ian Billinghurst. The BARF diet contains thoroughly ground raw and meaty bones, raw vegetables, raw offal and supplements. You can find these in patty form, which you can break up into bits when feeding your adult Whippet. Although Dr. Billinghurst suggests it is safe to feed raw meaty bones to growing puppies, some breeders and vets are against the idea, for reasons such as upset stomachs and the need to build them up to such a diet. He does however say in his book 'Give Your Dog A Bone' that he has successfully reared puppies on such a diet. He goes on to say that he would start them on minced chicken wings, bone and all, then soon after give them the whole chicken wing and so on.

If this interests you, please do refer to one of the excellent books I mention below. By the way, I am in no way affiliated or connected to the authors, they are books that many forum contributors recommend and that I have personally read and found useful and inspiring.

Many veterinarians have claimed that this diet helps dogs with skin disorders, which are allergic to grain, preservatives, and other added ingredients found in commercial brands.

There has also been some negative feedback about this diet, such as the threat of Salmonella and Listeria monocytogenes strains. This has been predominantly asserted by the FDA.

I have to say that I am a great believer in feeding raw meaty bones and there have been some excellent studies and books written. As mentioned, Ian Billinghurst an Australian Vet and Nutritionist originally proposed the idea that dogs have become ill and are dying prematurely because they have been deprived of their natural inheritance, 'raw meat and bones'. His books are still available but quite expensive, but his best seller 'Give Your Dog A Bone', is available reasonably cheaply as a Kindle download. The book is excellent and is well worth a read. I have only predominantly fed raw meaty bones and other raw ingredients to adult dogs, but I cannot comment on his assertion that it is perfectly acceptable to feed pups a BARF diet. In my experience, my dogs have not only looked much brighter, fitter and healthier, but their stools are more solid and their breath has been relatively odourless.

Other excellent books covering the subject include:

'Raw Meaty Bones' and 'Work Wonders' both by Dr Tom Lonsdale. 'Raw and Natural Nutrition for Dog, by Lew Olson PhD. Also 'Natural Nutrition for Dogs and Cats' by Kymythy R. Shultze.

I think if I have to sum up the message for BARF, raw meaty bones feeding, it is that you need to ask questions of the whole commercial food industry and that feeding a more natural primitive diet will provide your dog with greater health and longevity. Probably on a par with only buying puppies that come from reputable breeders who health test the parents, I would say nutrition is the other most important consideration regarding the health and happiness of your dog. Of course obedience training and knowledge of your dogs behaviour are important aspects for successfully keeping a happy relationship with your new friend. But I believe too much emphasis is placed on 'Dog Whisperers' and their training been the be all and end all. If your dog is not healthy, it will not be happy. Ask yourself the following questions: Would you rather spend a small fortune on regular visits to the vet over the duration of your dogs life? Or would you rather your dog is happy and healthy and destined to live a longer life, with far fewer visits to the vet? Please do consider the BARF diet at whatever stage of life your dog is.

Points to bear in mind with feeding a raw diet.

Chewing raw meat and bones exercises and massages the teeth and gums, above all keeping them clean. If the teeth and gums becomes diseased and infected, they create toxins and bacteria which will be ingested and contribute to ill health.

It is important that you keep any raw food separate from your own, for obvious reasons of cross contamination. This includes thoroughly cleaning surfaces and utensils with hot soapy water and anti-bacterial sprays suitable for food surfaces.

Fresh meat and bones will need refrigerating, but there is nothing to stop you buying in bulk and freezing portions. Any refrigerated food can be kept in seal-able food storage containers.

To a certain extent frozen food loses some nutritional value, but is far more beneficial than cooked/processed food.

Summarized list of raw BARF diet foods

» Raw meaty bones and muscle meat from: chicken, pork, beef, rabbit and lamb

» Offal/organ meats: liver, kidney, heart etc.

» Eggs

» Dairy produce: milk, butter, cheese, yoghurt.

» Seafood: All oily fish

» Vegetables: Dark green leaves, brassicas, root veg, salad veg etc.

» Fruits: Most fruits but definitely not grapes and the dried varieties such as raisins, sultanas etc.

» In addition brewers yeast as an excellent source of the B complex vitamins.

» The polyunsaturated oils mentioned.

Food separation and combination

Food combination and separation relates to the idea that food should be neither cooked nor combined in one complete diet. The premise of the commercially processed food is that the 'complete balanced' diet is cooked and contains a combination of food groups that the dog receives at each and every meal.

Ian Billinghurst suggests that wild dogs, feral dogs or whatever, will never eat a balanced meal (in other words, all of the food groups represented in one meal) and that a balanced diet is reached over time. So he suggests that one meal is likely to consist of entirely vegetarian in the form of the stomach contents or guts of a herbivore killed (This is usually the first thing a carnivore will eat, particularly if it is starving and needs to be nourished quickly). Another meal will be offal; liver, kidney, heart etc. Another will be muscle. Another, predominantly fat. Yet another will be entirely bones, which may well be one of the final parts of the animal eaten as all the rest is picked and stripped over a number of days.

So if the dog took this approach, day one would consist of all of the vitamins, minerals, carbohydrates and fibre mentioned as part of the vegetation food group. Day two is likely to be partly protein, but also the vitamins and other elements associated with liver and the other offal meats. Day three would be mostly protein. Day four would be mostly essential fatty acids via the fat. Day five would be mostly the minerals of the bones. So in this hypothetical scenario over a 5 day cycle the dog has received protein on mainly one day, vegetation on mainly one day, essential fatty acid on only one day. To be fair, vitamins, minerals and other elements will be present on each day, but not in the concentrations assumed for protein or carbohydrates or essential fatty acids.

Food combining is particularly problematic where calcium is concerned. As previously noted, calcium causes all sorts of problems with the absorption of essential minerals such as zinc, copper and iron. So it would be best to feed a product that has very little calcium but a good source of zinc, copper, iron and other minerals, separately from a relatively high calcium intake. Feeding offal, such as liver, kidneys, heart etc., allows your dog to feed in this way, similar to the way it would feed on a wild kill. It generally would have its daily feed of offal, and as offal is digested relatively quickly this should mean that any bone/calcium absorption should not interfere with the mineral absorption.

The advantage with a food separation diet is that certain raw foods that may seem high in certain elements are really not being given on a constant every day basis. One of the big problems with processed foods are that a lot of the same elements such as calcium and phosphorus, protein and salt, are given daily. The result of that is an overload of those nutrients and all of the consequential problems on various organs of the body, such as overworked kidneys, liver etc.

A lot of the food separation practice involves keeping proteins and starch foods separate and therefore promoting greater health.

Raw meaty bones should be fed separately from other elements such as the vegetables. The key to a healthy balanced diet is not the way dogs are fed on a commercially processed diet. In this case, they receive every element, i.e. protein, carbohydrate, fats, vitamins, minerals etc. all in one go, and on each day. This causes a lot of problems in the natural functioning of the dogs body. The correct, natural way should be to make each meal different and separate the different elements to ensure no overload takes place and no mixing of certain elements likely to conflict with each other.

Balanced diet in this case is your dogs natural eating habits take place, and not the artificially forced balance of commercially processed foods. In a sense, we are bound to eat different meals each day, but they are bound to be a combination of protein, carbohydrate and fat, with the associated vitamins and minerals of those foods. Dogs are not designed to eat that way.

Feeding bones to dogs

There seems to be a common misconception that feeding bones to dogs is dangerous. There are obviously many horror stories of bones splintering and causing internal bleeding, bones having to be surgically removed, impacted bones in the gut, dogs having bones hanging out of their rear end as they try to pass them, etc. Most of these problems however, happen with cooked bones. Bones that are cooked effectively dry out and lose their relative elasticity and become hard, brittle and splinter prone.

Raw bones

Raw bones, despite their hard, solid form are still living tissue full of nutrients. As well as marrow, essential fat, anti oxidant properties and enzymes, they also contain calcium and phosphorus in a perfect balance, necessary for a dogs needs. As previously noted the raw meaty bone/BARF diet is also suit-able for growing puppies as well as older dogs. In fact many owners and breeders insists this is their preferred way of raising puppies. This is particularly the case when we consider that puppies require sufficient phosphorus and calcium whilst growing and raw meaty bones take away the guess work of how much calcium and phosphorus you would otherwise have to feed if feeding processed food. Again, Ian Billinghurst states that bones actually contain the exact proportions of calcium and phosphorus needed. Again this has been a problem where some breeders over supplement calcium, when feeding a commercial diet.

Raw meaty bones also provide all of the essential amino acids your dog needs.

Incidentally, from the point of view of essential fatty acids, pork and chicken bones are a richer source than beef and lamb, which have relatively low amounts. That isn't to say that you should not feed beef and lamb bones also. They do have the same mineral and protein value, but lack the same high level of essential fatty acids that pork and chicken have.

Raw bones are also excellent sources of the fat soluble vitamins A, D and E. When bones are cooked, those vitamins are lost, which is another important reason why you should never feed dogs cooked bones. Cooking bones also destroys much of the nutrients of the bone marrow. Similarly to the A, D and E vitamins, the marrow is an excellent source of nutrients vital for a strong immune system. This not only fights infection and generally keeps our dogs in peak health, but also promotes longevity.

As well as the meat component, the bone in combination is said to provide the dog with its entire protein requirements. However, caution must be exercised where a dog has become obese. Please bear in mind that feeding raw meaty bones is an important addition for any dog. But because of the highly nutritious energy giving properties of raw meaty bones, giving too many will only add to the obesity. But again, please do include a moderate amount regularly as part of their diet.

It is suggested by advocates of raw meaty bones feeding that they will in themselves provide just about every nutrient your dog will need.

The benefits include:

» All of the important minerals

» Essential fatty acids

» Vitamins A, D and E (as previously noted, the K vitamin is manufactured in the bowel of the dog)

» Enzymes

» Antioxidants

» Optimum protein needs

» Most of the B vitamins (as well as vitamin C to an extent, dogs produce their own B complex vitamins)

» Blood forming and immunity benefits of marrow

A raw meaty bone diet is suitable for every dog whether Rottweiler or Pug. It is also suitable for every age group. In essence it is suitable for lactating female dogs, working dogs, growing pups, senior dogs, as long as their teeth are sound.

Buried bones

Raw buried bones will gradually decompose with their own natural enzymes, and should be perfectly healthy for dogs to eat. The cooking process of bones however, kills the enzymes and although they still decompose, it is bacteria that is involved, which in turn can produce toxins that could make your dog seriously ill. Incidentally, the likely reason your dog is burying bones is over feeding. So their natural survival instinct takes over, and any left over is saved for later.

Teeth cleaning

If dogs are not given the opportunity to chew, rip and crush bones, such as when they are fed soft processed food, their teeth and gums will suffer. The very action of chewing on meat and bones generally cleans the teeth, scrapes away tarter, massages the gums and teeth. The obvious advantages of this are a lack of gum disease, tooth decay, abscesses and a decreased chance of the body being poisoned via an infected mouth. In addition, the breath of bone chewing dogs rarely smells.

Problems feeding mostly organ meat

Constant feeding of heart, kidney, steak, tongue, liver etc., have been known in the long term to produce an imbalance and consequent disease. One such case involved the dog developing hepatitis which manifested in lethargy, arthritis, skin disease as well as high cholesterol. This type of diet produced an overload of protein, phosphorus, Vitamin A and a deficiency of calcium.

Problems feeding mostly fish

Certain raw fish contains an enzyme that destroys B1 vitamins. Oily fish fats affect Vitamin E. This is usually more significant if fillets of fish are given and not whole fish. The dog would benefit from eating the bones, head, internal organs that are all likely to contain the necessary B and E vitamins. Once again, feeding fish occasionally is perfectly acceptable, but as a main dietary source will cause all manner of complications.

Problems feeding mostly meat

A dogs diet consisting of mostly meat and in particular cooked meat, can result in diseases associated with skin diseases such as eczema, heart and kidney disease, arthritis and at worse cancer.

Similarly as above with an all offal diet, a meat only diet, is significantly lacking in calcium to the extent that they would only be receiving about 5% of their actual requirements. As you may well expect, the main problem with all meat is the concentration of protein. In addition, phosphorus levels are excessive. There would also be notable deficiencies of Vitamins A, D and E together with copper and iodine. The lack of calcium as well as the other vitamins and minerals deficiencies, in particular would also be extremely detrimental to a growing puppy. Even if these were supplemented in some way, it is never advisable and there are much better, safer ways of feeding them. But again, as with the other specific food only diets, in moderation meat is an essential component of a balanced diet.

e) Types of Commercial Dog Food

There are three main types of commercial dog food; wet, dry, and semi-moist. Dry dog foods are the most commonly used and they are also referred to as "kibble". This type of food is typically packed in a bag and they are usually extruded in the form of pellets. Dry dog foods come in a wide variety of flavours and formulas and they have a fairly low moisture content. Wet dog food obviously has a higher moisture content. They are typically cooked at very high temperatures to sterilize them and then packaged in pressure-sealed containers. Semi-moist dog foods come in the form of soft, chewy pellets typically packaged in pouches or sachets.

In addition to these types of commercial dog food there are a few other options. Dehydrated dog food is becoming popular among pet owners who want to feed their dog's fresh or raw food but who want a product with a longer shelf life. Fresh dog food comes in refrigerated or frozen varieties and it is one of the most expensive options when it comes to commercial dog food. Fresh dog food can also be freeze-dried to remove most of the moisture content (thereby increasing the shelf life) without resulting in a loss of nutrients by cooking.

The type of dog food you choose for your Whippet is largely a matter of preference. Most dog owners choose dry food because it is the most cost-effective option and because it lasts the longest. If your dog has food allergies or special dietary restrictions, a fresh or frozen dog food may be a better option because these foods are often made with limited ingredients. Senior dogs, who have trouble chewing dry food may prefer moist or semi-moist foods. You can also just soak dry food in water or broth to soften it.

Problems with dry food

Dried processed formulas are the cheapest and most convenient to use but are generally the worst of all the processed dog foods.

» Processed food, particularly dried 'kibble' has in some cases been found to contain an insufficient amount of zinc

» Generally made up of ground cooked bone and offal with cereal

» They have a low nutritional value and are hard to digest.

» Contain excess calcium and starch

» These large amounts of calcium can cause bloat and bone problems. Calcium is also responsible for zinc deficiency, because when calcium combines with zinc it results in a mixture that cannot be absorbed.

» Zinc is an essential ingredient and a lack of it can result in problems associated with growth, skin, infertility, pancreatitis, diabetes etc.

» Low in vitamins, minerals, protein, essential fatty acids and promotes tarter build up

» Lack of essential fatty acids contributes to skin diseases and problems associated with growth and reproduction

As most dry feed contains insufficient amounts of essential fatty acids this to large extent is a major contributory factor to severe skin conditions. The conventional drugs and medical treatments used to treat these conditions, generate massive revenues to the veterinary medical industry year in year out. Money wasted by you the consumer not to mention the discomfort and suffering to the dog.

» Fats and vitamins that are present, quickly deteriorate resulting in an even lower nutritional value after only a few weeks.

» Low in energy value and high in insoluble fibre

» Can cause bladder infections and stones which can result in difficulty passing urine and may require surgery or special diets to remove the obstruction

Problems with semi-moist food

This is considered to be marginally better than dry dog food. The energy levels are higher due to an increased carbohydrate content derived from ingredients such as corn syrup

They contain a low water content, about 30% and certain additives/preservatives to give them a greater shelf life.

As they have a similar composition to dry food, they are also associated with much the same diseases and other health issues.

Problems with canned food

There is a very high water content present in canned food, approxi-mately 80%. So in other words, what nutritional value that remains makes up only 20% of what you are buying.

The cost of buying tinned dog food in comparison to dry food is usually at least double. Again the ingredients are similar to the other processed foods, but in general the percentage of cereal is less and animal derivatives, more.

They are also in general more palatable to dogs than the others probably due to the moist meaty texture.

As with all canned products, their two main advantages are a greater shelf life and are extremely convenient. Other than that, they carry the same health problems as the other types of processed foods.

Problems with tarter build up

Where dogs are given the opportunity to rip, tear and crunch raw meaty bones their teeth are cleaned and gums massaged. With processed foods this function is lost. Even dry food where it is thought that the dry composition has an abrasive, cleaning effect. The result of chewing raw meaty bones, is that their mouth generally remains healthy and odour free. Contrast this with dogs fed on processed food and we take it for granted that the rancid 'dogs breath' is normal.

The high levels of carbohydrate and calcium in processed foods are thought to be a major contributing factor to tarter build up that attacks the teeth and gums. Eventually this leads to serious gum disease and tooth decay. Tartar harbours bacteria, which in turn feed off and thrives on the carbohydrates present in processed food. These bacteria attack and infect the mouth in general and specifically the teeth and gums causing painful gum infections and tooth decay, resulting in rancid breath and ultimately tooth loss.

In 1993 it was reported that 90% of dogs in the U.S.A ate processed dog food. In addition, veterinary dental treatment was said to represent over one third of vets income. In 2014 according to some surveys, processed dog food consumption was thought to be around 85%

Not only does this mouth bacteria cause serious localized problems, but the bacteria has a general toxic effect on the whole body, causing general ill health. The bacteria enters the blood stream and seriously affects the major organs of the body causing diseases of the lungs, heart, kidneys and reproductive organs etc.

As the legal obligation of manufacturers is that their 'complete formulas', contain a minimum level of certain nutrients, it is fair to assume that there isn't necessarily a specified amount. Some scientific analysis carried out in Australia showed certain foods contained less vitamins than the legal requirement. In some cases there was an excess. Obviously if your dog requires a certain level of nutrients for optimum health, if this is lacking they will develop diseases associated with a deficiency. In a similar way, an overload of certain vitamins or minerals can cause diseases and health problems. Excess protein for example can cause kidney disease. Excess sodium is associated with heart disease. As you know excess calcium causes zinc deficiency as well as growth problems and bloat. Over time, this can result in the devastating effect of major organ failure.

Why the complete/balanced diet, that commercial packaging promotes such as problem

The idea of having a complete balanced diet in one convenient package sounds like a great idea. The problem is, as we have already discovered, if certain elements such as calcium are allowed to interact with other essential minerals such as zinc and copper, they result in indigestibility of those minerals. The complete diet which effectively combines a whole host of nutrients means that if it is the only source of zinc or copper etc., then the body will likely not be absorbing those elements which results in a deficiency. The same problem occurs when B complex vitamins go through the heat process of cooking and also interact with other certain elements. They too can become immobilized and not ingested.

So the problem arises when we attempt to feed the dog all of the elements combined. Once again, by combining certain elements, they interact and interfere with their individual effectiveness. In its wild primitive state, the dog would be unlikely to ever get a chance to have all of those elements together in one meal.

There are similar problems when mixing protein and starch. Early scientific research into digestion feed trials for dogs, largely involved the separate feeding of starch rich foods and protein. Significant results were noted that dramatically altered the health of patients.

f) Reading the Ingredients List

Again, legal requirements state that food contains minimum recommended amounts of certain nutrients. Labelling does not necessarily have to state that the food will be the best option in terms of your dogs health, longevity, reproduction, growth. There will certainly be no mention that the food will probably lead to a premature death and a number of associated health issues.

Some of the reasons manufacturers process dog food the way they do include: greater shelf life and the ability to take questionable ingredients and make a product more appealing to the consumer, namely us the public.

As previously mentioned, in order to create this greater shelf life, most of the nutrients or everything that would otherwise benefit the dog, such as enzymes and micro organisms, have to be removed. The most efficient way of doing this is by cooking. Preservatives such as salt and sugar will be added which in addition to promoting a greater shelf life, also make them more appetising to the dog.

Having said that, as previously noted, commercially produced dog food seems to be the most popular option for dog owners. Like many other dog owners, you have the choice to feed your dog this way if you wish. As with most products, some are better than others. If you do opt for processed dog foods, whether as a temporary measure or otherwise, please do take the time to evaluate different brands and formulas. The best way to do this is by looking at the label and the ingredients list. For customers in the U.S.A, when you evaluate a bag of dog food for instance, the first thing you should look for is a statement of nutritional adequacy from the American Association of Feed Control Officials (AAFCO). The statement should look something like this:

"[Product Name] is formulated to meet the nutritional levels established by the AAFCO Dog Food nutrient profiles for [Life Stage]."

The American Association of Feed Control Officials is responsible for monitoring and regulating what goes into animal feed including pet foods. This organization has set standards that pet foods must meet in order to be considered nutritionally adequate for dogs in certain life stages; puppy, adult, and senior. If the dog food label does not carry an AAFCO statement of nutritional adequacy, you should move on to another option. On the other hand, just because a product carries the AAFCO statement doesn't necessarily mean that it is good for your dog.

In the United Kingdom, the Pet Food Manufacturer's Association (PFMA) exists to provide pet owners with guidance for selecting pet foods. This organization is the principal trade body for the U.K. pet food industry with more than 70 member companies, representing about 90% of the U.K. pet food market. The PFMA does not put a statement on pet food labels in the same way as AAFCO; but they do strive to raise pet food industry standards and to promote pet food products deemed as safe and nutritious.

However, there is also a new fact sheet on labelling with regards to the pet food ingredients list. As a Whippet dog owner you should always be checking and improving your dogs health, wellbeing, weight and shape. PFMA has a downloadable Dog Size-O-Meter that you can keep on hand. For more information, visit:

pfma.org.uk/dog-pet-size-o-meter/

Everything that we eat contributes to our health. The same will apply to your Whippet. He is entirely dependent on what you feed him. Keep in mind that although you may be thinking that your Whippet looks healthy enough, it takes years for a not so healthy dog food to take its toll on your Whippet's health.

For more information about pet food labelling standards in the U.K., visit the PFMA website here:

http://www.pfma.org.uk/labelling

The European Pet Food Industry Federation

This federation was formed in 1970 and represents the pet food industry in 26 countries. This representation is carried out via their network of 18 national or regional pet food industry associations. The main goal of this federation is to promote the views and interests of around 650 European pet food producing companies. Its goal is to make sure that all pet food manufactured is safe, nutritious and palatable. For more information, visit:

http://www.fediaf.org/who-we-are/

The U.S. Food and Drug Administration (FDA)

The FDA releases press releases regarding pet food recalls from the firms involved. The FDA is an organization that consists of the Office of the Commissioner and four directorates overseeing core functions of the agency. To learn more, visit:

http://www.fda.gov
also *http://www.foodsafety.gov/*

The best way to truly evaluate the nutritional value of a pet food is to examine the ingredients list. Dog food labels include a complete list of ingredients that is organized in descending order by volume. This means that the ingredients present in the highest quantity/volume appear at the beginning of the list. This makes it easy for you to get a quick sense of a product's nutritional value. If the first few ingredients are healthy ingredients, the product is probably a good choice. If however, the first few ingredients are low-quality fillers, you should move on.

When evaluating the ingredients list for a commercial dog food, you want to see a high-quality source of protein listed first. Fresh meats like chicken, turkey, beef, and fish are good options but do not be turned off if you see something like chicken meal. Fresh meats contain about 80% water so, once the dog food is cooked, their weight is much less than the original. Meat meals have already been cooked down to a moisture content around 10% so they contain up to 300% more protein than fresh meats. A high-quality commercial dog food might list a fresh meat first followed by a meat meal second.

In addition to high-quality protein sources, you should also look for digestible carbohydrates and animal-based fats in the ingredients list. Carbohydrates that are easily digestible for dogs include things like cooked brown rice, oats, and barley. Be wary of wheat and corn-based products however, because these ingredients often trigger food allergies in dogs and they are low in nutritional value. The number of carbohydrate sources on the ingredients list is also important to consider. Dogs do not require a great deal of carbohydrate. Only about 15% of your dog's diet should come from carbohydrates. Low-quality dog foods contain as much as 30% to 70% of this nutrient.

If you see an ingredient like chicken fat or poultry fat on the label for a commercial pet food, do not be turned off as it is a good thing! As you learned previously, fats are a highly concentrated form of energy and they play an important role in your dog's diet. Fats from animal-based sources are particularly beneficial so you should look for things like chicken fat and fish oil in your dog's food. Plant-based fats

like flaxseed oil and canola oil can also be beneficial but animal-based fats are more biologically valuable to your dog.

In addition to the main ingredients on a dog food label you also need to pay attention to the things near the end of the list. This is where pet food manufacturers like to sneak in things like artificial flavours, colorants, and preservatives. Avoid ingredients with the word "by-product" attached, as well as chemical preservatives like BHA and BHT. Be aware that these ingredients might be spelt out instead of abbreviated. You should also avoid things like corn syrup, MSG, food dyes, and low-quality filler ingredients like corn and wheat gluten.

So when you next look at a dog food label, as well as the ingredients, consider the following:

Does a food label or advertising assert that the food has been tested on dogs over a long term, and therefore state that the product supports long term health, a long life, effective for reproduction and growth? If not then you need to question why not? If they could state these long term health benefits then they would certainly be advertising the facts.

So in short:

» Will the food keep the dog healthy?

» Will the food fulfil the needs of growing puppies?

» Will the food aid dental health, produce healthy litters of puppies, ensure adult dogs remain healthy and live to a ripe old age?

In essence, is there proof via scientific data, that the food has been proven to promote health, longevity, dental health, delayed aging and absence of degenerative diseases. Obviously in order to prove that, clinical trials will need to have been carried out over a dogs lifetime. In other words, the claims made by manufacturers is not based on speculative assumptions. It would also need to be proved that the dog is in excellent health and this is due to being fed on this particular diet. The type of proof needs to demonstrate that trials were carried out by an unbiased independent laboratory. You would also need to see the actual food analysis found.

g) Whippet Feeding – What's in the Tin

The quality of commercially prepared dog food is a hot topic. The dog food industry is a high earning one and often owned by huge corporations that often put profit before the health of our dogs. Many dog food ingredients are not fit for human consumption and although vitamins are added to dog foods we cannot be certain whether they are of good enough quality to have an effect on the health of our dogs. Unless an ingredients list on a bag or tin of dog food is completely transparent the meat within dog food is usually rendered and described as 'meal'

or 'derivatives'.

But what do these hazy terms actually mean?

Rendering is a process which involves putting bones, carcasses, beaks, hooves and tails into a huge tub and heating it so high that any virus cells, bacteria or antibiotic content dies. The fat content rises to the top and is scooped away. The remnants are ground up into a hot pink sludge of body parts. And this substance is what will eventually become commercial dog food. Does it sound terrifying? It does, that's because it is. Rendered foods are permanently deemed unfit for human consumption for health reasons. Yet we unknowingly feed it to our dogs. After the food becomes kibble it is colored to look nice and then sprayed with fat, in order to tempt dogs to eat it. Tinned foods have a lot of salt added, as do the little pouches meant for small dogs, which is no good for the dog's heart.

Thankfully and due to many different investigations inclusive of the dog food project by Sabine Contreras many smaller business are developing better food, made from whole food ingredients that are much better for our dogs. www.dogfoodproject.com describes the entire investigation and is well worth a read.

Admittedly the following article relates to 2007, but it still makes scary reading as to how the so called safe dog food diets can infiltrate the food chain with contaminated supplies.

https://en.wikipedia.org/ wiki/2007_pet_food_recalls

Again, negative feedback about BARF diets, such as the threat of Salmonella and Listeria monocytogenes strains, has been predominantly asserted by the FDA. In 2011 as part of a study between 2010 and 2012, by the FDA Centre for Veterinary Medicine, 196 samples of raw dog food were analysed. This was in the form of frozen ground meat. 15 proved positive for Salmonella and 32 for Listeria monocytogenes. Again it is not fair to comment whether or not this sample represents a fair overall reflection of contamination threat in all cases. Or whether those figures would be the same with a different set of samples. My own personal experience of feeding raw meaty bones is that my supplier is a wholesale pork butcher and I receive this in 25kg bags approx. which I then portion up and freeze. I also purchase frozen supermarket chicken portions. I feed 1 portion of chicken thigh per dog per day, and in both cases the meat is served whole and not ground. I have never had any problem with either a sick dog or the suggested issues with feeding bones.

Once again, the dog owners who favour raw feeding and oppose processed foods, believe the contamination risks suggested by FDA outweigh the obvious benefits gained to the dogs health. Although the FDA do not recommend raw diets they do acknowledge that there are pet owners prefer to feed this way and furthermore suggest ways to deal with these possible contaminants

You can read the full article here:

http://www.fda.gov/AnimalVeterinary/ResourcesforYou/AnimalHealthLiteracy/ucm373757.htm

For additional information on processed dog food, please read the following:

http://www.dailymail.co.uk/news/ article-2546512/How-pet-food-killing-dog-feeding-parsnips-yoghurt. html

h) Quality Commercial Foods for Whippets

Once again, if you are considering trying commercial dog foods, you will find included here several brands to look at as examples of what you might consider quality dog food. The commercial dog foods available in your area might differ according to the pet store chains available as well as the distribution policies for certain brands. Below you will find a list of several commercial dog food formulas that are often recommended for active breeds like the Whippet: Again, this is not a personal recommendation or endorsement of these products. They are examples of the sort of thing you will be looking at and comparing.

Nutro Natural Choice – High Endurance Adult Dog Food

This commercial dry food formula is specially designed for physically active dogs, made with a 30/ 20 protein-to-fat ratio for optimal energy levels and improved muscle recovery. This formula lists chicken meal, whole brown rice, rice bran, chicken fat, and whole grain oatmeal as the top five ingredients. The fact that chicken meal is listed first means that this formula is very high in protein. Again, meat meals have already been cooked down to a low moisture level which means that they are a much more highly concentrated source of protein than fresh meats. Whole brown rice and whole grain oatmeal are both complex carbohydrates and generally considered to be good sources of dietary fibre for dogs. Chicken fat is also a good ingredient because it provides your dog with essential fatty acids.

Breeder's Choice Active Care Healthy Joint Dog Food

This dry food formula from Breeder's Choice includes brown rice, chicken meal, chicken cartilage, chicken fat, and flaxseed as the top five ingredients. It would be better if the chicken meal, were listed first and the brown rice second, but this formula is still perhaps a good source of protein and digestible carbohydrates. Both the chicken fat and flaxseed provide essential fatty acids. In fact, flaxseed is the richest plant source of omega-3 fatty acids. Overall, this product seems to provide balanced nutrition for your Whippet.

Earthborn Holistic Primitive Natural Dry Dog Food

This dry dog food formula from Earthborn is made with several high-quality sources of protein including turkey meal, chicken meal, and whitefish meal. It is also made with chicken fat for fatty acids and potatoes for gluten-free carbohydrates. Another valuable inclusion in this dry food formula is an assortment of chelated minerals. Chelated minerals are found in high-quality dog foods and they consist of minerals that have been chemically bonded to protein molecules which makes them more readily available for your dog's body to absorb.

Performatrin Ultra Grain-Free Dry Dog Food

Performatrin Ultra dry dog food states that it offers healthy, balanced nutrition, and has the bonus of being completely grain-free. The top five ingredients for this dry food formula are de-boned turkey, turkey meal, peas, salmon meal and duck meal. The fact that high-quality sources of protein are listed four times within the top five ingredients speaks of the high protein content of this formula. It is also worth noting that a number of fresh vegetables are included for dietary fibre as well as various vitamins and minerals. This formula also includes chelated minerals and probiotics to facilitate healthy digestion.

Again, I cannot say that any processed feeding regardless of so called quality would be a first choice or preference for me. However, my intention is not to dictate my opinion, but to give an overall picture of what is available. You are then free to make your own mind up and choose. My preference is to feed as natural and healthy as possible, a good quality BARF diet will provide this. Perhaps feeding occasional table scraps or commercial feed when you are pushed for time.

i) How Much to Feed Your Whippet

Apart from keeping our dogs fit and healthy by feeding its body vital vitamins, minerals and other nutrients, the main thing that food provides is energy. This energy is obtained from all the main food groups including carbohydrates, protein and fats. Again, they need to be given in the correct amounts for the dogs needs. Not enough of those elements would result in malnutrition, too many would naturally lead to obesity. It is all about when a dog most needs these food elements. This will be most needed for purposes of reproduction and puppy growth. Times of stress and extreme activity levels such as may be expected from working sled or farm dogs. Cold weather will also see a need for extra food resources. Strangely enough the opposite is not the case. Whilst we live on light meals such as salad during hot spells, dogs use a considerable amount of energy in order to cool down, by panting.

Where a dogs diet needs to account for these extreme uses of energy, it is necessary to bear in mind the energy values of the three major food groups. Weight for weight, fat is by far the richest of the three in terms of energy value, in fact this is actually double either carbohydrate or protein. If the dog needs an energy rich diet because it is a working dog, for example, then a fat rich diet would be appropriate. This type of feeding for a dog that is not burning the fat off, would result in an obese dog destined for health problems. In general, you should be very careful not to over feed your dog. Obviously the opposite of this is also true, you do not want to underfeed your dog, because being under weight is also unhealthy for your dog. It is not an easy remedy to keep your dog at an optimum weight. You can usually see if the dog is over or under weight. A more accurate way is to weigh the dog on a regular basis and feed accordingly. Again, I would personally take the ideal weight for your type of dog as a guideline and then as accurately as you possibly can, provide meals that will keep your dog at an ideal weight. And once again, routinely weigh the dog to see where any fluctuations occur. You will soon get an idea of whether your dog is getting enough food. Also remember to take into account periods of extra activity as mentioned previously.

As you have already learned, your Whippet's calorie needs will vary according to his age and activity level. When your Whippet is a puppy it is sometimes recommended that you allow him to eat as much as he likes. Please do bear in mind, that the type of food I refer to here is dry kibble type dog food, not perishable cooked or raw food that will quickly go off if left un-refrigerated all day. But again, refer back to the previous chapter and remember that he should be eating whatever the breeder has been feeding initially. But also remember that a lean breed such as a Whippet is highly unlikely to put too much weight on even as an adult. Most dogs are good about eating when they are hungry and stopping when they are full. In this respect, if you were to feed so many meals per day, you may find that your puppy will not eat certain meals. If your puppy isn't obviously ill, it is likely to be that he doesn't need the extra food. So do not worry too much about serving him a precise amount each time. If he leaves some it is fair to assume he is eating all the calories he needs to fuel his growth and development at that meal.

Generally, you may be told that from 8 weeks to 12 weeks their daily food ration should be split into 4 meals.

From 12 weeks to 26 weeks this should be reduced to 3 meals per day.

26 weeks to 52 weeks, this is further reduced to 2 meals per day. At one year and after, most dog owners will be feeding either one or two meal per day. I prefer to feed twice per day. Around 10 am I provide almost all of their daily requirement. On some days they eat everything and then perhaps the next day only half. If they eat everything, I do not give any extra now, but feed a second meal around 3pm. This is about half that of the first meal. They get nothing else, no treats etc., until around 10 am the next day. If however they have left some from 10 am, I refrigerate that and they get get along with some extra, perhaps not half as much again. They get fresh clean water all of the time which is changed at least once per day. Again, this is for two adult dogs. You could feed your puppy in the same way, but again with the extra meals included.

The important thing to realize is that you use a good quality puppy food. As to how much you give per meal, if you are splitting the meals, depends on the weight of your pup and the recommended amount stated on your brand of food. Again, a lot depends on the quality and therefore nutritional value of the product, which is why it is important to not skimp on price especially for puppy food.

But whichever plan you follow, once your puppy reaches maturity you should start rationing his meals. You can choose how many meals to give your Whippet each day, but again most dog owners recommend dividing your dog's daily portion into two meals. To help you determine how much to feed your dog, follow the feeding suggestions on the dog food package in relation to the previous calorie needs mentioned. Keep in mind that feeding suggestions are just that, suggestions, so you may need to make adjustments. Start off with the recommended amount for a few weeks. If your dog gains weight you'll need to cut back a bit. If he loses weight, you should increase his rations a bit. You can always ask your veterinarian for suggestions if you aren't sure whether your dog is at a healthy weight.

Keep in mind that during the puppy stage you'll need to:

» Ensure that your Whippet puppy is gaining weight steadily by frequent veterinary check ups during the puppy stage. You can also buy a scale and weigh him every week.

» Watch out for obesity, which is obviously something Whippets are not prone to, but they should not be permitted to over feed.

» Feed the correct puppy diet appropriate to instructions given by your vet or the dietary guidelines on the back of the food package you buy your Whippet.

» Avoid feeding only a one-sided diet of meat only. Mix with a quality dry food and other natural food stuff.

» Avoid feeding your puppy poor quality commercial dog food, any junk food or table scraps that contain empty calories

» Keep your Whippet away from dangerous foods like chocolate, grapes, candy and gum that can be deadly to dogs

Another factor you need to consider in regard to feeding your Whippet is how many treats you give him. When you are training your puppy, you should use very small treats. Even if your puppy eats a lot of them, however, it will not be a problem because he needs a lot of calories to fuel his growth. Once your Whippet is fully mature, however, you should limit the number of treats you give him to avoid going over his daily calorie needs.

Tips For Feeding Healthy Foods

» Feed a high-quality dog food that has been manufactured by a reputable dog food company.

» Always buy the best that you can afford.

» Feed the freshest fresh fruits and vegetables

» Dry dog food can lose its nutritional value as it ages with the fat content becoming rancid. Check expiry dates on each bag of dog food that you purchase.

For Whippets with ingredient intolerances or food sensitivities, choose a brand with a single-source of animal protein and real deboned meat as the first ingredient and a healthy, simple list of additional grain-free, gluten-free ingredients. Many health problems in Whippets can be avoided by feeding a high quality grain-free diet. Yet one needs to pay attention to the ingredient list even though it's labelled as grain-free.

Why Should Your Whippet Eat Fresh Fruits and Vegetables

"Artificial ingredients are often highly antagonistic, and can actually contribute to an animal's mental and emotional imbalance," according to Andi Brown, director of Halo and author of the Whole Pet Diet. *"Some additives can be so detrimental that they can actually have the same effect on animals as hallucinogenic drugs have on people."*

Seafood For Whippets

Seafood may seem an odd diet for a dog, but please read the following:

"Seafood is loaded with protein, minerals, and enzymes when fresh and also has lots of collagen", says Andi from Halo Dog Food. *"Spirulina and chlorella are a more concentrated source of chlorophylls than any other food. Both of these algae help reduce inflammation and are also rich in essential fatty acids."*

Feed salmon, sardines and other fish approved by your veterinarian. For more information, visit: *thewholepetdiet.com*

i) Toxic Foods Affecting Whippet Dogs

In addition to making sure that you provide your Whippet with a healthy diet, you also need to be careful NOT to feed him certain foods. It can be tempting to give your dog a few scraps from your plate but certain "people foods" can actually be toxic for your dog.

Below you will find a list of foods that can be harmful to your Whippet:

» Alcohol

» Apple seeds

» Avocado

» Cherry pits

» Chocolate

» Cocoa mulch fertilizer

» Coffee

» Garlic

» Grapes/raisins

» Gum (can cause blockages and sugar free gums may contain the toxic sweetener Xylitol)

» Hops

» Macadamia nuts

» Mold

- » Mushrooms
- » Mustard seeds
- » Nuts
- » Onions and onion powder/ leeks
- » Peach pits
- » Potato leaves/stems
- » Rhubarb leaves
- » Tea
- » Tomato leaves/stems
- » Walnuts
- » Xylitol
- » Yeast dough

If your Whippet gets into a food that he shouldn't have, you should call the Pet Poison Control Hotline, just to be on the safe side. The specialist on the other end of the line will be able to tell you if the amount your dog ingested is potentially toxic. If it is, they will walk you through the steps to induce vomiting to purge the item from your dog's stomach, or recommend that you take your dog to an emergency vet. You may also be able to speak to a licensed veterinarian on the phone for a fee around $65 (£42.25).

4) Toxic Plants Affecting Whippet Dogs

Not only do you need to be careful about which foods you keep out of your Whippet's reach, there are also plants that can be toxic to all dogs. If you have any of the houseplants listed below in your house, make sure you keep them well out of your dog's reach. For toxic outdoor plants, remove them from your property or fence them off for your dog's safety.

A list of toxic plants harmful to dogs can be found below:

- » Azalea
- » Baneberry
- » Bird-of-paradise
- » Black locust
- » Buckeye
- » Buttercup
- » Caladium
- » Castor bean
- » Chock-cherries
- » Christmas rose
- » Common privet
- » Cowslip
- » Daffodil

- » Day lily
- » Delphinium
- » Easter lily
- » Elderberry
- » Elephant's ear
- » English Ivy
- » Foxglove
- » Holly
- » Horse-chestnut
- » Hyacinth
- » Iris
- » Jack-in-the-pulpit
- » Jimsonweed
- » Laurels
- » Lily of the valley
- » Lupines
- » May-apple
- » Mistletoe
- » Morning glory
- » Mustards
- » Narcissus

- » Nightshade
- » Oaks
- » Oleander
- » Philodendron
- » Poinsettia
- » Poison hemlock
- » Potato
- » Rhododendron
- » Rhubarb
- » Sago palm
- » Sorghum
- » Wild black cherry
- » Wild radish
- » Wisteria
- » Yew

CHAPTER FIVE:

EARLY TRAINING

Every time I learn something new about the biology of dogs I realize how important puppy learning is. Those early stages not only build the body of your Whippet dog, but also his mind. Which is exactly why I wanted to share these stages of puppy learning with you now.

1.) The Stages of Puppy Learning

Dogs are, with no shadow of doubt, a mixture of their genetic influence and their prior learning. Learning and experiences go right back to conception too, shaping the puppy whilst he is still in the womb.

The influence on a puppy will begin with the hormones in his mother's body during her pregnancy, and end the day that the puppy dies an old and wise dog.

A stressed and insecure mother dog will be producing hormones such as cortisol and adrenaline whilst her puppies are developing in her womb.

Excess stress related hormones released during development has already been shown to change a puppy's behaviour, usually later as he grows into an adult dog.

Even with the most careful socialization schedule, a poor gestation period can lead to a less emotionally stable dog; another reason not to buy a puppy from a pet store or puppy farm.

So how does a carefully bred puppy develop when he has a happy and, well cared for and stable mom

a.) Your Neonatal Puppy!

When the mother dog is stable and healthy, she will usually give birth to healthy puppies. At the beginning, up until twelve to fourteen days old the puppies are in a stage of development called the Neonatal stage.

Their eyes are still closed and they are completely helpless, simply feeding and sleeping. At this point the puppy brain is not fully developed and many of the neurons still have some growing to do.

The puppy from birth does have a heat seeking nose and uses it to find the warmth of his mother if separated from her. The puppies are also stimulated to toilet at this point, by their mother's licking.

Tests have shown that puppies who are handled carefully for a few minutes a day, at this point, develop into dogs more able to cope with the world later on. This should obviously be carried out in the vicinity of the Mother dog and certainly cause her no stress.

Many professional dog training establishments utilize this knowledge now, and carefully handle puppies from birth.

b.) A Puppy in Transition

After the neonatal stage the puppies begin to learn about the world. This stage of development is called the transition period. This is a busy period for learning and change which lasts until the puppy is around twenty days old.

During this period the dog's eyes open, his ear canals form and he starts to use his senses. The puppy begins social learning and begins to bond with his siblings and mother. He will also protest if moved away from the litter. The puppy begins to learn appeasement behaviour, such as tail wagging and muzzle licking along with other forms of canine communication.

Again, the puppy will develop into a more confident older dog if he is carefully and kindly introduced to a variation of things during this phase. Toys, floor surfaces, noises and gentle handling all aid social confidence later on.

c.) The Socialization Stage

Socialization time lasts from the end of the transition period right through to the twelve week old point. This is crucial learning time that cannot be completely changed later on.

The dog's behaviour is shaped by this learning period and therefore this should be filled with positive social experiences that will shape a happy and confident puppy into adulthood.

A good breeder will ensure that the puppies in their care have as much positive social contact as possible. The new dog owner of an eight week old puppy will need to continue this careful social learning into adulthood.

The dog that misses out on proper social learning will struggle for the rest of his or her life. The Whippet dog that is poorly socialized will probably, eventually bark to warn away everything that is deemed scary. The poorly socialized dog may feel that he has to show defensive aggression.

Although behaviour modification can be carried out, a dog that has not been properly raised and socialized can never be truly 'fixed'. The owner will simply need to learn to modify the behaviour if possible, and manage it if not.

2.) Whippet Toilet Training

Do you remember the old saying 'rub his nose in it' For many years this was how house-training was carried out. Poor dogs. In this area of the book we are going to talk about puppy toilet training the right way.

Housebreaking a Whippet puppy need not be a difficult task. It is simply a case of teaching your dog, as soon as you can, that outside is where the toileting happens.

Whippet toilet training for success is a matter of putting everything that you can into that first few days. The more times your puppy gets it right in the beginning the quicker he will learn what you want from him. Whippets are generally known to be very clean, so hopefully you will have few if any accidents, and toilet training should take no time at all.

a.) What Will You Need

For perfect Whippet toilet training you won't really need a great deal. Some puppy pads or newspaper, an odour neutralizer and a sharp eye along with a swift movement if you notice your puppy needs to go.

I say an odour neutralizer because a generic cleaning product is not enough. General cleansing fluid does not rid the environment of the smell and the dog will always return to a smell when looking for a toilet area. Odour neutralizers literally take the urine into their own particles then disperse and destroy it.

b.) Good Toilet Training Practice

Get into your mind, the idea that for the next few days, you will be a puppy taxi. This involves ferrying your dog outside at least every hour to two hours. In addition, in the case of accidents, picking your little dog up and relocating him to the right place as he starts to toilet.

Similarly it is a good idea to expect to use puppy pads or newspapers in the beginning.

The idea is that in an ideal world, the puppy will go outside to toilet every time. It is still a good idea to have pads present though just in case you miss an opportunity to get him out. The puppy pads/newspapers, can be phased out later. But remember, your puppy has a tiny bladder at the moment and the puppy pad can help with any unexpected toilet mishaps.

You can gradually move the puppy pad toward the external door as the puppy becomes familiar with how to use them. Eventually when the dog heads for it, you can get him straight out of the back door.

Then in time, you may only need to put puppy pads down overnight until your dog's bladder and bowel matures.

Dog understanding, begins with knowing that a dog of any age will repeat any behaviour which is rewarded. Things get a little complicated when you look further into it but generally this is the baseline truth.

In addition, the act of rewarding something also teaches the dog to repeat it enough times for it to become a habit.

Putting this into practice, particularly where toilet training is concerned, is actually quite an easy – three step process as follows;

Step One

1. Get the environment ready for toilet training by working out where exactly the puppy will be expected to toilet outdoors and sorting out your puppy pads for indoors.

2. Place your puppy pads nearby indoors. Puppy pads can be used as the indoor toilet for now whilst your puppy is learning and through the night. As mentioned before, you can substitute pads for newspaper.

3. As a rule of thumb, approximately every hour your puppy may need to toilet. But you should commit yourself to look carefully at your puppy for signs that he may need to go at any point. You may see signs such as the following: he may lick his lips, yawn or glance at you. Or if you notice him wandering about, sniffing or circling, anticipate he may need to toilet. If you notice him about to go, it may also be an idea to say something like 'outside for toilets', or 'outside for a wee wee'. You will hopefully get to the stage where as soon as he hears this, he knows you want him to do his toileting outside and will wait at the door. Most dogs get to

the stage where they bark to let you know they want letting out to do their toilet business.

Step Two

1. Take your puppy outdoors every hour at least. Take him out after he has eaten, slept, played and had a drink because these are the times he will most likely need to go. Take him and wait with him until your puppy toilets, if he needs to.
2. Remember this is a baby in the big wild world and he is probably quite insecure. If you push any puppy outdoors to toilet, then leave him out there alone, you are teaching him something and it's not good toilet training.
3. So wait with your puppy until he has indeed done his business or he may just come inside and pee at your feet.
4. Taxi your puppy outside or to the pad at this point if he has an accident. If he toilets on the pad of his own accord then praise him, as this is a step closer to toileting outside and a step further away from doing it on the floor in the house. You can also begin to move the pad away gradually towards the external door.

Step Three

1. When your puppy 'goes' in the place you want him to,

it is vital to reward the behaviour. Remember that he won't know what you want from him unless you show/tell him. A carefully rewarded behaviour will always be repeated.
2. Watch your puppy for accidents. Any signs that he may need to toilet, then scoop him up to take him outside or to the nearest puppy pad. This is where you employ that puppy taxi habit.
3. Even if your dog has begun to go in the wrong place quickly and quietly ferry him along to his legitimate toileting area. This way you will be alleviating any confusion that he may have about the location of his toilet area.
4. Even if he does a tiny bit in the right area still reward him. It can be difficult to learn this for a puppy, particularly as his brain and bladder are still developing; so be kind and patient.
5. Keep your eyes peeled because the more successes at this point, the quicker your Whippet puppy will become housebroken.

Clearing soiled puppy pads/ newspaper.

You will need to clear away any soiled paper/pads on a daily basis. You will then want to replenish the area with fresh pads or paper. An important tip to use in the early stages of toilet training is to leave a piece of the soiled, damp paper. This is particularly important for any initial indoor training. The obvious reason for this relates to scent marking. They will naturally return to the area they can smell as scent marked. If you clear the soiled paper and put fresh unscented paper in its place, the pup may not remember where he last went to toilet, or be able to smell the odour. If you leave a piece of the soiled scented paper, he should instantly recognize this as the place to go. It is important that you that this is only in the very initial stages when you are trying to get the puppy to target the puppy pad. Again, once he is successful at this, the next stage is to move the whole thing outside. But again the scented piece will be useful at that stage. Once he knows were he should toilet, leaving the soiled paper will be unnecessary.

c.) No Punishment

If your puppy has an accident then you were either not watching him carefully enough or you have not taken him out enough. NEVER punish accidents. Simply clean up, and tell yourself that you will do better next time.

Punishment of accidents will cause anxiety around toileting for your puppy and this will simply lead to more accidents. Punishment may even lead to the puppy feeling he needs to eat his own poop. That's not a fair way to raise a puppy.

Older dogs can have house-breaking problems based on a few different things. If a dog has never lived indoors or been house-trained,

then he may toilet indoors. This is not his fault as he hasn't been taught the social etiquettes that we live by. You should therefore apply the steps above in the same way to show the dog what you want.

When you bring a rescued Whippet home, it's important to expect at least a couple of accidents, because he or she will be confused and nervous.

d.) Scent Marking

Male dogs may scent mark in the new home if they are un-neutered or particularly nervous.

Scent marking is the dog's way of showing other dogs that he is there, and can be a nervous reaction or a hormonal response.

Castration can help with the male dog that scent marks, but is not a definite solution as it can cause further insecurity in some worried dogs. It is worth speaking to your vet if you are having a problem like this.

e.) Elderly Dogs

Dogs can lose control of their bladder with old age. This is a sad situation and one which we have to adapt to because we love our dogs.

The vet can prescribe specific treatments for leaking and may need to check out your dog's overall health, if this is an issue.

Many dogs fail to make it through the night in the last months/ years without needing to go out.

Again, the best solution is to put down plenty of newspaper for him to go on. Cleaning this up in the morning is a small sacrifice to pay, as you need to make things as easy and comfortable for them as possible.

3.) Why Socialize

We have dealt with the importance of socialization earlier, but go into it a bit more detailed here. Socialization is a complete topic in itself. There are so many dogs in rescue shelters and homes that simply do not know how to react in social situations.

This is because they have never learned what to do in the company of other dogs, children and crowded areas or around other animals.

Stop for a moment and think of street dogs in Europe and similar places. You never see them fighting do you? They manage to get on with no tension and certainly no aggression. They never bark at cars or people.

The street dogs never seem to worry too much about their surroundings. Which points to the fact that there must be a specific reason for the behaviour. You guessed it, the reason for poorly socialized dogs is us humans.

We leash them up, stop them interacting, panic when another dog comes towards them and often keep them well away from social situations altogether. Then when a puppy gets to a few months old we complain about their social behaviour.

As mentioned previously, it is possible to grasp back some social skills with an older dog, after the socialization boat has sailed. Yet the dog that isn't positively socialized as a puppy, will never really be completely relaxed in new circumstances.

Positive socialization should incorporate everything that you possibly can into a dog's everyday life as early as possible. Not only that though, every experience should be positive.

A good socialization schedule will include positive experiences of and with:

Important!

» As many dogs as possible

» Buses

» Cars

» Children

» Domestic animals

» Farmed animals

» People of all ages

» Push chairs

» Sounds such as recorded thunder and fireworks

» The groomer (if you are to use a professional)

» Trains or trams

» Unusual looking people (those wearing hats and unusual clothing)

> » The veterinary surgery
>
> » Wildlife

Your dog will need to learn canine manners from other dogs. He is socialized with exposure to the aforementioned list, to build his personal confidence and ability to cope in new situations as he grows.

Although Whippets are known to be relatively placid, sensitive dogs, lack of social skills may easily become borderline aggressive behaviour because of a dogs genetic need to defend himself.

So introduce him to as many social situations as possible. He can then learn that most situations are nothing to be afraid of. When you do encounter any of the above, as with any training, always give him lots of praise and show him how pleasant these encounters can be.

4.) Other training considerations

a.)Avoid Over Attachment

When your puppy is feeling secure, it is vital to teach him that alone time is normal, even if your lifestyle dictates that the dog will never be left alone, because this prepares your dog for life. Remember the Whippet can live to a ripe old age, so who knows what the future holds.

Later on we will talk about separation anxiety and how it develops. Yet if you start leaving your puppy early in his life you can certainly minimize the risk. So set up times where you leave him for a short time

and try not to allow your puppy to trail around the house after you, following you into every room. This will be particularly important for some Whippets as they are known to be clingy.

The idea is not to allow your puppy to develop over attachment to you. When a dog becomes over attached they cannot cope with being left alone, simply because you are not there.

Practice leaving your dog with a stuffed Kong, the radio or television on and pop out for a few minutes every day after the first few days.

Make this a priority and part of your dog's learning program because by doing this you minimize the risk of your Whippet puppy developing distressing separation anxiety later on.

b.)Puppy Classes and Playtime!

Puppy classes can be so important to a young dog's social development that many veterinary surgeries offer them for free to new clients.

It is very easy to take a dog away from the litter and for the next few weeks only provide him with human contact. Particularly because vaccinations are given around the crucial socialization period and dog owners are advised to keep their puppy away from risky areas that may harbour disease.

The worrying thing with this, is that the time between leaving the litter and twelve weeks old is the crucial learning stage where social skills and canine manners are developed. No matter what we do, or how hard we try, we simply cannot replace another dog's place for the puppy who is learning social skills.

Puppy classes provide essential canine contact, play and sometimes even education for the developing puppy. Every Whippet dog should either attend a puppy class or get together with as many other dogs as possible, as he grows, in order to prevent fear and anxiety later in life.

c.) A Nice Relaxed Walk

Whippets are very adaptable, generally considered to be easy to feed and look after, and considered to be the the ideal dog for a lazy person. However, please do not take that to mean that they will be happy to sit at home all day and hardly ever exercise. Please do remember that these are very athletic dogs by nature. That isn't to say they need to spend all day racing around a dog track. But as well as regular, daily brisk walks, they should get the opportunity for off lead runs in a safe traffic free area.

If you do have a local enclosed park or field area, these off lead runs can be a great opportunity to introduce your puppy to the idea of chasing a lure. Even if you have no intention of taking up Whippet racing, this can still provide a great way for you to both interact. Simply tie some old fabric, preferably fake fur, to string or rope, and start to play with the pup, offering this to him. He will probably grab this straight away and want to chew and drag this about. Once he is familiar with this, start to walk and then run away from him to encourage him to give chase. Alternatively tie this to a broom handle or something longer and use that to get him to chase it and whip this away from him as he gets faster.

Again as he gets better and faster, use a mountain bike or similar to ride around dragging the lure. Be careful not to get this tangled in the wheel, and remember to let go after he catches it.

Taking your Whippet for a walk can be a wonderful experience or quite stressful all round. You will probably be starting this phase of his training after a few weeks of him being in and around the house and garden. Once this familiarization stage has taken place, by about 10 weeks old. It is actually a lot easier to improve behaviour on the leash than you may think though. This is also an excellent time to practice him walking and to encourage him to do his toilet business. The likely hood is that he will naturally go and do his toileting, whilst out on walks. But it is a good opportunity to praise him when he does, so that he knows that is a time when you particularly want him to go. There is no rush at this stage, so allow him plenty of time to get used to this walking and toilet training phase, before moving on to his basic obedience training.

Walking Equipment

Dog walking equipment should be introduced carefully, particularly to a puppy, and only the kindest collars or harness types should be used.

The harness is generally better than a collar, as it redistributes the weight of his body and naturally, immediately stops him pulling on the leash.

Dogs are far easier to control on walks when wearing a harness and there is no nasty pulling and coughing, as often happens on a standard collar and leash.

Generally there is never a need to use choke or metal collars on dogs. The same result is easily achievable by using humane equipment and the smallest amount of positive training.

When you first introduce a Whippet puppy, or older dog, to a collar or harness make it a nice and positive event. Pop it onto the dog and play for a while, then remove it again whilst the dog is still happy.

After doing this a few times, add the leash and allow the dog to trail it behind in the house or garden. Then your puppy should be sufficiently used to it and will be ready to go for a walk.

The following training steps are to help you prevent pulling on the leash. They are simply to make your Whippet walking experiences happy and relaxed forever.

The steps may take longer if the dog has learned to grab the leash in his mouth or fight against the tension, but if you persevere they will still work.

Training Steps:

1. With your dog on his leash, walk a couple of steps and if the leash stays slack say the command word ('walk nicely' or something similar. We will talk about the 'heel' command later, so probably the best word would be 'heel') you have chosen for an easy leash and click/reward in quick succession.

2. If the leash is tight you may need to change direction a few times to engineer a slack leash. As soon as any tension vanishes from the leash, carry out the command/click/reward sequence. I sometimes find that by simply stopping, thus breaking the sequence of him pulling, is often enough to make him realize he shouldn't pull. Please don't get into the habit that some 'impatient people' seem to do, and pull the poor dog back with enough force to pull him over. The dog is keen and excited to be out walking and sniffing about. Given the chance he wants to go off and do his own thing. So please be patient and considerate.

3. Just as an added note here, command/click/reward is referred to previously. If you are not familiar with clicker training, it basically means, as your dog performs a correct action, such as walk nicely you say the command word (so he

knows to associate the action with the word). You then use a clicker to mark the behaviour (you don't have to use a clicker, you can substitute this with the words 'good boy/girl'). You finally reward the behaviour with a treat to begin with, so he associates his action with something good and positive. You will be introduced to more detailed specific training procedures in the next chapter. For now however, simply initiate him walking nicely and as long as he is doing so praise/ reward him. I also like to keep repeating the word heel/walk nicely. But make sure he is actually walking nicely so he can associate his act with the word.

4.   Repeat and practice.

5.   Gradually increase the time between when you issue the command, and when you reward. This will keep him keen to carry out the action, as he knows that if he does what you ask, a reward will soon follow. Limiting/delaying the reward also makes it easier when you eventually phase out giving food rewards all together. We will talk about this later.

6.   Again, remember the 'release command' at the end of the session. (If you have come to this part first, without reading about 'release commands', the release is basically as follows: After successfully completing a piece of training, let your dog know they have completed it by releasing them. This can be done in conjunction with the treat stage, and you simply say "finished", "all over", or something similar. Again this is discussed in more detail in a later section.)

Teaching a Whippet to walk easily on a leash will probably take 3 to 6 training sessions in a quiet area. It will then need practice in various areas, gradually increasing distractions, to become a flawless command. This will require exposure to roads and busy traffic. You will need to get to a point of teaching him to sit and wait at the road side until it is safe to cross.

The time-scale to positive results of this particular lesson depend on how the dog has learned to walk on a leash in his life experiences so far.

CHAPTER SIX:

TRAINING YOUR WHIPPET DOG

In this next chapter we will cover specific step by step obedience training methods for your Whippet. The Whippet is a very intelligent breed that typically responds well to training but he can be easily distracted sometimes. For the best success, you should plan to keep your training sessions short and fun so that your Whippet gets something out of them each time. In addition to receiving step-by-step instructions for training your Whippet dog, you will also learn the basics about different training methods.

Please note that this is basic obedience that will be important to all Whippet owners. We will go into detail about actual Whippet racing and the specific training needs there. As that is not necessarily something that all Whippet owners will get involved in, the two chapters have been kept separate.

1.) Popular Training Methods

When it comes to training your Whippet you have a variety of training methods to choose from. Some of the most common training methods include positive reinforcement, punishment-based, alpha dog, and clicker training. In this section you will receive an overview of each training method as well as a recommendation for which option is best for your Whippet.

a.) Positive-Reinforcement Training

One of the most popular training methods for dogs today is positive reinforcement training. This type of training is a version of operant conditioning in which the dog learns to associate an action with a consequence. In this case, the term consequence does not refer to something bad, it is just something that happens as a result of something else. The goal of positive reinforcement training is to encourage your dog to WANT to do what you want him to do.

The basics of positive reinforcement training are simple, you teach the dog that if he follows your commands he will be rewarded. For example, you teach your dog to respond to the word "Sit" by him sitting down. In order to teach him to associate the command with the action, you reward him with a treat each time he sits on command. It generally only takes a few repetitions for dogs to learn to respond to commands because food rewards are highly motivational for most dogs.

The key to successful positive reinforcement-based training sessions is to keep them short and fun. If the dog enjoys the training, he will be more likely to retain what he has learned. It is also important that you make the connection between the command and the desired response very clear to your dog. If he doesn't understand what you want him to do, he will become confused. It is also important to pair the reward immediately with the desired response. This helps your dog to make the connection more quickly and it motivates him to repeat the desired behaviour.

b.) Punishment-Based Training

Punishment-based training is not as harsh as the word suggests. It is not exactly the opposite of positive reinforcement training, but it is very different. While positive reinforcement training is about encouraging your dog to repeat a desired behaviour, punishment-based training is about discouraging your dog from performing an unwanted behaviour. The goal of punishment-based training is to teach your dog that a certain action results in a negative consequence and thus the dog will choose not to perform that behaviour in the future.

The problem with punishment-based training methods is that it is generally only effective in teaching your dog to stop doing something rather than teaching him to respond to a certain command. It is also important to note that punishment-based training can have a negative impact on your relationship with your dog. Even though your dog may stop performing the unwanted behaviour, it may not be because you taught him that the behaviour is undesirable. He will likely only associate the behaviour with fear and pain (depending on the type of punishment you use).

In addition to learning not to perform the behaviour in question, your dog will also learn to be fearful of you. If you know anything about dog behaviour, you may already know that in most cases, aggression is born of fear. Even the most even-tempered dog can become aggressive if he is afraid. If you use punishment-based training methods you not only risk teaching your dog to fear you, but there is also the possibility that he will become aggressive with you at some point in the future.

Note: I would like to point out here, that if you adopt this style of training, you should NEVER, under any circumstances hit your dog. It is not only cruel, but an unnecessary action on your part. If you are ever having recurring behavioural issues with your dog, you should either seek an alternative approach or in extreme cases, seek the help of a professional dog trainer.

c.) Alpha Dog Training

You may be familiar with this style of training in conjunction with the "Dog Whisperer," Cesar Millan. Cesar Millan is a famous dog trainer who has published a number of books including three New York Times best sellers. Mr Millan's dog training methods are based on the idea that dogs are pack animals and that the dog owner must establish himself as leader of the pack. In doing so, the dog will become submissive and will submit to the owner's will.

According to Cesar Millan's style of training, you should never let your dog walk through a doorway before you and he must wait until you've finished your meal to receive his dinner. Though Mr Millan has a great many followers, there are also many who believe his training methods to be extreme and inhumane. In fact, the RSPCA issued a statement saying that "Adverse training methods which have been seen to be used by Cesar Millan can cause pain and fear for dogs and may worsen their behavioural problems". It is not my intention to discredit Mr Millan or his methods and I cannot personally comment about the effectiveness of his methods. If you are at all interested in this or any other approach, then I urge you to do your own research and make your own mind up. Again, providing you act with kindness, are firm but fair in your dog training approach, then I am sure you will have success which ever method you use.

d.) Clicker Training

Clicker training, as described previously, is a type of positive reinforcement training. With this type of training you use a small clicker device to help your dog form an association with a command and the desired behaviour. Because this is the most difficult part of positive reinforcement training, clicker training is often a very quick and effective training method. To use this method you follow the same procedures as you would for positive reinforcement training but you click the clicker as soon as your dog performs the desired behaviour and then give him the reward. Once your dog identifies the desired behaviour you then stop using the clicker so he does not become dependent on it.

A quick idea of how this works is to firstly get your dog associating the clicker with getting a reward. Usually as soon as the dog hears the clicker he will prick his ears and look towards the clicker or you. When he does, quickly give him the treat, and keep repeating this a few times. You next say the command so if this is sit, say sit and the moment he sits you click and reward. That is basically how this works and how you proceed to other commands.

If you want to get a visual idea of how clicker training works, there are some excellent videos on YouTube, you may wish to check out. Just type clicker training and take your pick. If you are interested in much more detailed information about clicker training, books by Karen Pryor are usually recommended, although I am sure others are useful also.

e.) Training Recommendations

It is completely your decision which training method you choose to utilize with your Whippet but most dog trainers recommend some form of positive reinforcement training. As the Whippet is considered to be a sensitive gentle personality, you are certainly not recommended to use any harsh treatments. Whippets are a very intelligent breed so they typically pick things up fairly quickly. Using a clicker may help you to speed up your training sessions as well.

2.) House-training Your Whippet Using the Crate.

This is covered in a previous chapter, but is used here in conjunction with crate training

When you bring home a Whippet puppy, one of the first things you must do is house-train him. Puppies have very little control over their bladders and bowel movements, so house-training can sometimes be tricky. If you use the crate training method however, you can not only reduce the frequency of accidents, but you may also find that your puppy becomes house-trained fairly quickly. All you need to crate train your puppy is, of course, the crate, patience and some time.

You have already learned a little bit about the benefits of crating your puppy but in this section you will receive more detailed information about the crate training method. In order for this method to work, your puppy's crate, needs to be just big enough for him to stand, sit, lie down, and turn around in comfortably. If it is too much larger, your puppy might give in to the temptation, and have a toilet accident. You also need to understand that puppies cannot hold their bladders for more than a few hours until they reach six months old. So do not force your puppy to remain in the crate for longer than he can physically restrain himself. In this respect it is probably best to leave him with his crate door open, over night and simply leave paper down. Of course after about six months he will be able to hold this, and you can perhaps close his crate door. But you may find he doesn't soil the paper anyway, if you simply leave the door open, even as an adult.

Before you actually begin crate training your puppy you need to get your puppy used to the crate. If you skip this step in the process, your puppy may learn to associate the crate with bad things, such as you leaving the house. Instead, you should teach your Whippet puppy that the crate is a good thing.

PLEASE NOTE: Whippets generally like their own space, and they are generally known to like the crate so the crate should not be a problem to him. Also please note the comfort factor here. Again, although Whippets like being in the crate, they do not enjoy hard surface, even carpeted. So please do make sure the crate contains lots of bedding such as nice soft blankets etc. Also be aware that even in doors they will quickly feel cold if there is a draft. In essence, please make sure that this new den is as appealing as possible, warm, quiet and draft free. I would also suggest draping the crate with a large thick blanket, perhaps leaving the front open so he can see out easily.

To do this you can follow these steps:

1. Take the door off the crate, if possible, or prop it open so that it does not close while your puppy is in it.
2. Bring your puppy over to the crate and talk to him in a soothing voice as he explores it.
3. Toss a few treats in and around the crate to encourage your puppy to go inside of his own free will. If treats don't work, try a favourite toy.
4. Start feeding your puppy his meals in the crate. Ideally you should place his food bowl in the back of the crate so he has to go all the way in to eat.
5. Once your puppy is comfortable eating his meals in the crate, you can start to close the door while he is in it. Open the door again as soon as he is finished eating.
6. Each time you feed your puppy in the crate, leave the door closed a few minutes longer until your puppy remains in the crate for 10 minutes after eating.
7. Once your puppy gets used to this, you can start leaving

the room for a few minutes after he has already been in the crate for 5 minutes.

8. Slowly increase the amount of time you spend away from your puppy while he is in the crate. If he starts whining or crying, you may have increased the duration of your absence too quickly.

Once your puppy is able to remain in the crate quietly for 30 minutes you can begin crate training. The process of crate training is really quite simple. Your overall aim is to leave your puppy in the crate overnight and when you leave the house. (Some people find that the Whippet is so well behaved that crates are not necessary. I would still suggest doing the crate training anyway as it can be a useful tool, even if you find you do not really need to use it.) While you are at home, give him plenty of opportunities to do his business outside. If your puppy never has the opportunity to have an accident inside the house, then crate training will not be a chore. It is possible that during the night, your puppy may need to do his toilet business. In this case I would advise lining the crate with newspaper or puppy pads. Most dogs I have known will bark, asking to go out. If it is possible, please do attend to the dog as it will be uncomfortable for him to be expected to hold this until the morning. If you prefer not to keep your dog in his crate overnight then leave him somewhere such as a kitchen with a tiled floor and again plenty of newspaper/puppy pads that

can easily be cleaned up.

Follow the steps below to properly toilet train your puppy in conjunction with crate training:

Once again, I realize that details of the following have been covered previously. I apologize for repeating certain steps again. The point is, that when you first bring your puppy home you will need to start toilet training immediately. You will not necessarily immediately start him with crate training. You are now utilizing the crate and need to be aware of how this fits in conjunction with toilet training.

1. Choose an area of the yard where you want your puppy to do his business. Housetraining will be easier if your puppy learns what you expect of him when you take him outside to that particular area.

2. Take your puppy outside to the special area every hour or so to give him a chance to do his business. If he doesn't go, take him right back inside. The reason you take him back inside straight away and not leave him to his own devices, is so he knows that this is training.

3. When you take your puppy outside and lead him to the special area, give him a verbal command like "go pee", "outside for a wee wee", or "toilets" etc. It is a good idea to choose and

use the same command until he gets the idea. Using several different commands may confuse him. Once your puppy is successfully house-trained you'll be able to just open the door and give him the command. Eventually, your puppy will also get to the point where he stands at the door and gives a little bark, asking to go out.

4. If your puppy does his business, praise him excitedly and offer him a treat. Be very consistent about this to make sure your puppy learns what you expect of him.

5. When you are inside, keep your puppy confined to whatever room you are currently in. This will help to reduce the chance of accidents.

6. If you notice your puppy sniffing the ground or turning in circles, it is a sign that he has to go and you should take him outside before he has an accident.

7. Place your puppy in the crate overnight and when you are away from home so he doesn't have an accident. Hopefully at this point, he will know exactly what is expected, and be able to refrain from needing to go until the morning. However, if you are woken in the early hours, with his short, "asking to go out",

bark, he may need letting outside. Again please don't ignore this, as it will likely be uncomfortable for him to have to hold it until the morning.

8. For the first few weeks you will need to let your puppy out every few hours until he is old enough to hold his bladder overnight. If you work a full-time job you may need to ask a friend to stop by or hire a dog sitter.

9. Let your puppy outside immediately after releasing him from the crate, and always give him a chance to go before you put him in it.

If you follow these simple steps you will find that house-training your Whippet puppy is really quite easy. In many cases, house-training only takes a few weeks. The key is to be as consistent as possible in letting your puppy outside as frequently as you can and in rewarding your puppy for doing his business outside. Your puppy has a natural desire to please you, so praising him for doing his business outside will teach him that you like that behaviour and he will be eager to repeat it.

3.) Obedience Training - Teaching Basic Commands

By the time you start your puppy with his basic obedience training, he should be about 12 weeks old. By this time he should be very familiar with his toilet training and generally walking about on his lead. While your puppy may not be able to comprehend complex commands right away, you should be able to start basic obedience training at a fairly young age. There are five main commands which form the basics of obedience training; Sit, Down, Come, Stay and Heel. In this section you will receive step-by-step instructions for teaching your Whippet these five basic commands.

PLEASE NOTE: The type of collar you use when training your puppy is important for keen, excitable breeds such as the Whippet. By all means, start him with the regular collar you have purchased or the harness if prefer. If you have no problems with your puppy surging or lunging forward or hanging back, then fine. If you do find him lunging forward and weaving about, you may find an absolute must is a variety of choke chain. The name does suggest something inhumane, but it can be a lot less damaging to the dogs neck or throat, than a regular collar. Again, in these early training stages a harness, although very beneficial later on, will not allow you the control you need when walking your dog at heel for example. The idea with a choke chain is that you give little sharp tugs, in the direction you wish him to go. This short sharp shock does not hurt the dog as such.

A lot of trainers seem in favour of 'prong collars', as a better alternative to the choke chain. I must admit, when I first encountered them, they appeared to me like some sort of medieval torture implement. They do look quite severe to say the least. However, having read more into these, they do work in a far more humane way than you would imagine. The idea is that the choke chain attachment, evenly draws the prongs around the dogs neck. The choke chain or regular collar, applies pressure in a limited area, usually more so across the throat area. The prong collar, on the other hand, actually applies less pressure at various points of the neck. The prongs are blunt and arranged in such a way, that they should not be able to break the skin of the neck. I have personally used these on two mature rescue German Shepherd dogs who had received very little obedience training and were head strong to say the least. As the dogs were what you might consider as excessive lead pullers, I would only ever lead them with a harness. A couple of times I attempted the standard choke chain but found they would literally choke the dog if they saw another dog, and surged forward in an attempt to greet the dog. I would also find that whilst on country walks, on the odd occasion a rabbit suddenly bolted out of a hedge, the dogs would lunge with such force, that I felt they were about to pull my arm out of its socket. It was at that point, I decided I needed to try a prong collar. I have to say, that for these dogs, it was the best thing I could have done. It wasn't a total cure, but I had much more control, and I also only had to give odd relatively gentle tugs on the lead. After using these for some time I decided to test the effectiveness, in comparison to the original choke chain and harness. I have to say it had made no difference in their obedience as they reverted to lunging and pulling. But as long as I used the prong collars the dogs were fine. They also showed no sign of distress or aversion to my putting the collars on.

My example is probably an extreme case and prong collars are not for everyone, and certainly be unnecessary for every dog. However, as a training aid I was very impressed how effective they can be.

I emphasize again, if you are having problems with pulling behaviour, I suggest you look into using one. The only other thing I would add, is never apply more than gentle pressure or a soft wrist tug. You will probably find, that is all you will need to do anyway. The other thing is, never attempt to put these over the dogs head as they are. You should always un-clip the links and then re-attached on the dogs neck. I would also strongly suggest, anyone interested in using one to have a look at some of the excellent videos on this subject on YouTube.

Again, a lot of people are appalled at the very thought of something like a prong collar or choke chain. In this case my recommendation is to use one of the special wide Whippet collars. I have to say that it is highly unlikely that you will need to resort to any such metal collars with a sensitive Whippet. But I have to give you options and there does seem to be mixed opinions. Some insisting on flat collars others a mixture of both types.

If this is something that intrigues or concerns you, please do a Google search for something like [Whippets and Prong Collars]. You may also be interested to read the following articles among others.

http://www.whippetworld.net/ board/viewtopic.php?f=2&t=1628

http://www.whippetworld.net/ board/viewtopic.php?f=21&t=216

You are probably best to start with a gentle flat collar or a harness, and see how you get on. There is no point taking drastic measures if this is unnecessary.

However, before we get started with those basic training commands I want to firstly remind/introduce you to a couple of useful preliminary aspects of his training. In the initial stages of training, please make the training sessions relatively short. Ten or Fifteen minutes of good concentrated practice should be fine initially. When you feel he is keen to carry on, extend these lessons. Or practice these commands frequently at odd times around the house, rather than appoint one session for a designated time. The idea is that you can use the training at a moments notice when required anyway.

a.) The Release Command

This is covered in the previous chapter, but again, if you are coming to this section first, then an explanation is in order. The 'release command' is particularly useful for a number of reasons. It first of all lets your dog know that he has successfully completed a part of his training. It also hopefully lets the dog know the difference between the serious business of sitting as you come to a busy road for example, and when it is time to play or run off lead in a safe area.

So, it is important to teach this from the moment that you start teaching your dog anything new at all. The release command is, as mentioned in a previous chapter, a word or words that you use at the end of each session or piece of training to let him know the training has finished. This can be, **'finished'**, **'all over', 'training over'**, or something similar. But again please be consistent here with the term you use.

Some people will prefer to issue the release command at the end of each piece of training so that the dog/puppy doesn't become bored with a lot of discipline. This may be necessary in the early stages, and will ensure the puppy remains focused. Others will simply issue the final release command after your training session is complete.

b.) Focus On Me

We teach "focus" as a preliminary command for a very specific reason. A dog that is focused elsewhere is less likely to pay any attention to your requests.

When a dog is focusing on you, the other commands are much easier to teach.

Similarly the dog is far easier to control, when he is not focused on the rest of the environment.

Training Steps:

1. Take a really tempting treat and place it at the end of your dog's nose so that you have his attention. You may find you have to pinch it between your fingers in-case he is tempted to snatch it. Or let him sniff it, and then hold it in your hand, so that he knows it is there, but can't take it.

2. Move the treat gradually away from the dog and over your head; making sure that the dog's eyes are following your hand.

3. Bring the treat down at the back of your head in order for your dog's eyes to meet yours.

4. At the moment your eyes meet, say the command that you will use for asking your dog to focus, so for example say 'focus'. You then click if you are using the clicker method or say good boy/girl to mark the behaviour and finally give him the treat. All of this needs to be done in very quick succession in the beginning, almost all at the

same time. But make sure that you mark the behaviour with the click or praise, only when, at the very moment the dog fulfils the command, in this case focusing on you.

5. Again, if he has completed this successfully, give him the release command. Remember, with the release command, you can just use this at the very end of the training session. However, in the initial stages of training I prefer to use it often and therefore make this habitual as soon as possible. You can then phase this out as his concentration develops, until you only issue it at the very end of the session.

6. Repeat and practice.

7. Gradually increase the time between command, act and click/reward delivery. In this way he will retain focus longer and longer, until you finally give him the reward.

8. Practice, then eventually begin to use variable reward; that is, you gradually phase out giving him a treat, but always praise him with 'good boy' or whatever your praise word is.

Teaching a Whippet to focus on you will probably take 3 to 5 training sessions in a quiet area. It will then need practice in various areas, such as a park with more dogs about to distract him. Therefore gradually increasing distractions, until it becomes a flawless command.

c.) Sit

For the dog that sits naturally, it is simple to capture the behaviour with a click (or **_"good boy/girl"_**). Whilst it is also possible to easily lure the act, so that the dog is in the sit position.

This is a position that comes so naturally to a dog that most Whippet dogs, as they are so naturally intelligent, will pop into the sit position if you show them something that they want.

As previously noted, this command is the best one to start with because sitting is a natural behaviour your dog performs anyway. All you have to do is teach him to do it on command.

To teach your dog to sit on command, follow these steps:

1. Kneel in front of your Whippet and hold a small treat in your dominant hand.

Pinch the treat between your thumb and forefinger so your puppy can see it.

2. Hold the treat directly in front of your Whippet's nose and give him a second to smell it.

3. Say "Sit" in a firm and even tone then immediately move the treat forward, away from you, toward the back of your dog's head. I prefer to keep saying the word sit until he sits. This is a technique known as leading, in that you lead your dog to perform the required action.

4. Your dog should lift his nose to follow the treat and, in doing so, his bottom should lower to the floor.

5. As soon as your dog's bottom hits the ground, click with your clicker or praise him excitedly with good boy/girl to mark the 'sit' behaviour and finally give him the treat.

6. Quickly release your dog, (remember the release word previously noted) repeat and practice.

7. Repeat this sequence several times until your puppy gets the hang of it.

8. Once your puppy does get the hang of the sequence,

you should not have to lead anymore and just say 'sit' and he should sit.

9. If after all this, you find that he doesn't seem to be getting the idea, you can apply gentle pressure to the top of his hips, all the while saying 'sit'. This should hopefully encourage him to sit down.

10. Gradually increase the time between command, act and click/reward delivery. In this way he will retain focus longer and longer, until you finally give him the reward.

Teaching a Whippet to sit in this way will probably take 1 to 3 training sessions in a quiet area then it will need practice in various areas. Gradually increase distractions, to become a flawless command.

d.) Down

Teaching a dog to lie down is another useful command. This can be used for anything from settling your dog when visitors come to the home, right through to telling him to drop at distance in an emergency.

The easiest way to teach a dog the down position initially is to lure the position. After a few goes, he will be offering to get into the position very quickly if he thinks you have something he may want.

What you are effectively doing is to take a treat and pop it onto the end of your dog's nose and lure him to the ground. Here, you are drawing the treat down to the ground. It usually works in between his legs or as near as.

Again, once you have taught your Whippet to sit, teaching him to lie down is the next logical step.

To teach your dog to lie down on command, follow these steps:

1. Kneel in front of your Whippet and hold a small treat in your dominant hand. Pinch the treat between your thumb and forefinger so your puppy can see it.

2. Hold the treat directly in front of your Whippet's nose and give him a second to smell it.

3. Give your puppy the "Sit" command and wait for him to comply.

4. Once your puppy sits, immediately move the treat quickly down to the floor in between your puppy's front paws. It is important at this point to add the word

"Down", or "Lie Down". I often prefer to keep repeating the word "Down", so that he hears it often enough to know that this new action relates to the word.

5. Your puppy should lie down to get the treat. The instant he does, again mark this with a click or praise him excitedly and give him the treat.

6. If your puppy stands up instead of lying down, calmly return to the beginning and repeat the sequence.

7. Again, once he successfully carries out the command, quickly release your dog, (remember the release word previously noted) repeat and practice.

8. Repeat this sequence several times until your puppy gets the hang of it.

9. You should be able to get to the point of skipping the 'sit' command and simply say 'Lie Down', to get the desired action from him.

10. There are some extra options for the dog that is simply not getting the idea. You can sit on a chair and lure your Whippet under your outstretched leg. What this does is to make him crawl under your leg,

which should leave him in the down position.

11. Be patient here, but if after countless attempts, nothing seems to be working then try the following. As you go through the sequence above, if his back end is sticking up in a beg position, gently apply some pressure to his hips. As you gently push down say the words, 'down' or 'lie down'. Again, as soon as he does it, and doesn't immediately get up, click or praise to mark the behaviour and reward.

Teaching a Whippet to lie down will usually take 3 to 6 short training sessions in a quiet area. You will then need to practice in various areas, gradually increasing distractions, to become a flawless command.

e.) Come

Teaching your dog to come to you when called is incredibly impor-

tant. Say, for instance, that you open the front door of your house one day and your Whippet rushes out before you can stop him. Your dog does not understand the danger of a busy street but if you have taught him to come to you when called, you can save him from that danger. In an emergency situation, your down command or the stay command will come in very handy. Using either one of those will hopefully stop him in his tracks. You can then call him back and away from any danger.

The Whippet needs to be taught to come back when called as soon as possible and in careful stages.

Most dogs can either be super responsive to recall or happy to leave you standing all day, calling his name in vain, whilst he chases rabbits or squirrels around the park. Regardless of his behaviour outdoors though, this breed really needs a free run every day in order to be truly healthy.

Even the very best behaved pet that is happy to settle in the home, whether he has been for a run or not, will suffer if he isn't given the opportunity to stretch his muscles. A bored Whippet dog can easily become depressed, destructive or even aggressive.

Owners give many reasons for not giving a Whippet the free run that he needs, most of the reasons are fear in one way or another. The main concern is that the dog owner is scared of their pet running away and never coming back.

Recall training can be broken down into easy steps and recall games added to strengthen the behaviour. The exact same approach is taken when teaching recall as when teaching anything else to the dog. You always set the dog up to succeed; never allow room for failure; therefore building his confidence high.

With recall you need to make certain that your dog sees you as the most interesting and attractive prospect in the area. If you are red faced and shouting his name with frustration he is less likely to want to come back. He will naturally think you are angry with him.

There are some very specific habits that you can procure when teaching recall;

Ideally you should allow your dog off the lead to run or do recall training in an isolated area and certainly not near a busy road were there is a risk of him running across the road and possibly being run over. Please do remember that Whippets do have a reputation to take off after rabbits, and some generally run away. Always be on your guard to potentially hazardous areas and therefore avoid accidents. I once had a situation with an Irish Setter that took off across a field, after she had picked up the scent of something. I literally shouted my head off and fortunately she came to her senses and came running back. Dogs can easily give chase to rabbits and if you are near a road there is a chance the rabbit may cross, along with your dog. Please preempt and avoid this from happening. If in doubt, keep your dog on a long 5 or 10 meter training type lead.

If you get a situation as described above, never punish your dog when he gets to you. Always be welcoming and friendly, no matter how frustrated you are, or he may not come back at all next time.

Never chase your dog. The only time you should give chase is if an emergency situation is apparent. If possible run the other way if he is ignoring you. By being the most interesting thing in the area and rapidly disappearing into the distance you are most likely to attract the attention of your Whippet. Giving chase can be seen as a game for the dog and you giving chase adds to their excitement.

Set up positive results. When your dog is looking for the next thing to do this is the best time to call him and show the treat. Yes, it's trickery but it will convince the dog that he comes to you each time you call.

Whether your dog is ten weeks or ten years old, puppy recall steps will work in the same way.

For complete success it is vital not to move on from the present step unless it is absolutely 100% learned and established. Remember we are aiming for success even if we have to manipulate it at first.

Whether you have never allowed your dog off his leash or he runs away every time you do, these stages will help. It is much better to go too slowly though. You want to avoid giving your dog the idea of running away.

To teach your dog to come to you on command, follow these steps:

1. Work out an extra motivator involving your clicker and some tasty treats of course. Also carry a squeaky toy or something of equal fascination to your dog. Save the toy for recall and only allow short play periods and limited use by your dog. This will ensure that it is a "magic toy" in his mind. Again, the thing to bare in mind is that it needs to make him keen enough to want it.

2. I would always advise you to do this in a secluded open field, preferably away from any road. You may have success with this in a secluded part of a park field, perhaps early morning. It is also a great idea as previously mentioned, to get hold of one of those long retractable leads or a 10 meter plus training lead. That way you can let him off at some distance, but you still have him safely attached, in case he decides to take off.

3. Now simply let him go off, all the while allowing the lead to extend. Stop, and call him back with your recall command (I would advise using his name along with 'come' or 'come on' or 'come here'). The moment he is heading back towards you use a click/praise then take his collar and give him the treat, and always use the release command.

4. It is vital to take the dog's collar every time you give him the treat because this prevents the act of 'grab and run'. Do not be tempted to ask your dog to sit or do anything else at this point, he came to you and this is enough for now, adding extra commands is adding pressure to the recall command and may put your dog off.

5. Only when your dog is coming back every single time using the extended leash, enlist the help of a friend. Your helper is going to hold your dog and you are going to show the dog a treat. Take a few steps away and call the dog. Your helper is then going to release him as you call. As he runs toward you, click/praise, take his collar and treat in exactly the same way. Release him as before.

6. Then, when the above steps are established you can increase the distance that you go before the dog is released. You can start to run away and hide. Eventually you can start to allow the dog off leash and practice

calling him back a few times each walk.

This whole process may take a few weeks but do not be tempted to let your dog off the long leash too soon as he may ignore your call and this can easily develop into a habit of running away.

f.) Stay

After you have taught your dog to come to you on command, the next logical step is to teach him to stay or wait until you call him.

To teach your dog to stay on command, follow these steps:

1. Kneel in front of your Whippet and hold a small treat in your dominant hand. Pinch the treat between your thumb and forefinger so your puppy can see it.

2. Hold the treat directly in front of your Whippet's nose and give him a second to smell it.

3. Give your puppy the "Sit" command and wait for him to comply.

4. Now say "Stay" in a firm, even tone and take a step or two backward away from your puppy.

5. Pause for a second then walk back up to your puppy. Now click/praise to mark the fact that he has stayed put. Finally reward him with a treat. You do not want to release him until you have walked back and he has successfully remained seated throughout.

6. Repeat the sequence several times, rewarding your puppy each time he stays.

Each time you practice this, aim to increase the distance between you and your dog. You can measure this in paces if you like, so two steps to four, then eight and so on. Once I get some distance between me and the dog, I like to add the release so that he comes back to me. So start him in the sit position as before and say 'stay'. I usually keep repeating this as I walk backward. Once you have walked back quite a few paces, stop and pause as long as you feel he is concentrating. Then call him back to you, with 'come on [his name]', praise and give him the treat as before.

g.) Heel

Teaching a Whippet to heel is easy. Or it should be if you have been using this initially when you started his general walk. I always teach walking to heel with him on a leash first then off leash in a safe area. To a certain extent, you will probably have already introduced him to this in the early training as mentioned previously when you started him on his walks. We will extend and add to that training here.

When you are teaching a dog to walk to heel it is important that you focus on the position and never on the leash.

To keep pulling the dog back from a tense leash, to a slack one, whilst stating the command to heel will never work, or may turn into a form of harsh training, which we want to avoid. The dog is not actually learning anything positive with this approach.

Training Steps:

1. Some people prefer to start the puppy in a sit, stay position, and then move to either the right or left hand side of the dog.

2. It is important that you have the loop of the lead through whichever is your preferred lead hand, so it hangs on your wrist. Your puppy should then be on the opposite side to that. So if you hold the loop of the lead in your right hand, have the dog walk at your left side. This is more for control and safety of your puppy in these initial stages. With the other hand, in this case your left, grip the lead, so that it is close to your dog, again giving you greater control. This will also act as a guide or restraint to let your puppy know where you want him, should your puppy surge forward or hang back.

3. Next give the command to "heel", whilst starting to walk. Hopefully your puppy will follow you at your side. All the while say the command "heel", not just once, but keep repeating this.

4. If at this point your puppy has walked with you, without surging in front or lagging behind, and staying at your side; then you can stop click/praise to mark the behaviour and again give him his treat. That is the ideal scenario. However if he doesn't do that, simply stop and start again.

5. Remember, at whatever point he successfully walks at heel and you have praised him, release him before you continue. Once again, only release him, off

lead, in a safe area. If you are doing this training by a roadside, by all means use the release command, but always retain control with the lead.

6. Now do exactly as before, only this time try and go further, perhaps walking several feet or yards. Again stop when you are satisfied he has improved and as before, click/praise, reward and release.

7. Eventually you will have him walking nicely at your side without pulling forward or holding back.

8. When you've completed the session, praise your dog with your usual release command, indicating that you have finished, so that he understands he has been successful, you are pleased and that training is over.

Once again, when training a young puppy who pulls strongly at the leash, you'll need to stand still until your pup understands that he's not going anywhere until he listens. Once your puppy understands that he only receives praise when he begins to respond appropriately, it will only take a few days before he's walking right next to you without pulling on the lead.

Once you get him successfully walking at your side, you can in-crease the difficulty of the exercise by suddenly turning at a right angle, or do a complete about turn. This is more or less what happens in agility training and dog shows. The dog follows precise paths at your side.

As mentioned at the beginning, you can increase the level of difficulty with this exercise by eventually practicing this without the lead. However, only try this in a safe area, and certainly not near a busy road.

Teaching a Whippet to walk nicely at heel will probably take 4 to 6 training sessions in a quiet area. It will then need practice in various areas, gradually increasing distractions, to become a flawless command.

If you follow the steps listed previously, teaching your puppy to respond to the five basic commands should not be a difficult or lengthy process. Make sure to keep your training sessions short. Only about 10 or 15 minutes to ensure that your puppy stays engaged. If he starts to get bored or distracted in the middle of a session, stop for now and pick it up again later.

4.) Incorporating Hand Signals

Once your Whippet is consistently responding to the five basic commands you can start to incorporate hand signals. The process is a little bit different for each command, but you should be able to follow the same basic steps to incorporate a hand signal. Make sure that the hand signal you choose for each command is easily distinguishable from the others so your dog doesn't get confused. You can of course incorporate hand signals along with your training.

Follow these steps to incorporate hand signals:

1. Kneel in front of your Whippet and hold a small treat in your non-dominant hand.
2. Hold your other hand in front of your puppy's nose as if you were holding a treat.
3. When you have your puppy's attention, give the "Sit" command and shape your hand into a fist then move it forward toward the back of your puppy's head just as you did earlier with the treat in hand.
4. When your puppy's bottom touches the ground, click/praise as before, release him and praise excitedly and offer him the treat from your other hand
5. Repeat this sequence several times until your puppy responds consistently and associates the fist/hand signal with the sit command. You should then be able to simply clench the fist without moving it over his head, and he should sit each time.

Use this same process to teach your dog a hand signal for the "Down" command. Holding your hand out flat, parallel to the floor, move the palm up and down while you say the word "Down" or lie down

For "Stay", I would recommend holding your palm flat and as near vertical as possible towards your dog. This is not dissimilar to a traffic officer holding out their palm to get motorists to stop.

Again taking the traffic officer analogy, use the same signal they use to beckon traffic towards them, for when you need him to "Come to you".

For the "heel" command I usually pat/slap the side of my leg to indicate, that is where you want him to be.

Once you have taught your puppy to respond to hand signals as well as verbal commands you can move on to the next step which is to phase out the food rewards.

5.) Phasing Out Food Rewards

Food is a highly motivating reward for dogs. But you do not want your Whippet to become dependent on a food reward indefinitely to perform the desired behaviour. Once your puppy starts to respond consistently with the right behaviour, when you give him a command, you should start phasing out the treats. Start by only rewarding your puppy every other time then cut it back to every third time and so on. Even though you are phasing out the food rewards you still need to praise your puppy so he knows that you are pleased with him. You may even choose to substitute a food reward for a toy and give your puppy a brief play session with the toy as a reward instead of the treat. Do not feel guilty that your poor dog is looking sad, disappointed and bewildered by no longer receiving his treat. All dogs are only too happy to please their owner, and he will soon get used to no longer getting the treat every time. Of course you are free to treat your dog occasionally. But you are doing his long time health no favours by constantly giving him treats. Also please be aware that there are dog trainers who do not use treats at all and successfully train happy dogs.

6.) Swapping

If you are training any dog, then it is a good idea to teach swapping very early on.

Every dog should know how to swap because this is a good and fair way to take something away from the dog that he shouldn't have. Obviously if this is something dangerous to the dog, then I would not recommend being so polite. In an emergency you would have to snatch this immediately and take it out of harms way.

However, in non dangerous situations, proceed as follows.

1. Whilst your dog is playing with a toy, have another one to hand
2. Offer the new toy in front of him, say the word 'leave' or 'swap'; you may have to repeat the command word until he drops it.
3. Hopefully he drops the one he has, ready to take the one you have. At the point

he drops it click/praise, and reward; allowing him to carry on with the new toy.

Retrieving with balls is a really good way to practice this. You can show the dog that you are happy to throw the next ball just as soon as he has handed over the one he just fetched back.

If your dog doesn't want to give something to you then you can change your approach and convince him that the item is pretty much worthless. If he thinks you don't care about an item then your dog is far less likely to care about it either. Even the most precious thing often loses value very quickly with lack of human interest.

7.) Further Training

There are many options for further training with the Whippet. The choices are endless for sports and fun classes, particularly for the fit and healthy members of the breed. The next chapter discusses Whippet racing, which for some is THE reason for becoming guardian to a Whippet. For others not interested in Whippet racing, there are still a number of excellent activities to consider.

On that note, it is vital that you ensure your own dog's joints are sound before asking too much of him physically.

Sporty dogs can join agility classes, flyball teams and even CaniX, where owners run with their dogs. All of these are great fun and perfect for the more active dogs and owners amongst us.

Flyball is a team relay that includes a mixture of hurdles and speed.

Agility is a sport where the dog encounters a series of hurdles, weaves and similar obstacles in a timed race against the clock. The sport is great fun and a lot of dogs excel at agility.

Competitive obedience is an art where the dog is taught sharp obedience that looks great in a show ring. The more modern forms are heelwork to music or dancing with dogs. You will no doubt find that your dog makes an enthusiastic obedience partner.

Therapy dogs, a job for the older steadier pet, are assessed and taken into homes and hospitals at visiting times. If your dog is kind and you want to do more with him, or her, then registering them as a therapy dog will change both of your lives.

8.) Discipline Whilst Training.

We have now talked a lot about positive reinforcement training, as opposed to any punishment based methods. I always advocate a firm but fair approach and dislike the idea of 'disciplining' a dog. But it is worth clarifying your approach to training. Most dogs behave perfectly well and respect you as their carer. Some dogs however, can have a wilful personality and they will sometimes test you and misbehave. Again, I would never advocate hitting a dog nor would I advocate being a strict disciplinarian for the sake of it. But if your puppy does appear to be de-

veloping wilful disobedience, the following will be worth bearing in mind.

1) Remember a well behaved adult is the result of a correctly trained puppy, given firm basic training.

2) Your dog will respect you when you are firm but fair, and when you say 'No', they should know this by your tone of voice. You obviously do not want to become a sergeant major, barking commands. But if say for example, you tell your dog to stay or wait and he starts to move before you have given the word, then tell him in a slightly disapproving voice, 'No'.

Do not feel bad, or that you are being cruel and do not forget that this training could potentially save your dogs life in an emergency situation. In this respect, I would not advise shouting at your dog whilst generally training your puppy. However, if you are in an emergency situation shouting may be the only way to shock or frighten your puppy into realizing something is seriously wrong. If you shout all the time, he will probably see this as normal, and be unable or unlikely to differentiate when something is seriously wrong.

Sometimes he will need to know that he is doing wrong with a firm 'No'. It will be even more satisfying to him, when you shower him with praise. Also remember some personalities need and respect someone who they take as a strong leader. Again, without wishing to get into a debate about 'alpha dog' training, dogs generally respect you when you are firm but fair.

CHAPTER SEVEN

WHIPPET RACING

Although Whippet racing still remains popular amongst enthusiasts, this popularity has to a large extent over the years, been superseded as a sport by Greyhound racing. If this is something you are keen to get involved in, hopefully this chapter will inspire you to get started.

Around the early 1900's, Whippet racing was so popular that in certain areas, it was almost on a par with horse racing.

1) Whippet Racing

In the UK Whippet racing is administered on behalf of the Whippet Club Racing Association (WCRA). There are twelve clubs that are affiliated with the Association. These are spread from Scotland to Cornwall.

The main focus of Whippet racing is to have fun and to accommodate all standards. Most Whippet racing clubs will race on a Sunday afternoon. Racing will usually last for a couple of hours, and you'll be able to watch other dogs compete. New Whippet racers have extra time to get introduced to the sport. Most races are usually handicapped to give all Whippets a fair chance.

Owners of Whippets that race, tend to focus more on their dog's weight than on height for racing. Although the WCRA does now enforce strict rules regarding the height of dogs limited to 21 inches and bitches to 20 inches. The Whippet Club, which also happens to be the oldest Whippet Breed Club in the UK, formed a committee, The Whippet Club Racing Association, (WCRA)

to promote pedigree Whippet racing. The ruling within the club did not allow for Whippet racing to involve prize money; this was to maintain the amateur status of pedigree Whippet racing in the UK. After both Greyhound and Terrier blood was introduced into dog racing, these cross bred Whippets ceased racing for the Whippet Club Racing Association. The non-pedigree Whippets were much faster, and UK owners could crossbreed with other hound breeds to have a larger gene pool. There are currently clubs which incorporate both pedigree and non pedigree dog racing.

Whippet racing is still popular today. Most participate in Whippet clubs, with their own special racetracks. Many Whippet dog owners aspire to win the Championship weight group that their dogs compete in.

For more information about UK Whippet racing, visit:
thewhippetclub.com/whippet-racing/ or wcra.btck.co.uk.

For more information on American Whippet Racing, whippetracing. org

Americanwhippetclub.net/awc-events/national-specialty

a) Whippet Racing in a nutshell

In general most Whippet clubs meet on a regular basis and mainly on the weekend. You will probably find that if there are several clubs in a close geographical area, they will ensure the meets do not clash.

Whichever Whippet club you join whether this is affiliated to the

WCRA or not, you are likely to experience the following:

Once you join a club, you will usually meet on a weekend and expect the whole event to last an afternoon, some may be all day. Whippet racing is considered a family event and you will no doubt find everyone is friendly and accommodating.

You will no doubt have an event calendar for scheduled races throughout the year. You will probably kept well informed of your inclusion in a race or possible cancellations.

Again, although most clubs follow a similar format and rules, these are likely to differ between clubs. These variations usually include the type of race track, i.e. distance, whether straight or oval, as well as variations to calendar meetings.

b) A typical race meeting

Set Up

Many clubs do not have the luxury of a permanent track, and quite often a communal playing field may be used for the afternoon. So in this case, everything will need to be set up including the traps, lure, etc. The traps alone can take time and they can be heavy and bulky. Also if the traps are set for handicap, then these will need measuring and placing, whereas a scratch race has all of the traps together in a line.

Weigh-Ins

Weigh ins can take time also, as each dog has to be weighed and handicapped, if this is the method used. Some clubs impose strict time limits to weigh ins, in other words if you turn up after this time, chances are you will not be permitted to race. Also, as there is generally waiting around whilst other dogs are weighed, any race fees may be collected at this time.

Schooling Trials

These are separate races for younger dogs to gain experience racing, so are generally kept separate from the actual races. As a beginner your Whippet will probably start in these schooling races, which can often take place with experienced dogs that haven't raced for a while.

Races

Once your Whippet is in a position to take part in normal racing, again depending on club variations, you can expect between two and four runs.

The race format may well involve heats broken into quarter, semi and then final. Usually 5 dogs will race at one time and similarly to athletic track events, first and second place will progress to the next round. The dogs not qualifying are generally placed in yet another race, ensuring that the dogs are competing throughout the meeting.

Open events.

Chances are, once you join a club you will be happy to just take part in those club meetings, perhaps because you have limited time available. However, other clubs sometimes allow non members to race at open events. These are a great opportunity to test your dog against other perhaps faster dogs. For example, although the WCRA is a governing body for Whippet racing it does not hold regular meetings in the same way that a club does. However, they do hold championship meetings that are 'open events' and are well worth attending. These meetings are held four times per year, but you do need a WCRA passport to enter (the passport is just a document with all of your dogs details such as KC registration etc.). These are races on straights as well as bends and are not handicapped as such. But weight categories are adhered to, and similar dogs are grouped to race.

That is Whippet racing in a brief nutshell. Obviously there are specific details relating to each club. So once you have established a club in your area then the first thing is to find out more about their rules and regulations and apply to join.

c) The racing Whippet

The Whippet bloodline is historically/genetically related to the Italian Greyhound. However, what is known as the 'hackney gait', a trait of the Italian Greyhound, is not considered desirable for either showing or racing. In particular the high 'hackney gait', is known to be detrimental to the speed of the racing dog. Having said that, the dog with a 'hackney gait', will still be a fast runner, but perhaps not able to compete as well as dogs without the characteristic.

Other than the aforementioned physical impediment above, characteristics of a show type will not nec-essarily be important for the dog with racing potential. The most important considerations for the race dog are stamina and speed. However, without proper training, your dog is unlikely to reach its full potential in racing.

For anyone wishing to purchase a pup for its racing potential, this is largely a matter of luck. Of course genetic breeding stock from past champions have a good chance of also becoming racing champions, but there is no guarantee. In fact it is not until the puppy is at around six months of age, that the future race potential will be evident.

Race track training

Once you have had success at this and he has gained sufficient experience, you are now ready to consider his race track training.

Remember that it is important, as with any form of training, to set your dog up to succeed. In this respect training is best done whereby you initially race him with an older slower dog. One thing is for certain, it is always best to use a muzzle, as chases can develop into play fighting and at worse, fighting. This is often due to initial inexperience and over excitement. As the Whippet becomes more experienced and less distracted, this becomes less of a problem.

As with any kind of training, it is best to build up the distances raced in gradual stages. It is usually considered that a good starting distance is around 20 yards (18.3 meters). You then build up gradually until he is comfortably covering 100 to 200 yards. (91.5 to 103 meters). He will then be in a good position to cover a full race distance quite comfortably.

Conditioning your whippet for racing

In an actual race, it is not advisable to allow your dog to feed at least eight hours before they are due to race. For general training, there is no need to be so strict, but please do leave as much time as possible, between when they feed and when they train.

Most Whippets keep themselves in top shape by running around their yard or property. However, it's best if you schedule planned sprints regularly. Sprinting will help develop stamina and good footing required for the 200-yard race course. If you're planning to race seriously, you'll need to walk, run and train your Whippet a few times a week. It's more fun if you take a friend with you. In that way you can get your Whippet to run from one person to the next.

Remember that if you are serious about Whippet racing, you need to view their training as seriously as any athlete. It is therefore important to regularly exercise him and not allow him to get out of shape and become idle. This conditioning will not only help with his ability to race, but for his own health benefits, will keep him fit and healthy.

Using a Muzzle For Racing

As mentioned previously, for racing, your Whippet is going to need a muzzle. The excitement of the race and competitive nature of Whippets can result in a mass dog fight unless the muzzle is worn to prevent this. You also do not want them grabbing the lure should they catch up to it.

You can start showing your Whippet puppy the muzzle once you start your training sessions. This should be at around six weeks before you start taking him to schooling races. In the beginning your Whippet will resist the muzzle when it is placed over his mouth. You'll need to place it securely, and allow him to wear it for about 5 minutes the first few times. After that you can gradually extend the length of time that he wears the muzzle. In the beginning he'll scratch and try to pull the muzzle off. Trainers recommend slowly increasing the time until your Whippet wears the muzzle until he can bare it for around 30 minutes. He needs to get to the point where he totally ignores the muzzle.

After Racing

Again, baring in mind any athletic activity, it is important to cool down after a race as well as any training session. It is important to not let him cool off too quickly. So as soon as the race or training is over, cover him in a blanket and rub him briskly to remove excess sweat. Keep him covered to ensure he doesn't chill and remove his muzzle. You can now allow him to take a drink of water if he wants. However, make sure he does not drink all he wants, just a small drink, as too much can lead to colic or other complications. You should then walk him around, with the blanket or his coat on, for several minutes. If he has just raced, he should be sufficiently cooled and settled to place him in his crate/carrier.

Training for racing

Formal race training of Whippet pups usually starts around 8 to 10 months of age. So there is no need to panic about specific training as soon as you purchase your pup. This will allow you plenty of time to ensure he has received his obedience training. What is usually recommended though, is that you socialize your pup at club meetings. By doing this on a regular basis, it allows the pup to get used to race meets and the whole event.

There are no set rules as to when puppies should actually start schooling, so again it is best to check with your designated club. However, clubs affiliated to the WCRA do not permit puppies less than 6 months old to chase a mechanical lure.

d) Early Race Training

Puppies in general will want to chase and play games and this is the best thing you can do to get your Whippet started. So build up his interest in chasing balls or by getting him to chase toys or fur/fabric pieces as you run away from him.

Lure Training

Lure training is a simple matter of dragging some sort of rag or furry object along the floor, which the Whippet hopefully takes an interest in and chases. This is not always as easy as it sounds and some Whippet pups need extra time and patience to get the idea that they chase the object. Quite often, if the pup seems disinterested you simply need to use a favourite toy to get the same interest. Do not be tempted to give in to the pups desire to get hold of the lure/toy. As long as you only do this for several minutes or so, you will not feel you are being unfair and cruel. Again, just remember that it is simply an aspect of his training.

You would need to continue lure training until your Whippet is well experienced in this. Only then should you consider entering your dog for competition races. Depending on where you live, and the competitions for your area, puppy races can take place when the pups are aged 6 to 12 months. Over 12 months of age, the Whippet transitions from puppy-hood to adult and consequently competes in adult races.

Some trainers prefer to build up the Whippets interest in the 'lure', by placing the dog in their cage and showing them or dragging the lure, but not allowing them to touch the lure. This is seen as teasing by some, but it certainly encourages the keenness and interest of the Whippet. You should only do this for short periods of time and should be stopped if the dog becomes overly excited and keen to get at the lure. Obviously the idea is to gain the dogs interest but not to overly disturb or arouse a problem behaviour. Again, this should not be done everyday either. Once or twice per week for several weeks should get the desired effect, for when he races on a track.

If you have already seen a Whippet or Greyhound race, you will know that the dogs are lined up in cages with a wire fronted trap door. The dogs are then waiting in anticipation for the door to open and the chase to begin. At this stage the dogs are full of excitement and anticipation as they have been trained to know what is coming next. As a mechanical lure passes in front of the cages, the trap doors are released and the dogs begin the chase. This initial training is designed to replicate that anticipation and excitement.

Once you gain this interest, you take this a step further by using the same object as a lure. It is only really practical to do this with someone else, or if you have a mechanically operated lure.

So ideally you take the dog into an open field, or similar area that is safe from distractions

and use the following steps:

1. You hold onto your Whippet, by his collar and leash.

2. Your friend walks away at a sufficient distance in front of you, with a long line attached to the lure.
3. Have the lure a few feet in front of your Whippet, but not too close for him to grab it.
4. Hopefully the Whippet should be keen and interested to try to get hold of the lure.
5. At this point have your friend start to run away and when they are some distance away, but not too far, release your Whippet.
6. If he chases the lure, then your training has been a success.
7. Alternatively, try releasing your dog as the lure gets further and further away each time.

Always be safety conscious when releasing him, as you do not want him to get distracted and start running off, towards an open road or something. In the initial stages, I prefer to use a long training line and have a third person standing in the distance to the dogs right or left. The training lead is attached to the dogs collar and is not left loose in the path of the running dog. The third person then runs along so that your Whippet is not impeded in his chasing the lure.

Once the puppy reaches at least 6 months of age he can then be introduced to the mechanical lure. If your previous chase games have been regularly carried out, he should have no trouble chasing the lure. These sessions with the lure are not full on races but built up over short distances to give him the best chance of success. Incidentally he is not introduced to the trap just yet, but held and released by hand.

Training with the trap

The trap may be frightening to a pup, so care is needed and introduction given in stages.

1. He may panic if immediately confined in the trap so the first step is to have the back and the front open and allow him to wander in and out at will.
2. You next introduce the lure, by ensuring he is in the box and then drag the lure a short distance which he hopefully chases. The lure should start at the front of the trap so that the puppy can see this straight away and then see it move.
3. Once he is used to the idea of chasing the lure from inside an open trap, you progress to closing the trap. Again do not shut the box at both ends but keep the front down and the back open in case he panics and wishes to back out. It is also advisable to hold him or at least place a reassuring hand on him whilst he is in the trap. Initially it is best to release the front without a spring in place as this could frighten the dog. Once he has successfully exited the

trap without the spring, put the spring back on but again lift manually. The spring will probably make a noise, but not to the extent that will frighten him.

After a few attempts like this, move on to closing the back and allowing the trap door to spring open mechanically.

Training with other dogs

As previously mentioned, it is often advisable to run a pup with an older experienced dog. The main reason for this is that the older dog will know exactly what to do and hopefully this will encourage the pup to follow suit. It is also advisable that the older dog is potentially slower, again to instil confidence and independence about racing to win. You would then need to progress with more dogs and introduce handicaps. There are bound to be other club members who will help you with this and race their dogs with you.

Official race trials

Up until now this initial training has emulated actual race conditions but not quite an official race. Your next step is for the club to officially clear and approve your Whippet to race. Remember that if you are connected to the WCRA this will be no sooner than 12 months of age. So at this point, your training will have been a 6 month or so duration. This is something that is specific to a club in terms of rules and regulations but the general idea is to prove that your dog is mature enough and well behaved in order to race. Upon acceptance and successful completion of this trial your Whippet can now enter actual races

Training for bend racing

This again progresses on from straight racing and does require careful training. It is usually recommended that bend training and consequently racing is only carried out once a dog has regular experience of straight races. Bend races do put strain on the dog that normal straight runs do not, and so the risk of injury is greater.

Once you are happy to commence bend training, as always this should be carried out in gradual steps. Hand slipping (holding the dog wherever you want to start him) is usually carried out and is usually either actually on the bend or just before. The outside lane is also a preferred start point to allow the dog more room for error as it reads the bend. You would also need a helper to 'catch' the dog as it exits the bend and doesn't go flying off round the track. You would then increase the start distances so that he gets used to running the bend at greater speed.

Keeping fit

Whilst doing this extra training your Whippet should be permitted at least 1 hours exercise per day. This does not necessarily need to be in one go, and can be either a brisk walk on the lead or preferably off lead sprints also. This is usually considered to be ample to maintain race fitness.

However, do be careful not to over work your dog, particularly if he is racing on a regular basis each week. This is especially important as the dog ages. You do not want to wear him out, particularly as he starts to stiffen with old age and perhaps be afflicted with early stage arthritis to some degree. It is also recommended that bitches are not raced after the finish of their season, and this is usually up to 13 weeks.

d) Whippet racing clubs

Modern amateur Whippet club races generally take place on a straight grass track of between 140 and 200 yards (128 meters to 183 meters). The dogs start the race in traps, either wooden or metal, similar in construction to professional Greyhound racing traps. They would be either manually operated with a lever to lift the front gate, or electronically operated. In the past, lures would be colored onion bags and were used mainly for practical purposes of durability, easily washable as they can collect mud, and importantly they are easier for the dogs to see. Being sighthounds, Whippets when racing are vision oriented as opposed to scent. The lure itself has to travel fast enough to evade capture by the racers.

Modern lures are usually mechanical, motor operated. However, it is still possible to construct a perfectly workable apparatus from a converted bicycle. The bike can be set up similarly to an exercise bike so that the rear wheel is converted by removing the tyre and some sort of a guard welded to accommodate the rope as it winds the rope back around the wheel, avoiding any tangles in the wheel hub. Motor driven pulleys have also been cleverly converted using for example car starter motors. These can easily be mounted and converted with a suitable pulley wheel to wrap the rope as it is driven. The whole thing can be run in remote areas using a 12 volt car battery.

Races would then be timed using either simple stop watches or sophisticated timing equipment, depending on finances available to the club. Without electronic timing equipment timing is reliant on human judgment and in many cases two people are employed to accurately take the times. If a unanimous judges decision fails to establish the winner, a photo finish may be required or failing that a split decision may result in a re-run. There are usually two other judges, the trap or starter judge who would ensure that the dogs have been correctly prepared with muzzles fitted etc. A second judge would be positioned mid way to ensure no infringements take place as the dogs run.

In addition to straight tracks, some Whippet clubs have the luxury of bend racing similar to Greyhound racing. In some cases, clubs will use the actual Greyhound tracks for their race meets. The distances can vary from 220 yards to 350 yards (201 to 320 meters), and handicapping may well be utilized as discussed next.

Handicapping

Whippet club handicapping has several methods depending on club

rules. However, the common forms are based on either the weight of the dog or a time handicap. The various types will be explained as follows.

Weight Handicapping

Handicapping of dogs based on weight is not the same as other sports where competitors have the same or similar weights. With Whippet weight handicapping a race may have several dogs ranging from 18 to 25 pound in weight. The rule applied is usually 1 pound of the dogs weight is equal to 1 yard or in some cases half a yard. To give you an example if you took a 20 pound dog and a 23 pound dog, you obviously have a 3 pound difference between the two. So taking the 1 pound to 1 yard rule, the 20 pound dog would be given a 3 yard start on the 23 pound dog. If there was an 18 pound dog, this in turn would be place 5 yards ahead of the 23 pound dog and 2 yards ahead of the 20 pound dog. But as this is not an exact science, should the 18 pound dog run far quicker than expected, it would not be given the same lead next time. Any dog that loses will either retain their original starting position or be given an extra yard or so to improve their chances of winning. So you may eventually establish that the 18 and 20 pound dogs could start neck and neck (at scratch) and the 18 pound dog still wins, because it has a greater athletic ability.

Time Handicapping

Time handicapping is the approach used for Greyhound racing and is commonly used for Whippet racing. A dog would be given a solo run around a track or over a straight distance and whatever time they finish will establish where he starts. The way the handicapping works is that the per yard handicap would be established according to 1 yard equalling either 0.06 seconds or 0.07, depending again on the club rules. The dog that races the fastest time over the distance is known as the scratch dog? So if that particular 'scratch dog' has run 150 yards in 9.10 seconds, and the new dog had covered the 150 yards in 9.40 seconds then the 9.40 second dog would be given a 5 yard start on the 9.10 second dog. The way this works is if we take 0.06 seconds and divide 0.30 by that 0.30/0.06 = 5, so the 9.40 second dog gets a 5 yard start on the 9.10 second dog.

The whole point of handicapping is to give slower less able dogs a chance of winning a race. If the handicapping has been set/established correctly, the dogs would all cross the finish line roughly at the same time. Again if a dog loses it will be given a better handicap (greater chance of winning next time). If that dog then wins, the handicap it had is reduced.

Some clubs do not operate the above handicapping in the strictest sense but may use a mixture of the two. So one week it will be weight based, the next week time based. In some cases all dogs will start together, which some see as the natural way races should be run, in other words, the best dog wins. But this can be very discouraging for dogs that are slower and would perhaps never win a race without handicapping.

Grading

An alternative to races where a mixed bunch of abilities start a race together is grading. In this case, dog of relatively similar ability are grouped to race together. So the fastest dogs would be group A, next fastest group B and so on. Sometimes handicapping may be used for faster dogs, or consistently faster dogs within a group would move out of that group into the next higher. Again the idea is that you end up with a group of relative equal ability. This would then give any one of them a chance of winning a race, perhaps because it has built up more strength and stamina over the weeks. Grading is usually the preferred method in the U.S.A

e) Competition Whippet Racing

PLEASE NOTE: The following is a basic guideline for registering a Whippet to race in the UK as an example. In the U.S.A these rules will vary depending on the organization, but the idea is usually the same. Again the purpose here is not to go into specific detail of rules and regulations for Whippet racing in different countries. A whole book could easily cover the various Idiosyncrasies, so again please refer to the specifics of your chosen race club.

Registering to race

There are many clubs around the country and different rules and regulations apply depending on the club in question. However, to give you a rough idea of what to expect I have summarized registering and passport application with the WCRA the full details can be found at *http://www.wcra.btck.co.uk/Co nstitutionandRules/3Registration.*

You will also find much more information concerning their rules of racing much of which is covered above.

First and foremost their rules on registration may seem strict and other clubs may suit you better with less strict rules and procedures. In most cases a race passport is needed which is basically all of the details about the dog including KC registration, height of the dog etc.

To register with the WCRA, you would need the following:

1. KC registration
2. DNA testing and Five generations of registered breeding acceptable to the WCRA and Whippet Club committees
3. A Whippet should be at least 1 year (12 calendar months) old.
4. A Whippet cannot enter or compete in a WCRA race until the dog is registered with a passport.
5. A dog Whippet must be no more than twenty one inches high and a bitch no more than twenty inches high.
6. At 12 months of age the Whippet must weigh at least (minimum) 14 pounds.

7. A Whippet can only be WCRA registered having undergone the following vaccinations: distemper, contagious hepatitis, leptospira canicoln, leptospiraicterohaemorrhagiae and parvovirus

Once again, this is a brief introduction to Whippet racing. If this is something that is of interest to you, I would highly recommend researching the resources chapter at the end of the book. You will find website links to most of the organisations connected with Whippet racing in both the UK and USA.

CHAPTER EIGHT:

GROOMING YOUR WHIPPET

Grooming a Whippet is easy. This breed has a tight, short coat, which does not carry burs, and also does not tangle to form nasty mats. Your Whippet should always have a good coat, with very little shedding. Proper grooming will help to keep your Whippet looking and feeling his best. Regular grooming also helps to prevent health problems related to poor hygiene.

1) Grooming and Parasites:

Before we get into the actual grooming and bathing, it is worth mentioning parasites that you may encounter whilst grooming. We will talk more about parasites in another chapter, but as you are most likely to notice fleas and tics etc., whilst grooming we will discuss dealing with those here. Fleas, tics and mites are the most likely culprits you will encounter. Fortunately, as the coat of your Whippet is relatively short, fleas in particular are not as problematic as longer, double coated dogs. Fleas prefer to bury and hide themselves in a relatively thick coat. They are therefore bound to feel more exposed, vulnerable and less safe on a thin, less dense coat. They will also be much easier to pick out with fine toothed flea combs.

The added problem with fleas, is that they can also set up home in the dogs bedding or the furnishings of your home. It is therefore necessary to not only treat the dog, but their bedding and your furnishings. If you ever get a particularly bad infestation, it may be necessary to call in professional pest controllers. I have never had to experience this, but have had experience with a minor infestation. I found that fumigating the house with a good smoke bomb did the trick. All I then had to do was to keep on top of any fleas invading either the dog or house with the occasional flea spray or powder on the bedding, and a number of remedies on the dog.

It is up to you what remedies you use on your dog. So called 'spot on' treatments are commonly recommended by vets. They do work, but a lot of dog owners, who are more organically inclined, are against the idea of applying these because of a potential toxic effect to the dog. It is not for me to comment about the long term affect of any such toxins to the future health of the dog. What I have also noticed is that long time market leaders such as Frontline have recently been proved to not be as affective as they once were. The vet that I currently use recommends a product called Stronghold as a much better alternative. I have to say that I have used this product and it does seem to work, with only the occasional flea showing up. My dogs appear perfectly healthy, vital and seemingly unaffected by this product. I hasten to add here, that I am in no way recommending nor endorsing any product, but am merely speaking about veterinary advice I have been given and personal experience. Other vets or individuals may well disagree with this information.

If you use a 'spot on' treatment, they are generally affective for one or two months depending on the product. It is also worth bearing in mind that although there are shampoos that claim, to be effective against fleas, I would never rely on these as a regular flea treatment remedy. As we have stated above, regular bathing with shampoos is not recommended. By all means use a shampoo that offers flea treatment, but only for when you bathe your dog.

I have also used natural remedies to treat parasites such as fleas. In the past I have used natural oils such as neem, cederwood, lemongrass and citronella. To be fair, I am not convinced that they are effective on all dogs. I have generally applied those once per week, and it seems they are more effective with shorter coated dogs such as Whippets. But I have found that double coated dogs such as German Shepherds have still had episodes of scratching obvious flea bites. They have probably helped considerably, but I am not sure they are a 100% effective alternative for all dogs. Again, I am only speaking from experience and other users may well have had a better outcome. What I have found to be an effective, useful application is diluted lemon juice. I generally use the bottled lemon juice available from supermarkets, rather than actual lemons. Be careful with the dilution for Whippets. As they are prone to skin sensitivity you may be better starting with a dilution of 1 part lemon juice to 10 parts water. The point is, it needs to be strong enough to not necessarily kill the fleas, but at least to repel them. But again, not too strong that it starts to affect the skin of your Whippet. You will also find, that any bites your dog does suffer, the lemon juice soothes any itching irritations.

Tics and mites will be discussed later, but generally, insecticides available from either your vet or pet shop will be needed to deal with them. Fleas seem to be a common problem for most geographical areas, but tics are not a problem for all. So again, not everyone will have a problem with all parasites.

2.)Grooming Tools and Methods

Some dogs do not react well to grooming because they do not like being held still. Because grooming is so important however, you should get your puppy used to grooming from an early age. Brush your puppy for a few seconds at a time several times a day until he no longer seems bothered by it. Then you can cut back to one longer brushing session each day and then as I said, perhaps once per week will be all that is needed. You should also frequently touch your puppy's paws and ears so that once you start trimming his nails and cleaning his ears he will be used to this kind of handling.

When grooming, always be gentle and brush or comb, with slow careful strokes. The last thing you want is for your dog to start shaking and be left traumatized, or the very least, disliking the experience. Whippets are generally a clean breed so they may not require a lot of bathing.

Again, the adult Whippet requires a weekly brush at the very least to keep their coat in good condition and prevent hair around the house. Daily grooming with a fine bristle brush is recommended by some owners and particularly when they shed usually around spring and then winter time. You will hear different stories from different owners as far as hair shedding. Some report a high frequency and some hardly any at all.

Be careful not to use grooming brushes/rakes more suitable for thick double coated dogs. Remember the Whippet has a relatively thin coat. A brush that is too harsh will hurt your Whippets delicate skin. This will also make the grooming experience unpleasant and at worse traumatic.

A massage with a rubber hound glove should follow, and this keeps the Whippet's coat smooth and his skin healthy. Your puppy Whippet should become accustomed to being groomed every day if needed. Some Whippets may struggle in the beginning, but most Whippets learn to enjoy the bonding and close contact.

I would suggest preceding grooming with the following:

1. It is entirely up to you, but I prefer to regularly hand rub the coat and skin, first of all. This serves two purposes, firstly you are effectively massaging your dog as well as removing any dead loose hair and skin. Secondly, it allows you to check your Whippet for any lumps, bumps or sensitive skin parts that may require attention. Remember to take your Whippet to the veterinarian if you notice any unusual lumps or skin irritations.

2. This is then followed with a good brushing, preferably with a bristle brush that isn't too stiff. In order to remove as much dead skin and hair,

do this against the lay of the coat. This effectively roughs up the coat, but is a lot more thorough than simply brushing with the lay.

3. You can finish by brushing back the coat, with the lay, using the bristle brush. Some people prefer to use hound gloves if you can get one, or a rubber curry comb.

4. Also check for any long hairs that appear around the legs or muzzle. It is best to trim these with a pair of blunt ended scissors, to avoid accidentally stabbing your dog as you trim.

Rubber Curry Comb: The curry comb fits into your palm and contains flexible rubber nibs. It works by loosening your Whippet's undercoat, and brings all the grime to the surface of your Whippet's coat.

3) Bathing your Whippet

On occasion it may be necessary to bathe your Whippet, in particular if whilst outdoors he gets muddy. As a matter of routine, I always use an old towel to dry my dogs legs and feet, on damp, wet outings. You will usually find that this sufficiently dries and cleans any soiled areas.

Organic or Natural Shampoo: Whippets do best with an organic or natural, chemical free shampoo. Since they are prone to skin sensitivities, dry skin, or flaky skin. Because of this it is best not to wash your Whippet very often and certainly not every week. If you have to wash mud from their legs, feet or coat, please do this with warm water, but no shampoo. You can then either towel dry and or use a hair drier to ensure your do does not get chilled.

Avoid bathing your dog on a regular basis as this strips the skin and coat of natural healthy oils. Remember that your Whippet's skin has a pH of 7.5, while humans have a pH of 5.5. That said, never use human shampoo on your Whippet. This will lead to scaling and skin irritation. There are numerous dog shampoos available for various canine skin problems.

Remember also that Whippets dislike being cold, or generally getting wet. Be sure therefore to always use warm water, but not too warm and never hot. Your Whippet needs to have a positive experience with water when being bathed.

Don't forget that your dog relies on natural oils to keep the skin soft, healthy and free from drying out. The oil also has the benefit of protecting the coat and retaining its water resistance. It is tempting to consider how grubby and uncomfortable us humans feel when we don't bathe regularly. However, you cannot take that same viewpoint where your dog is concerned.

Some Whippet owners advocate rubbing olive oil into the coat prior to bathing. This is especially useful if the dog has an obvious skin problem. This is fine, but I would further add that it is probably a good idea to do this after wards as well, until he replenishes his natural oils once more. I wouldn't advise using too

much though, as you do not wish to have oil all over your furnishings. A few drops that you brush into the coat after he is dry, is probably all you need. Or if you are aware of any sensitive areas, then perhaps apply a little oil to those parts only.

To bathe your Whippet at home follow the steps outlined below:

1. Give your Whippet a good brushing before you bathe him to get rid of accumulated loose hair.
2. Fill your bathtub with a few inches of lukewarm water. You may also want to put down a rubber bath mat so your dog doesn't slip in the tub.
3. Place your Whippet in the tub and wet down his fur with a handheld hose or by pouring water over him.
4. Avoid getting your Whippet's eyes and ears wet when you bathe him. Wet ears are a breeding ground for bacteria that could cause an ear infection.
5. Apply a small amount of mild dog-friendly shampoo to your Whippet's back and gently work it into a lather along his neck, back, chest and legs.
6. Rinse the soap thoroughly out of your Whippet's coat and use a damp washcloth to clean his face.
7. Some professional groomers at this stage advise that whilst the dog is still wet,

to give a brisk rub with a hound glove or rubber grooming glove to remove excess hair

8. Use a large fluffy towel to towel-dry your Whippet, getting as much water out of his coat as possible. If it is warm you can let him air-dry the rest of the way.

If your Whippet seems to be cold you can use a hair-dryer on the low heat setting to dry him the rest of the way.

You can bathe your Whippet if he gets dirty, but you should avoid bathing him when it is not necessary. Over-bathing a dog can dry out his skin and lead to skin problems. In some cases you may be able to brush dried dirt and debris out of your Whippet's coat instead of bathing him.

4.) Trimming Your Dog's Nails

Puppy Nail Clippers

The best clippers to use on a Whippet puppy will be cat nail clippers. These are made especially for thin, small nails. As your Whippet grows older, you'll learn to alternate and use the regular dog nail clipper. These cut thicker adult canine nails. When buying nail clippers, pick up some styptic powder, which can be used on any bleeding caused from a too-closely clipped nail. It also works as an antiseptic. Obviously try not to nick the quick when cutting your Whippet's nails.

Trimming your Whippet's nails can be challenging because you need to be very careful. A dog's nail contains a quick; the vessel that brings blood to the nail. If you cut the nail too short you will cut the quick. This not only causes your dog pain, but it can bleed profusely as well. When you trim your Whippet's nails you should only cut the very tip to remove the point. Depending on what colour your dog's nails are, you may be able to see the quick and use it as a trimming guide.

It is generally recommended that you trim your Whippet's nails every two weeks. If you do it this often then you will only need to clip the slightest amount off the nail each time. This will reduce the risk of cutting the quick. Before you trim your Whippet's nails for the first time you should consider having a veterinarian or a professional groomer show you how. You also need to be sure you are using real dog nail clippers for the job. Please also be aware that you shouldn't attempt to clip your dog's nails routinely every two weeks, just for the sake of it, as he may not need it. You should notice that if your dog walks on pavements or your concrete yard, he will to a certain extent be filing them down anyway.

5.) Cleaning Your Dog's Ears

Your dog's risk of ear infection increases significantly if you get the ears wet, such as during a bath.

Cleaning your dog's ears is not difficult, but you do need the right supplies. Gear up with a bottle of dog-friendly ear cleaning solution, preferably recommended by your vet, and a few clean cotton balls.

1. Gently hold your dog's ear and squeeze a few drops of the cleaning solution into the ear canal.
2. Massage the ear canal, around the base of the dogs ear, to spread the solution then use the cotton balls to wipe it away.
3. Be careful not to put your fingers or the cotton ball too far into your dog's ear or you could damage his ear drum.

Please also avoid cleaning with cotton buds as again they could cause internal damage. The frequency with which you clean your Whippet's ears will vary but you should aim for once every week or two.

6.) Brushing Your Whippet's Teeth

Please be aware that if you adopt the type of diet advocated by vets such as Ian Billinghurst, this nest step is likely to be unnecessary. The idea of brushing your dog's teeth may sound strange but dental health is just as important for your dog as it is for you. In fact, periodontitis (gum disease) is five times more common in dogs than in humans. Gum disease is incredibly serious but it often goes unnoticed by pet parents, especially since many people think that dogs are supposed to have bad breath. Bad breath, or halitosis, is one of the most common signs of gum disease

and could be indicative of a tooth abscess. Once again, please note that dogs regularly chewing on suitable raw meaty bones have relatively odourless breath. If you suspect an abscess, or anything un-toward, seek a veterinary examination as soon as possible.

To brush your Whippet's teeth, follow the steps below:

1. Select a soft-bristle toothbrush to use. Most pet stores stock special toothbrushes for dogs.
2. Choose a toothpaste that is specifically made for dogs, never human tooth paste. They come in a variety of flavours, so select one your Whippet will like. He will probably like them all. Again, never use the tooth paste you use. These contain chemicals that can be harmful to dogs.
3. Get your dog used to having his teeth handled by gently placing your finger in his mouth against his teeth. Carefully manipulate his lips so he gets used to the feeling.
4. If you find he doesn't particularly like this, try dipping your finger in peanut butter or chicken broth so your dog learns to like the treatment.
5. When you are ready to brush, place one hand over your dog's mouth and gently pull back his lips.

6. Apply a small amount of toothpaste to the brush and rub it gently over a few of his teeth.

7. After a few seconds, stop brushing and give your Whippet a treat for good behaviour.

8. Slowly increase the length of your brushing sessions over a few days until your dog lets you brush all of his teeth in one session.

In addition to brushing your Whippet's teeth at home you should also make sure he gets a dental check-up from the vet every 6 months.

CHAPTER NINE:

HEALTH CHECKS AND FIRST AID

Before we get into the main health issues affecting the Whippet, this chapter will deal with important preventive care. There is also useful and sometimes vital advice on health checks and first aid.

1.) Choosing a Veterinarian

You may already know this but not all veterinarians are the same. They are only people after all. So to find a good vet that you get on well with, may take some time and effort.

Dog owners in most geographical areas tend to gravitate towards a particular vet. It is usually someone who is good with dogs, trustworthy, great at the job and also has a good bedside manner with worried dog owners.

It is vitally important that you are completely happy with the vet that you choose for your dog. This person may need to lead you through some very difficult times. So a veterinarian who is hazy when sharing information or blunt towards you, may be very stressful for your entire family if you have an ill dog.

A good way to find a popular vet in your local area is do some community research, ask other dog walkers, go onto Facebook and find community pages of dog owners in your local area. Find out from other people what their experiences are and learn from them.

As holistic care is growing in popularity, a number of holistic veterinary surgeons are becoming available. This is an option that I personally would urge you to consider; though it is usually more expensive, it is well worth it.

The holistic vet has learned about veterinary science via the conventional route but has, in addition, put a lot of effort into learning natural health-care too. They will often treat symptoms with a mixture of less invasive therapies and conventional medicine, rather than simply use pharmaceutical options.

In short the holistic vet is more likely to look at the entire dog, diet, lifestyle and external influences on the health of your dog, as part of an overall holistic approach of care and treatment.

2.) Daily Health Check: Essential Handling

You will get used to seeing your new friend on a daily basis and quickly get used to his quarks and how he generally behaves. It will therefore become very obvious to you if something is wrong health wise. If you suspect that your dog is ill, just remember that most serious illnesses occur simultaneously with a rise in body temperature. It therefore makes sense to take your dogs temperature, which if you haven't already got one, please do get a rectal thermometer. If your dog is used to standing, you can probably do this yourself by holding his tail and with a small amount of Vaseline or similar, insert the thermometer into his rectum. If he wont stand for you doing this then obviously you will need someone to help you hold him whilst you insert the thermometer

A normal average temperature for a dog should be about 101.5 °F (38.6°C). If there is a rise of even a few degrees and this isn't the result of a sudden burst of exercise or similar, then assume there is a problem and consult with your vet a.s.a.p.

Preventative care

From the very minute that you purchase your Whippet puppy, you will be responsible for his care. The only way to tell if your Whippet is becoming ill, is to be in tune with him. You'll need to take a few minutes each day to do simple health checks. Some of these can be done while grooming, such as feeling for bumps or loss of muscle. You will no doubt be able to see if your puppy looks ill, or seems weak and listless for no reason.

Daily examinations will include examinations for:

»   Bleeding, swollen, or pale gums, loose or broken teeth, mouth ulcers, or bad breath

»   Discharge from the eyes or nose

»   Ears having a bad odour, redness or discharge

»   The skin for parasites, hair loss, hot spots, crusts or lumps

»   The feet for abrasions, bleeding, broken nails or misaligned toes

Many Whippets that are a safe and healthy weight look thin to other dog owners. These dog owners are not used to the sighthound family of dogs.

You should be able to feel at least two vertebrae at the top of the Whippet's spine. Ribs should not protrude, but you should be able to feel these beneath the skin. The Whippet's hipbones should not be sunk into fat, so that he has dimples.

A Whippet that has the right amount of daily exercise in the form of off leash runs on the beach, dog park, long walks, games that include chasing a ball or flying disk, will have strong muscle tone and strong connective tissue. This will reduce the likelihood of many injuries that are expensive to repair surgically. Veterinary bills run high during emergencies, so bare in mind that prevention is always better than cure.

Hip and elbow dysplasia don't often occur in Whippets, and are generally unknown in the breed. Arthritis and spinal cord problems such as Fibrocartilaginous Embolism (FCE) do tend to affect some older Whippets. However, Whippets are an active breed until they become older. Older Whippets need more warmth, particularly outdoors, so make sure you have a Whippet coat handy for when you go on outdoor walks.

What Will Early Handling Establish?

Handling your dog early on will teach him that being touched and health checked is a perfectly normal part of his life. This makes life so much easier at the vets along with making nail clipping and similar activities stress free. Handling in this way will also give you the chance to see what is normal for your own dog and his health. This way you will be able to recognize and catch any problems quickly.

Physical Manipulation

If you live with a young puppy, lift the dog up and cradle him in your arms on his back. There is no real reason for this position other than it's quite a difficult place for a dog to relax in, because it exposes his belly. Therefore by enjoying it, he is learning to be relaxed when handled regardless of what is going on. You will probably not be able to manage this with older Whippets. In this case you should really just attempt handling in whatever position is comfortable for them, whether sitting or lying them down on their back, or front. The important thing is that you handle them. Also be initially wary of an older rescue dog until you know that they do not mind you handling them.

Next, take hold of each paw and look at the underside of the pads by squashing them open. This will help to check pads for cuts and foreign articles when you really need to. If you find any sharp object stuck in there, do your best to carefully pull this out preferably with tweezers. If this looks difficult, then you are probably best taking him to the vet, as soon as possible, to get them to extract it.

Ears

Take a good look into the dog's ears. They should be pink and clean with no thick or smelly discharge. Look out for signs of redness and swelling.

Try to make the ear examination similar to one he will have at the veterinary surgery. Again if you notice anything untoward, do not delay in taking him to the vet.

Ear Care

Eyes and ears should be checked every day. A Whippet's ears should look clean on the inside, and have no foul smell. As previously noted your Whippet shouldn't suffer too many ear problems if at all. However, if your Whippet's ears appear dirty, then get some cotton balls and wipe them softly. You may wish to get hold of a commercial ear cleaner, or use something natural such as olive oil. Never probe deep into a dog's ear. This could easily damage the inner ear. If you suspect that your dog is suffering an inner ear infection or you see a large wax build up, then make an appointment with your vet for a proper examination.

After any type of water exposure, dry your Whippet's ears. The inside part, under the flaps, cannot dry on their own. When your Whippet comes in after a long hike in the woods, or from running out in tall grass, check for ticks, foxtails and seeds from other grasses that may work their way down his inner ear, and cause an infection.

Signs of an Ear Infection

If your Whippet's ears are inflamed, look reddish brown or carry a black substance, this could be ear mites or an ear infection. Watch for signs of your Whippet shaking his head, pawing his ears, or holding his head at a strange angle. If he does not let you touch his head area, that could possibly indicate an ear infection. Contact your veterinarian if you notice any symptoms of an ear infection.

Natural ear cleaners for Whippet's usually contain witch hazel, yucca, aloe Vera, tea tree oil (be careful with the use of tea tree oil as this can be toxic to dogs. If in any doubt, do not use this oil), chamomile, rosemary, and many other plant-based ingredients. These gently remove ear wax and promote healing.

http://www.vetstreet.com/care/ chronic-otitis-chronic-ear-infection- in-dogs

Signs of an Ear Infection Include:

» Inflammation

» Discharge

» Debris

» Foul odour

» Pain

» Scratching

» Shaking of head

» Tilting of head

» Circling to one side

If there is extreme pain, it may be indicative of a ruptured eardrum. Ear problems can be hard to cure if you don't see a vet right away.

Bacterial and Fungal Infections

Bacterial, fungal infections, ear mites ticks, inhalant allergies, seborrhea, or hyperthyroidism and foreign bodies can all cause problems. Grass awns are a common cause of ear infections for Whippet's that spend time outdoors, particularly whilst running in long grass.

If you suspect bacterial or fungal infection, keep his ears lubricated with mineral oil, and seek veterinary treatment without delay. Ear problems in Whippets can only get worse without proper treatment.

Eyes

Carefully examine your dog's eyes for swelling or redness. A small amount of sleep is normal. If you live with an adult or an older dog any blueness or blurring can be a sign of cataracts.

You can check your dog's sight by holding his face gently forward and dropping a balled up tissue or feather on the edge of his vision at each side of his head. If his vision is fine he will notice this straight away, if not, he may have a problem. Again a trip to the vets will be best for further investigation.

Eye Care

Check daily around the eyes for any signs of discharge. If your Whippet's eyes appear to be cloudy or red or show signs of discharge, contact your veterinarian for a complete examination. Healthy Whippet eyes are bright and have a glow to them. They will have a natural dull pink mucous membrane.

http://www.vetstreet.com/care/the-ophthalmic-exam

Teeth

Next check your dog's teeth right to the back of his mouth. As previously mentioned, it is a good idea to start brushing your dog's teeth early. If you are doing this on a daily basis, you will soon notice any problems that will need checking at the vets.

Preventing Tooth Decay in Whippets

http://www.animalwellness-magazine.com/articles/alternative-dental-care/

Dental sticks are often used and are supposed to do a similar job to brushing. However, be careful as some contain sugar, and as well as being bad for the teeth and gums can add to your dog becoming overweight. Many people swear by fresh bones, but be careful not to give cooked bones as they can splinter easily and cause intestinal problems. Also it can be very painful for dogs to pass. If your dog ever suffers any problems associated with eating bones, then obviously avoid giving your dog bones. There is much debate about bone consumption for dogs. But weighing up the pros and cons, in most instances bones are probably healthier than manufactured dental sticks, if perhaps not as safe. Your dog will love them in any case, so the choice is yours.

Feet

Then check each of the paws, checking the nails, and as previously mentioned, cut any that seem to have overgrown. We have already covered this to an extent in the chapter on grooming, but it is worth mentioning again.

The toenail of a dog is slightly different to that of a human so will need very careful handling. The nerve grows into the nail, which can easily be seen with white toenails but is more difficult with dark ones.

It is completely up to you whether you clip your own dog's nails or find a professional groomer or vet to do it. If you decide to clip them, then you will need to buy specific clippers and only take the very tip away with the clippers, or you may hurt the dog. If you would like to try this yourself, but are nervous at first, ask someone to show you or watch one of the many YouTube videos for instruction.

Anus and Genitals

After the feet, simply check the anus area and genitals for any abnormal discharge or swelling then finish by physically running your hands down the puppy's tail.

a.) The Worried or Reactive Whippet

If you are bringing home an older Whippet then it is important not to push your luck with handling. Remember that the dog will be confused and maybe even quite stressed.

A good way to carry out handling with a worried dog is to do it a few minutes, or even seconds if necessary, at a time and reward with treats, then stop.

The idea is to show the dog that handling and checking his ears, eyes and teeth etc., is a pleasant experience that brings nice food rewards.

Never force the worried dog beyond his limitations. Always stop whilst he is still relaxed and try to understand that this may all be brand new to him.

b.) Basic Massage and Muscle Care

Basic Massage can also be carried out when handling your dog of any age. By taking a few moments to first massage the dog's ears, where there are a lot of relaxing acupressure points, then moving your hands down his body in even strokes, you will be able to check his muscle balance and well-being.

Any uneven muscle balance will show that there is a potential skeletal problem below the surface. This is something that can be carefully monitored and should really be checked by the vet.

Any heat or swelling in the muscle areas may show a deeper problem. Similarly if the dog licks his lips, yawns or tries to move when you touch a certain area of his body, then he could have some type of pain beneath the surface and is displaying calming signals as a response to your touch. It could also be nothing to worry about and the dog displays calming signals because they perhaps do not like been handled.

3.) First Aid

As the owner of a Whippet dog it is a good idea to have at least a basic idea of canine first aid.

General first aid and its universal lesson is currently using the Acronym Dr's ABC. By memorizing this you have at least a basic idea of what to do if you ever find yourself in a first aid situation.

Danger

Remove the animal from any further danger, and be aware of danger to yourself in the situation.

Response

Check the response of the dog, is he conscious?

Summon help

Shout for help, ask someone to call the vet if possible.

Airway

Check the dog's airway, can he breathe Is there an obstruction

Breathing

At this point there may be a need to re-trigger breathing for the animal. Holding the mouth closed you can gently breath air into your dog's nostrils. Try to visualize the size of his lungs and not over inflate them, try to mimic how your dog would pant.

Cardiac compressions may be necessary at this point. The dog should be laid on his right side and the heart massaged in a similar way to CPR compressions for a human but carefully at a ratio of one breath to every two to five compressions depending on the size of the dog. The average Whippet would be around three compressions per breath. The heart is approximately located in the chest area above his front left leg. They usually have a stronger beat on the left but can be felt on both sides.

The basic sequence for CPR is as follows:

1. Check for signs of breathing which should be noticeable around the chest or by placing your cheek to your dogs mouth.
2. Check for a pulse which if this is not noticeable around the heart area, can be felt via the femoral artery. This is located on either of the back legs, on the inside of the leg, near to the top of the leg. By feeling inside that area, if there was a pulse you would feel it quite strongly there. It will be worth you detecting that now, so that you know where to look and how it should feel.
3. If neither breathing nor pulse are detected, start chest compressions. With the heel of your hand, press reasonably firmly, but in the case of the Whippet, not too firmly that you risk cracking a rib. Count about three compressions
4. Now move over to your dogs mouth/nose and

steadily blow into both and you should see the chest expand.
5. Again move over to the chest and compress three times again.
6. Keep repeating the sequence until he starts to breath.

Please read the following article for additional information:
http://www.petmd.com/ dog/emergency/common- emergencies/e_dg_cardiopulmo- nary_resuscitation
If you prefer a visual demonstration, please search YouTube using a search term such as[CPR on dogs]

Circulation

In an emergency, the dog's pulse and circulation will need to be checked. If bleeding is apparent then the wound will need to be put under pressure and elevated if possible in order to contain the bleeding.

After first aid has been carried out, the Whippet should always be taken to see the vet as a matter of urgency.

There are some particular conditions that can develop very quickly can cause rapid health deterioration; which as a Whippet owner it is important to be aware of. One of these is heat stroke or heat exhaustion.

4.) Heat Exhaustion

Dogs can only pant to cool themselves as they don't sweat like people do; except to a certain extent from their paw pads.

In the warm summer months it is vital to keep your dog away from hot sun. Because he only cools his body on the inside by taking air from his surroundings, the dog in excessive heat, loses the power to cool himself at all. This will quickly lead to heat exhaustion which can be a fatal condition.

Dogs should never be left in hot cars, full sun or hot areas from which they cannot escape.

The symptoms of heat exhaustion are as follows:

Important!

» Panting (however, dogs do this naturally anyway and in most cases is not indicative of a problem)

» Restlessness

» Loss of focus in the eyes

» Deterioration of consciousness

» Staggering

» Collapse

If you suspect that your Whippet dog is overheating it is vital never to take the panicked action of immersing him in cold water, as this can cause shock or even heart failure. Remove the dog from full sun and either drape damp towels over his body or dribble water over him to cool his overheated body gently.

When the body has overheated, then it is vital to get your dog checked by the vet for symptoms of long term damage.

A relatively new invention in the dog equipment world is the cooling vest. It can be placed in water then put onto the dog in hot weather.

The water wicks the heat away from the dogs body as a process of evaporation. If you believe that your dog is particularly susceptible to hot weather, then a cooling vest is a really good investment.

Another good idea for the warmer months is to provide your dog with a stock pot iced pop. Simply pour stock into a big bowl, add some treats of varying types and freeze the entire thing. Then on a hot day turn the ice pop out into the garden and allow your dog to lick away happily. You may want to place this on some sort of a tray in case the whole thing melts before he has chance to consume it.

5.) Essential Exercise

Every Whippet dog needs daily walks, and will certainly not be happy at home all day. The adult Whippet ideally needs a good walk every single day or he may develop problem behaviours. The excess energy build up can easily cause destructive or even aggressive behaviour.

As the Whippet is more active than most dogs, some off lead runs in a safe area, at least twice a week and more if you can, will certainly go a long way to keeping your Whippet happy and healthy. Try to leave a gap of about 2hrs between eating and any off lead run, as the Whippet will not just be casually galloping about, but no doubt hurtling as fast as he can.

The first sign that your dog is not getting enough exercise is weight gain, which admittedly will not be particularly noticeable as they are obviously a thin breed that are not known for weight gain. But you will get used to his normal fit looking size and quickly notice any changes.

Many dog behaviour problems are sorted out very quickly when the dog's food is changed (food causing allergies or just poor food quality lacking necessary nutrients) and the daily walks are increased in time and intensity. Many of the most problematic behaviours stem from a lack of suitable exercise.

If you are out at work for a full day then why not consider a doggy day care or professional dog walker for your Whippet dog. A good professional canine caretaker will wear your dog out and meet his social needs all at once.

Please be aware that Whippet puppies along with other puppy breeds, need to be broken in gently to exercise, as their bones are soft whilst they are still growing. Your regular, long walks will begin when your puppy is a few months old.

Puppy exercise should involve gentle short walks; the UK Kennel club advises;

*"**Puppies need much less exercise than fully-grown dogs. If you over-exercise a growing puppy you can overtire it and damage its developing joints, causing early arthritis. A good rule of thumb is a ratio of five minutes exercise per month of age (up to twice a day) until the puppy is fully grown, i.e. 15 minutes (up to twice a day) when three months old, 20 minutes when four months old etc. Once they are fully grown, they can go out for much longer.**

**It is important that puppies and dogs go out for exercise every day in a safe and secure area, or they may become frustrated. Time spent in the garden (however large) is no substitute for exploring new environments and socializing with other dogs. (Make sure your puppy is trained to recall so that you are confident that he will return to you when called)"*.

See more at: *http://www.thekennelclub.org.uk*

The Whippet reaches adolescence at around 10 months old and adulthood, or maturity, comes quickly after-wards. So by the time your puppy is a year old he should be fine to walk as long as you like, within reason.

It is important that you still socialize your puppy throughout his first few months, simply by carrying him a lot of the time and putting him onto the ground to socialize when the opportunity arises.

If you are having trouble keeping the puppy still without walking, then you can always do some training. Getting creative with some circuit training is a great way to tire any dog out. The training sessions you are already familiar with can be combined to make a circuit training session. You are probably familiar with dog owners that throw a ball or whatever for the dog to chase and retrieve. This again is a great way to get him racing off after the ball and then racing back again. Unfortunately though, not all dogs are immediately responsive to this and may need some initial training to get them used to the idea.

Again, try finding an activity such as agility or Frisbee for your Whippet to enjoy. All Whippets enjoy mental challenges, and that one-on-one time spent doing fun activities like dog puzzles, rally obedience, scent sports, tracking or agility, will be time well spent. These can be combined with daily walks, trips to the dog-park or beach. When the weather is cold, most of these can be done indoors.

Frisbee

So many Whippet owners expect that their Whippets will leap into the air and catch a Frisbee right away. This does not always happen first time around. Some Whip-

pets have been known to duck and wince at the sight of a flying Frisbee. Most dogs, Whippets too, have to be taught how much fun catching a Frisbee can be. This is not done by throwing a Frisbee and hoping that your Whippet will catch it. You'll need to start this with baby steps, just like any other forms of dog training, and reward with dog treats.

1. Start off by having your Whippet chase after a rag lure dragged across the ground. This is usually the preliminary method used for training whippets to race or take part in coursing runs. You can start with someone running ahead with the lure on a line. This can then be advanced using some sort of mechanical winding mechanism.

2. Allow your Whippet to catch the lure, and then bring it back to you.

3. Praise your Whippet and reward with a treat.
4. Next, try getting your Whippet to chase a ball. Allow your Whippet to catch it in the air. Attach the lure to the ball, and try getting your Whippet to catch it.
5. When training during this phase, you can begin introducing the Frisbee by rolling it along the ground on its edge. Praise your Whippet for bringing it to you.
6. Throw treats above your Whippet's nose. When the treats hit the floor, grab it before your Whippet. Soon your Whippet will realize that the only way he can get it is by catching it before it touches the ground.

Agility Exercises

Your Whippet should enjoy this sport whereby both dog and handler are timed as they negotiate a fun course of obstacles. Some of these will include ramps, brightly coloured tunnels, candy striped weave poles and jumps. This is a fantastic way to keep your Whippet mentally stimulated and physically fit.

You don't have to be competitive, and there's no initial investment required for all the agility equipment. Start off by building fun courses at home. This is extremely fun during the Autumn (fall) and can benefit a dog that's used to being busy, but is being kept indoors due to bad weather. Try hiding some stuffed Kongs around the house during these times and create a game of hide-and-seek with your Whippet.

Whippets are one of the fastest and most agile breeds of dog. They can jump, sprint, climb, balance, and weave with an unbelievable nimbleness. The Agility Club is the UK's largest Kennel Club registered agility club. It was formed in 1983, during the early days of agility, with the purpose of giving all competitive dog handlers a voice in the sport. For more information, visit: agilityclub. org

For fun agility pet products for your Whippets, visit:

petsperfect.co.uk/pages/agility

For UK International Agility News (UKI), visit:

ukagilityinternational.com

6.) Stress

a.) Short Term Stress

Stress is a biological response to a perceived threat. Biologically the dog's body is programmed to keep the animal safe by reacting in a certain way to fear. The natural reaction, at a very basic level, involves the release of very specific hormones into the dog's body which prepare the animal to deal with a threatening situation.

The subconscious preparation that happens within the body of the dog involves sending adrenaline to each of the muscles thus preparing the dog for a fight or to take flight.

In addition to this, the dog's body redirects energy to the places that will best provide immediate safety. The heart rate raises whilst digestion, immunity and reproductive organs are literally 'switched off' as each of these are secondary functions to the need for basic survival.

The dog's decision at this point will usually depend on a mixture of genetic responses and his experience of life so far. Similarly the things that a dog gets stressed about will be determined by the animal as an individual.

Some dogs, for instance, will get stressed in the car whilst others are stressed and fearful during fireworks season. Dogs that have not been properly socialized will often get stressed in the company of other dogs, simply because they don't know how to react.

b.) Long Term Stress

So now we know, in very basic terms, what an immediate stress reaction does to the dog. We will focus further on the dog's immediate reaction later. But for now let's take a look at exactly what long term stress does to a dog.

Long term stress leads to dysfunction in digestion, loss of general condition and eventually many illnesses because the immune system is busy elsewhere.

c.) What Causes Stress

This is where it gets really interesting. Stress can be caused by anything at all. This is a subject where dogs and humans are very much alike.

Just as we are all different and some of us can deal with a lot of stress before we cave in, dogs are exactly the same. Some can cope with anything at all and others deal

with things by becoming stressed about them.

Common causes of stress are:

» Allergies

» Under socialization

» Lack of training

» Insufficient exercise

» An insecure environment

» Excessive noise

» Over exercise

» Agility and other sports that cause adrenaline release in the body of the dog.

Your job as the guardian and friend of a Whippet, is to recognize any stressors in the life of your dog and make changes.

For instance, if your dog eats food with known allergens then change his food type. If your Whippet is worried about other dogs, do some careful socialization training. If your friend is completely stressed during firework season, take some precautions to help him through it, such as Bach Flower remedy, or simply comforting him and not leaving him alone.

7.) Natural Therapy and Remedies

Natural therapy is often passed over because conventional medicine has become such a big part of our lives. This is a pity in many ways as remedies, hands on therapy and a mixture of the two can have such amazing results.

Before conventional medicine, ailments were treated with herbs, flower remedies and massage. This type of treatment healed many and let's face it conventional medicine is based upon the same approach but is far more complex.

Natural therapy is inclusive of flower remedies used for emotional balance. Herbal remedies are created from plants to support the body and immune system. Homeopathic remedies are created directly from disease at a cellular level in order to provoke immunity.

Physical therapy includes massage, hands on healing methods such as canine touch, hydrotherapy (the strengthening of muscles with the use of water) and re-alignment techniques such as canine chiropractic treatment.

All of the above have an undisputable place in the health and well-being of your Whippet dog. So whilst the veterinarian may prescribe painkillers, a parallel natural hands-on treatment is also an option that should be considered.

As the guardian of a Whippet it is vitally important that you do not put his health completely into the hands of someone else, not even the veterinarian. Of course in an emergency situation the vet is the most important person to turn to. However, for routine, perhaps less serious conditions you are perhaps better placed to work out what is best for him on a holistic basis.

Your veterinarian can diagnose, treat with drugs and give you advice. But it is up to you then to go away and explore all of the options available to you and your dog.

In the book **Veterinary Secrets: Natural Health for Dogs and Cats,** (2014) Dr Andrew Jones talks through the place of veterinary medicine in the life of your dog and this book is a welcome addition to the care kit of any Whippet dog. Similarly the book **The Veterinarians Guide to Natural Remedies for Dogs** (2000) by Martin Zucker, is also a fantastic resource for any dog owner.

CHAPTER TEN

PARASITES, WORMS AND COMMON ILLNESSES

This chapter deals with the unfortunate subject of parasites and common illnesses that can affect your Whippet. Please do not skip this chapter as it is important that you are aware of these parasites and conditions and can therefore deal with their treatment and prevention.

1.) Parasitic Worms

A huge concern within the digestive process are parasites.

Worms are known as internal parasites of which there are plenty that can affect the Whippet dog and Whippet puppies. It may surprise you to know, but puppies are actually born with worms present. Having purchased from a reputable breeder, your puppy is bound to have already been wormed. You should check when this was, and the dose and type used, which will indicate when he needs worming next. Please do not neglect regular worming whether a puppy or adult as these parasites can seriously affect their health and in some cases lead to death. Also be very careful and stick to correct doses, as this can cause intestinal damage and again at worse lead to death.

a.) Roundworms

The most common worm type is the roundworm, of which there are a few variations. Symptoms of a roundworm infection include itchiness in the anus area, worms in the dog's faeces and loss of condition.

A mother dog can pass roundworms on to her puppies and all Whippet puppies, bred and raised well, will be wormed properly by the breeder before being sent to their new homes. Worms usually live in the dog's digestive system and some are actually symptomless, whilst others can have serious consequences for the health of the Whippet dog.

Hookworm and whipworm are also roundworm types that cause pain and digestive upset in dogs. The hookworm grips onto the stomach wall causing constant and severe discomfort to the dog.

A roundworm infection within the digestive system of the dog can affect general condition, though roundworm larvae has far more sinister potential.

Roundworms are a zoonotic parasite which means that they can be passed between species.

If roundworm larvae is ingested by humans it can become confused within the body and head for the eye area. The aim for the worm is to eat its way out of the retina causing blindness.

b.) Tapeworms

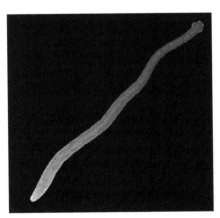

The tapeworm is a type of parasite which can sit in the intestine without doing any damage, other than consuming nutrients that your dog should be consuming. They will also grow to a large size throughout the intestinal tract. The tapeworm reproduces by shedding parts of its long and segmented body, which is passed with the faeces or drops from the anus of the dog. The tapeworm is happy to live in the digestive system of both dogs and people. Again the main problem here is that it will consume a considerable amount of ingested food and obviously grow as a result. As you can imagine, your dog will not be getting sufficient nutrients and will suffer as a result.

Basic worming tablets will keep the chance of infection under control. As a routine these should be administered about every 3 months. Be careful that you are giving your dog the correct dosage. This is usually gauged by kilo weight of your dog. Also be aware that different brands suggest a different number of tablets. This is probably because of the size or potency of each tablet.

c.) Lungworms/Heartworms

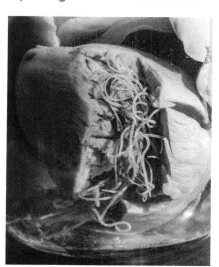

The other type of worm, and one which has serious consequences, is the lungworm/heartworm.

The larvae for this type of worm, when it gets into the body, migrates to either the lung or heart of the animal. It then quickly breeds to fill the major organ with worms, as illustrated above. By the time that the symptoms of this type of infestation appears, the damage to either the heart or lungs will be well underway.

Symptoms are excessive coughing and loss of heart or lung function. This parasite type is becoming more common, and currently being diagnosed in geographical areas where it has not previously been seen.

The larvae of this parasite enters the body via a mosquito bite or ingestion. Dogs that eat slugs, snails and their eggs are particularly susceptible to an infestation of heart or lungworm.

With quick spreading infection, has come preventative medicine. If you are in an area that is high risk, I would urge you to consult with your veterinarian about preventive measures.

As a matter of routine, you are strongly advised to check with your vet, the general type of worms your dog may be susceptible to. Worming tablets can be bought at pet stores and many general stores seem to stock these now. Once again, always make sure you choose the correct type and dosage for both your dogs size and age.

2.) External Parasites – Fleas and Other Suckers

The other type of parasite that can potentially affect your Whippet dog is the external parasite.

a.) Fleas

The flea is an inventive little jumper that can hop up to half a meter and jumps onto dark areas. Therefore if your dog walks passed a flea on the ground the little insect is likely to hop on.

As soon as she finds her host the female flea will begin to lay eggs and in her lifespan of up to a month, she can easily leave up to 800 eggs on your dog and in your living environment. Eggs will wait for months, until the time and temperature is right before hatching which is why in the springtime there is a big increase in fleas.

Symptoms of fleas are grit like dirt that turns red in water and a profusion of itchy bites. Please remember that fleas can transmit tapeworms.

Many vets will advise that chemical treatment will need to occur every few months as a preventative measure. This is usually in the form of a spot on treatment applied to the back of the dog's neck.

Holistic veterinarians advise that a dog will only need chemical treatments in the event of an actual infestation and I'm inclined to agree with this. The logic behind this thinking is to avoid exposing the dog to a chemical substance unless it is absolutely necessary. If you find your dog is not constantly under attack in the summer months, just apply when you notice symptoms and not routinely for the sake of it.

If you keep your Whippet healthy, well fed, clean and rinse him in a lemon juice or apple cider vinegar solution (mixed 1 part lemon/vinegar to 10 parts water) once a week, then that should keep your dog, flea free, without any need for stronger chemicals.

I also like essential oils such as cedar-wood, lemongrass, citronella, neem and rosemary among others. There has been a lot of talk on the internet about the benefits of using these as natural flea/tick repellents. There are also some interesting videos on YouTube from people uploading their favourite remedy.

Today there are advances in flea and tick control. Always contact your vet as to the best products to use. Some products are much stronger than others, so it's really important to try and choose a formula that is not harmful to your Whippet. There are plenty of flea and tick products that are natural and environmentally friendly. These will repel and kill fleas, ticks and mosquitos with a natural botanical formula like geraniol and eugenol. Sprinkling borax powder, around the home is a known flea killer. However, salt is known to do a similar job. Again, avoid direct contact of the animal as this can dry the skin and possibly have a toxic affect.

b.) Ticks

Ticks can be found anywhere on a Whippet, but are mostly found on the neck, chest, and between the toes. They are often found in the US. Ticks will transmit Rocky Mountain spotted fever, tick paralysis, Lyme disease, babesiosis, and tick fever. (Erlichiosis)

Ticks are a completely different type of parasite. They do not live on the dog but simply wander onto the animal in order to feed then drop off when full.

An empty tick looking for food (blood) is not actually much bigger than the head of a pin, and then ex-pand in some cases to resemble a small pea. After finding a suitable spot on the body of the dog, the tick dives in by burying its tiny head under the skin and sucks as much blood as it can take, then drops off, (unlike the flea who sets up home on your dog). This is when you find them in the crate, dog bed or on the floor.

Ticks do not differentiate and will happily bite people, sheep, deer and cattle alongside dogs. They are usually only around in the summer months, but in areas of plentiful wildlife or farming environments they come in force during the warm weather, particularly when the grass gets long.

To remove a tick it is important not to squeeze its body whilst it feeds. This can cause the stomach contents and innards to be pushed into your dog's body. It is also important not to just pull, as this can leave the head under the dog's skin even if you remove the body. Be careful, because if the head is left attached this can easily lead to infection. If this happens, seek veterinary attention without delay.

Pet stores sell small hooks, which can be put between the tick's body and your dog's skin for careful removal, this will safely remove the parasite completely.

There is advice, mostly on the internet that suggests all sorts of cigarette burning and similar harsh approaches that aim to shock the tick into releasing its grip, all are best avoided for obvious safety reasons.

I would suggest either getting a friend or vet, who has experience of how to remove ticks to help you, or watch a step by step video from YouTube. The tick attaches itself in a spiral clockwise direction. So with tweezers or one of the specially designed hooks to grip the body of the tick you then gently twist in an anti-clockwise direction. This effectively unhooks the tick and avoids you accidentally twisting the head off.

You may wonder, if the tick eventually drops off anyway why go to all this trouble of removing it. Well the main concern with ticks is that in some geographical areas they carry Lyme disease which will most certainly need veterinary and medical attention. Symptoms of the disease are fatigue, muscle pain and joint problems. People alongside dogs are susceptible to Lyme disease if bitten by a host tick.

c.) Mites

Mites are everywhere. Generally they do us no harm, yet some can cause problems for the Whippet dog, particularly the mange mite.

Mange mites burrow under the skin of the dog and cause itchiness and general hair loss. Left untreated the mange mite will affect the general health of the animal and result in eventual baldness.

The immune system of the dog is severely affected by the presence of mange mites. If not treated, the seemingly simple mange infestation will be fatal.

Any dog that is suspected of carrying mange mites should be treated by conventional veterinary medicine. The condition can be really difficult to get rid of and the course of treatment may be long and slow.

If your Whippet is itchy in the autumn time, then he may be suffering with a reaction to harvest mites, particularly if you live on or near farmland. Other than irritation, these little mites are harmless and can be washed away with soap and water.

d.) Ear Mites

Ear mites cannot be seen by the human eye but are easily visible with the use of a microscope. These little mites grow and reproduce in the dog's ear and create a very smelly brown discharge. Ear mites are usually easily treated with drops.

Ear Mites

Ear mites, are often found in puppies, and are very contagious and irritating to dogs that have them. Whippets that are affected with ear mites will shake their heads, and carry their head sideways. Again, the ear mite's signature is a waxy, dark build-up that looks like coffee grounds in the ear canal. This usually occurs in both ears. This material is actually dried blood that is mixed with earwax. Ear mite infestations are best taken care of by your veterinarian.

http://www.vetstreet.com/care/chronic-otitis-chronic-ear-infection-in-dogs

e.) Flies

Flies in the summer are a real hazard if your dog has any open wounds or sores. The big flies are continually looking for somewhere to lay eggs, which quickly grow into maggots and eat their way beneath the flesh. This is a condition called 'fly strike' which often affects pet rabbits and similar animals.

So if your dog has anything from a small flesh wound to sore anal glands ensure that the heat does not leave him vulnerable to this particular nasty parasite.

3.) Other common Illnesses

Whippet health is something that every owner of the breed should be aware of. Dogs get sick sometimes, they have off days, and they are susceptible to passing bugs, just as we are.

To have a basic understanding of the way that these things affect the body of your dog, will put you in the best position to help him.

a.) Diarrhoea

Diarrhoea is a common occurrence and not normally one to worry too much about.

If the Whippet dog does display symptoms you can simply withhold his food for 24 hours, to allow the stomach and bowels to rest, then re-introduce it gradually. Diarrhoea can also be indicative of many illnesses, and is fairly common in all dog breeds. Sometimes, it's trivial, but may at other times be due to something more serious. It is usually caused by digestive problems, and will cease when the food causing it is changed or withdrawn. A common cause of diarrhoea is a sudden change of diet. All dietary changes need to be made gradually. Water needs to be made available at all times.

Many Whippet owners will add a spoonful of glucose powder to the water. When resuming feeding, offer boiled chicken and brown rice, or fish with brown rice. Start off by feeding small amounts, gradually increasing the quantity until your Whippet is back to his normal diet. Look out for blood in the faeces, and contact your vet immediately if you see any signs of blood. There could be a number of causes of this including Canine Parvovirus infection or Hemorrhagic Gastroenteritis.

If the following symptoms occur, then it is important to visit your veterinary surgeon as soon as possible;

» The dog has eaten something potentially toxic such as chocolate or artificial sweetener

» The dog is lethargic or staggering

» The dog's gums are very pale or very dark red

» When pinched, the back of the dogs neck does not spring back into place – this is a sign of dehydration

» The condition does not clear up within a few days

» The dog is passing blood

b.) Vomiting

Dogs vomit by choice, so a one off incident is usually nothing much to worry about. You will see them eating grass for instance, and then sometime later you may notice a pile of chewed up grass and mucous/stomach contents. Although eating grass doesn't always lead a dog to vomit, it may be one of the reasons you may see them vomit. It is generally thought they may vomit if they feel ill and need to empty their stomach, much the same as we may need to vomit and then feel much better afterwards.

Yet if the following circumstances are associated with vomiting, then the dog should be taken along to the veterinarian:

> » The dog could have been exposed to poisons.
>
> » The dog's airway is obstructed either alongside or as a result of vomiting.
>
> » The dog has not long been chewing a bone or toy that could possibly be stuck in his digestive system.

Constipation

This is generally caused by a lack of dietary fibre, so try changing your Whippet's diet, and adding some fresh green veg and fresh fruits. Other causes of constipation will include consumption of bones particularly if these are cooked; bone fragments, which can damage or block the colon causing hard faeces. These are difficult to pass. A dose of Castor oil helps and should clear the blockage. If your Whippet is still having problems, consult with your vet.

Often a Whippet will suffer from constipation because he has not had enough exercise and has been indoors for too long. Whippets need to go outside a few times a day. When travelling by plane or car, be sure to adjust your feeding schedule, and also to add plenty of fresh fruits and vegetables.

Anal Glands

Although this isn't a disease as such, it is still an internal condition that affects most dogs and needs to be dealt with. Whippets do not generally have problems with their anal glands, but it is a potential problem. The anal glands are found on either side of the anus. Symptoms of anal gland problems include bottom-shuffling on the floor, and chewing the area around the tail. Your vet can easily empty your Whippet's anal glands that have become impacted. Interestingly feeding raw meaty bones has the effect of clearing anal glands as the stools are generally quite hard, but not hard to pass.

Cystitis

Cystitis affects only female Whippets. She'll show signs of wanting to go outside, and will squat often as though urinating. You will need to take your Whippet to the vet because this is an inflammation of the urinary tract, and if left untreated, is not only painful, but dangerous. It is usually caused by a bacterial infection. Female Whippets recover quickly, but only under good veterinary care.

Balanitis

Male Whippets can suffer from a very similar condition called balanitis. This is an infection of the Whippet's penis. You'll notice a discharge from the sheath and your Whippet will have problems urinating. Your Whippet will need antibiotics for this, so it's important to visit your vet as soon as possible.

If any of the previous conditions are worrying you to excess, or seem too severe to ignore, even if your concern is caused by an instinctive 'gut' feeling; this should result in a check-up with the vet.

You know your dog better than anyone else. If you are overly worried, then it is a good idea to listen to those concerns. Your Whippet dog's health may depend on your instinct at some point in your lives together.

CHAPTER ELEVEN:

KEEPING YOUR WHIPPET HEALTHY

Even if you give your Whippet a healthy diet and a safe environment, he may still be prone to developing certain health problems. Familiarizing yourself with the health problems to which this breed is prone will help you to identify them early on. You can then be better equipped to provide your dog with the necessary treatment. In this chapter you will find valuable information about Whippet diseases, vaccination information, and pet insurance etc.

PLEASE NOTE: The following is intended for informational purposes so that you are aware of potential diseases that can affect the Whippet. Although you will read here about many diseases and illnesses that a Whippet can be susceptible to, please do not assume that the Whippet is bound to contract all or any of these diseases. You can read veterinary guides on certain breeds and you will find, in the case of some dogs pages of diseases that at some time a particular breed, or specific dog has been affected by. Do not worry unduly about this as most dogs will get only a few mentioned and some none at all.

1.) Whippet Health Surveys

Again, all dogs are prone to developing certain diseases and congenital conditions can be passed from the parent dogs to the puppies.

"Without good health, nothing else really matters." Heather Dollygroves
Pencleave Whippets, UK.

Introduction to health care

The Whippet is considered one of the healthiest purebreds with very few health problems that will require long-term veterinary care or lifelong medication. In this respect they carry hardly any potential hereditary diseases, and a few relatively minor disease predispositions. If

you take good care of your Whippet, and he's given the right veterinary care, proper nutrition and regular exercise, your Whippet may live up to 15 years or more.

The Whippet is not generally prone to frequent ear infections, hot spots, skin allergies, joint problems, food related allergies that affect many other breeds, although these can of course occur.

The following will give you some idea of a number of current health surveys and initiatives carried out, that you may wish to have a look at.

Whippet admirers and owners that are dedicated to the long-term health of this breed formed the Whippet Health Foundation (WHF) in1999. All WHF members are also members of the American Whippet Club. It is an independent non-profit organization sustained by donations. The Whippet Health Foundation has close ties to the American Whippet Club. This club includes the organization of popular Whippet health clinics every year at AWC National Specialty, and the promotion and sponsorship of research projects and other studies of interest, which are of importance to Whippet breeders and owners.

WHF are centering their research on mitral valve disease, cleft palates, hemangiosarcoma, and other birth defects. The American Whippet Club feels that generally they are a healthy breed; however they feel that there is a need to monitor certain heritable health conditions. This is done by testing for heritable diseases and defects, and sharing these results and diagnosis. The WHF feel that members should participate in these studies via WHF's database and other online databases like CERF and OFA. All Whippet owners are encouraged to do so, regardless of whether they are breeding or not. For more information, visit: americanwhippetclub. net/about-whippets/whippet-health

In 2004 The Kennel Club conducted a health survey of all purebred dogs. This was a nationwide survey in the UK with the intention of identifying specific health conditions of purebred dogs. Questionnaires were issued via breed clubs to members of dog owners. The type of questions posed were intended to identify the dogs health, breeding, causes of death and birth defects.

Please note that the KC suggests that caution needs to be taken when interpreting the results and figures. In the case of the Whippet, of all the forms sent out only 24% were returned and this represented 1214 living dogs. 486 deaths were reported, a median age at death of 12 yrs 10 months was established and this was within an age range of 2 months of age to 18 years and 2 months.

Of the 1214 living dogs, 920 (76%) were reported as healthy. The remaining 294 representing (24%) were reported with at least one health condition, in some cases more. Of the 294 a total of 440 conditions were reported.

The cause of death and disease tables relating to this survery are shown on the next two pages.

The full 7 page PDF report is available at the following link
http://www.thekennelclub.org.uk/ media/16790/whippet.pdf

Once again please bear in mind the warning made by the Kennel Club regarding interpretation. As the number of cases is not every Whippet in the UK, nor is it all historical cases, it is by definition a statistical sample. In that respect, although the information is very useful it is not definitive nor conclusive.

However, the sample does indicate that 76% of the living dogs were healthy and without disease. The remaining 24% had one or two conditions. There were several serious conditions such as MVD, heart failure, pyometra etc. But most of the diseases were less serious and only a few incidences. Incidences of Cancer were relatively low.

Regarding causes of death, old age represented over one quarter of cases. Again cardiac disease and ultimately failure was relatively high in the list, as was cancer, but neither represented a particularly large percentage.

Whippet Breed Council Health Survey 2005 -2012

According the the WBC, the main health concerns affecting Whippets are cardiac related with trauma not far behind. There are several other health conditions that affect Whippets relating to neurological, orthopaedic and musculoskeletal conditions.

Of the 61 dogs, (7.5%) of the total number of dogs reported to have/have had cardiac conditions,

The Cause of Death	Number or dogs affected	% of total 486 dogs	Specific causes
Old age	130	26.7	Old age
Cardiac	67	13.8	MVD, Unspecified heart defect, cardiomegaly, Heart failure, heart attack.
Cancer	50	10.3	Brain tumour, Unspecified throat, lymphoma.
Urologic	31	6.4	Kidney failure
Trauma	28	5.8	Spinal injury, road traffic accident, attacked by another dog.
Cerebral vascular	26	5.3	Cerebral vascular accident , Stroke
Neurologic	23	4.7	Unspecified spinal disease, Seizures, IVDD.
Immune mediated	13	2.7	Thrombocytopaenia, AIHA.
Gastrointestinal	11	2.3	Pancreatitis, gastroenteritis.
Endocrine	9	1.9	Diabetes mellitus, Cushings disease, Addisons disease.
Hepatic	9	1.9	Cholangiohepatitis, Liver failure.
Reproductive	6	1.2	Prostatic disease, Pyometra.
Behaviour	5	1	Rage syndrome, aggression.
Musculoskeletal	5	1	Joint pain, Arthritis, brittle bones due to steroid use
Respiratory	5	1	Lung lobe torsion,

Disease	Number of cases	% of the 440 cases	Specific conditions noted
Reproductive	78	17.7	False pregnancy, pyometra, dystochia (uterine inertia>physical blockage), cryptorchid, infertility.
Cardiac	57	13	Congestive heart failure, Heart murmur, MVD
Musculoskeletal	49	11.1	Fracture, lameness, arthritis
Gastrointestinal	36	8.2	IBD, pancreatitis, vomiting, diarrhoea, colitis, gastric dilatation.
Dermatologic	32	7.3	Interdigital cysts, mites, alopecia, ringworm, dermatitis.
Respiratory	31	7	Long soft palate, asthma, rhinitis, coughing, kennel cough, bronchitis
Neurologic	27	6.1	Meningitis, IVDD, seizures
Ocular	24	5.5	Conjunctivitis, KCS, cataracts, corneal ulcer, epiphora.
Immune mediated	18	4.1	Thrombocytopaenia, allergy, autoimmune disorder.
Trauma	14	3.2	Spinal cord, hind limb, urinary tract, skin, forepaw, tail, spine.
Urologic	13	3	Kidney stones, cystitis, incontinence.

specific information was given for 56 instances of 10 conditions, broken down as follows:

Bradycardia	1
Cardiac(not specified)	4
Cardiomyopathy	4
Congestive heart failure	3
Enlarged heart	1
Heart Attack	2
Heart Failure	2
Heart Murmur	36
Mitral Valve Disease	2
Pulmonary Valve Malfunction	1

This health survey is not 56 separate Whippets, as one dog may have/have had one or more of the conditions listed either at the same time or different times.

"Murmurs are by far the most common Whippet cardiac condition reported. The majority of these dogs with murmurs were neither on medication, nor showing clinical signs, and most lived to normal life expectancy." Caroline Osborne. Breed Council Health Coordinator.

Whippet Cardiac Health Project Update 2014

Whippets have been known to have an increased risk of mitral valve disease (MVD). That said, they are also an extremely athletic breed that participate in many dog sports like coursing, straight track racing and agility, and generally do so without any associated problems. Many other dog breeds that are considered athletic, also have MVD. Whippets often have soft systolic heart murmurs associated with athletic training or body conditioning.

These murmurs are not related to cardiac abnormality, and veterinarians think that they represent the sound of blood ejecting from the heart in athletes. Murmurs in Whippet athletes are easily heard by veterinarians because athletic Whippets are deep-chested with a thin conformation.

Having said that, in non-athletic Whippets functional murmurs are sometimes heard, and also do not represent disease in Whippets. For more information about the Whippet Cardiac health project, 2014, visit:

whippethealth.org/WhippetCardiacHealthProjectUpdate_2014.aspx

What is COI?

This stands for Coefficient Of Inbreeding. It measures the breeding line from the sire and dam, and will show the probability of how genetically similar they are. This is very important. Inbreeding can maintain some good traits, but there is plenty of danger related to the possibility of keeping the bad genes too.

Health and good temperament are top priorities in any breed. Breeders should also aim to keep inbreeding levels, or COI levels of their litters to those recommended by the Kennel Club, less than 10% calculated to 8 generations.

For more information, please visit: *dogbreedhealth.com/a-beginners-guide-to-coi/dog Breed Health:*

dogbreedhealth.com/a-beginners-guide-to-coi/

2) Diseases known to affect Whippets

The following will offer details of most of the specific diseases noted in the surveys. It will also include certain diseases not covered in the surveys but published elsewhere.

The following diseases and disorders have been known to affect the Whippet breed:

The more you know about these diseases the better equipped you will be to handle them if they occur. The earlier your Whippet receives a diagnosis, the more effective the treatment will be, and the greater his chances of making a full recovery.

a) Mitral Valve Disease

Your dog's heart is divided into four chambers – top, bottom, left, and right. There are a number of valves which supply blood to the heart and keep it flowing from one chamber to another in a specific direction. Blood first travels into the right atrium then through the right ventricle into the lungs where it is oxygenated before passing into the left atrium then through the left ventricle into the rest of the body. The mitral valve of the heart is found between the left atrium and ventricle and it serves to prevent the back-flow of blood into the left atrium.

This disease is caused by the degradation of the mitral valve which keeps it from closing completely. As a result, small amounts of blood leak into the left atrium which causes the heart to work harder to pump blood.

Eventually, this will lead to congestive heart failure.

The cause of MVD is still unknown, but it is known that it most commonly affects older small-breed dogs, and obviously affects Whippets. There is strong evidence to suggest that this disease is genetic and the good news is that it can be screened for. What this effectively means, is that any affected dog should not be used for breeding.

One of the first signs of MVD is a heart murmur – you can only hear this using a stethoscope and it might be slight and hard to detect. In many dogs, a heart murmur is the only sign of MVD and the dog may appear healthy otherwise. As the disease progresses, however, the murmur will get worse and the dog may show signs of heart failure.

As your dog's MVD gets worse, he will develop symptoms like coughing, lethargy, high blood pressure, reduced exercise tolerance, and fainting. Treatment options vary depending on the severity of the condition. Once again, unfortunately there is no cure for MVD and replacement of the valve can be very expensive and risky. Typical treatment involves medications to manage the heart failure. Treatments such as diuretics may help strengthen the heart and make the flow of blood easier. Sometimes switching the dog to a low-sodium diet is helpful as well.

Please refer to the following for additional information:
http://whippet-health.co.uk/#/heart-disease/4531648499

b) Epilepsy

Canine epilepsy is a very serious condition known to affect the Whippet breed. This condition is the most common neurological condition seen in dogs and it can affect as much as 5% of the canine population. Epilepsy is not actually a single disease. A diagnosis of epilepsy generally refers to any of a number of conditions characterized by recurring seizures. Seizure conditions in dogs can be genetically inherited, caused by anatomical abnormalities in the brain, or they may stem from an unknown cause in some cases.

There is a widely-accepted classification system for seizures in humans but one has not yet been adopted for dogs. There are several different types of seizures such as those that involve involuntary muscle movements or motor seizures which affect localized areas. An automatism is a type of motor seizure which often looks like a voluntary behaviour like chewing or barking. Non-motor seizures do happen in dogs but they are more difficult to detect as they often involve the perception of a sensory stimulus that isn't actually present. You may therefore observe the dog biting at non-existent flies or staring off into space.

Unfortunately, there is no cure for canine epilepsy but there are a variety of treatment options available to help control the disease. Anti-epileptic drugs like potassium bromide, phenobarbital, and felbamate are commonly administered to reduce seizure activity. Research is still being conducted regarding the causes of canine epilepsy, both inherited

and acquired, in order to make treatment options more effective.

Epilepsy affects all dog breeds, but again can occur in Whippets as the forum address below will confirm. Symptoms involving seizures usually occur when the dog is sleeping or in a relaxed state. The first epileptic fit may occur between one and three years of age. It begins with a period of stiffness, followed by shaking and muscular spasms. These progress to involuntary paw paddling which may last for a few minutes. Your Whippet may recover very quickly after that and seem fine. Sometimes epileptic fits last longer. If your Whippet ever suffers a fit, he will seem disoriented for many hours after-wards. Call your vet in case of emergency and in the mean time create a safe haven for your Whippet where he cannot hurt himself. Give him plenty of care when he does come through.

For further information:

http://www.dogforum.co.uk/topic/45932-epilepsy-in-whippets/

Please remember epilepsy in Whippets can be controlled by medication, so that your Whippet can reach his golden years. Get an accurate diagnosis from you vet because seizures can be caused by brain tumours, blows to the head, distemper, and even liver disease.

c) Corns

Corns are circular, hard and painful growths found on the digital pads of dogs. This condition is found predominately in Greyhounds and can be the source of significant lameness.

Corns are a condition that mainly affect Greyhounds and Whippets. Corns are hard, painful, circular growths found on the paw pads that can result in lameness. There isn't a great deal of veterinary information on the condition and the general cause is unknown. Being athletic dogs, they are likely to be at greater risk because they are likely to exercise more. Although this could be a factor, popular theory points to a lack of fatty tissue within the pad that would normally protect the pad and act as a shock absorber. It is also speculated that other causes include: Wounds to the pad that as they heal, leave a hard fibrous scar; the possibility of a papilloma virus infecting the area and forming the corn.

The presence of the corn will be easily diagnosed and although a growth will be present, this will be either painful requiring further treatment or painless requiring no further treatment. Should the corn be problematic and require treatment there are a number of options such as surgical removal. As a very last resort, removal of the affected digit may be the only option. In some cases a silicon injection into the area can be applied which may reduce any recurrent growth.

There are actually boots available that you can put on your dog, which act as protection for their paws/pads. This would no doubt act as a great preventative aid and I would recommend doing a Google search such as [boots for dogs].

d) Gastric Torsion (Bloat)

Also known as bloat, gastric torsion is a condition that commonly affects large-breed dogs though it has also been known to affect the Whippet. This condition occurs when the dog's stomach dilates (swells) and then it rotates on its short axis. This torsion can result in a number of serious conditions such as pressure within the abdomen, progressive distension of the stomach, and damage to the cardiovascular system. Decreased perfusion may also occur which could lead to damage to the body's cells and a potential for organ failure.

The symptoms of gastric torsion often include pale gums, appearing sluggish, a pained expression, depression, anxiety, distended or swollen abdomen, abdominal pain, pacing restlessly, shallow, laboured breathing, excessive drooling, vomiting and dry heaving, producing only excess saliva when vomiting As the condition progresses the dog may also experience an increased heart rate, a weakened pulse, unable to stand in later stages of bloat and possibly collapse. Do not always assume that any or all of the symptoms are indicative of torsion. However, as always, seek veterinary assistance without delay.

The causes of this condition are largely unknown, unfortunately though, dogs that have a parent or other relative who have experienced the disease, are at a higher risk. Deep-chested breeds are also at an increased risk for gastric torsion.

Because gastric torsion can quickly escalate and lead to emergency conditions, it is essential that you seek treatment for your Whippet as soon as you suspect the condition. Hospitalization is generally required, especially if your dog is experiencing cardiovascular symptoms. Once the heart problems have been treated, the pressure in the abdomen will be released through orogastric intubation. After this happens, surgery may be performed to correct the position of the stomach. Additional treatments may be required in some cases to correct additional organ damage.

Torsion is not as common in Whippets as it is in Greyhounds. Nonetheless, as they are a similar breed there is the potential of this occurring and again, it is a life-threatening condition. Consult with your vet immediately if you see any symptoms mentioned previously.

As previously said, it is rare for Whippets to be affected, but it is possible. As a preventive measure it is probably best to feed your Whippet small meals on elevated dog bowls. Also restrict access to lots of water after vigorous exercise or immediately after and before feeding. Try resting your Whippet after he has eaten.

e) Megaesophagus

Megaesophagus is a condition which results in a dilated oesophagus and can affect both puppies and mature adults. It is common for puppies to naturally recover from the condition but less so for adults. Puppies also have the best chance of having the problem corrected by surgery and medication can treat

the condition if it is the muscles and nerves that are affected by disease. It is effectively the nerve supply, which would normally cause a peristaltic wave to push the food along the oesophagus to the stomach that is defective and therefore causes the problem. The food simply sits there until it is eventually regurgitated and if large amounts of food are held long enough, this can stretch the oesophagus more so, further exacerbating the problem.

Symptoms of the condition typically include a cycle of vomiting, hunger or in some cases appetite loss and consequent weight loss. Drooling or a nasal discharge can occur as can halitosis, coughing and possibly aspiration pneumonia, whereby food or liquid enters the lungs. Where there is a risk of food or liquid inhalation, it is recommended that the dog remains upright for up to 15 minutes after eating. It is also advised that water and food vessels be elevated at a manageable height for the dog. Veterinary diagnosis and possibly laboratory testing are likely to confirm the condition. Unfortunately there is no easy cure and often the dog requires on-going care and therapy. The important thing is that the dog receives sufficient nutrients. As solid food is difficult to pass, small meals generally in liquid form must be administered whilst the dog stands upright.

f) Cushing's Disease

There have been instances of Cushing's disease in Whippets due to the adrenal glands over working. It is more common in mid to old age dogs. The condition manifests itself with symptoms such as an increase in thirst and consequently urination; muscle weakness with lethargy; a hairless pot belly with the swollen belly thought to be related to enlargement of the liver; increased appetite. The cause of the condition relates to a tumour that affects either the pituitary or adrenal gland. Once again a veterinary diagnosis and treatment should take place without delay.

Excessive cortisone drug treatment has been known to exacerbate the disease. This has also been linked to dogs drinking highly chlorinated water. If you live in an area where the water contains high levels of chlorine, consider using bottled or filtered water, rather than tap water.

g) Cancer

Statistics today indicate that one in two dogs will be affected with cancer, most notably in later years. Early detection of cancer in dogs can save a dog's life. Your veterinarian will no doubt recommend seeing an oncologist if they detect any abnormality when your Whippet is examined during his bi-annual exams. By following certain dietary guidelines, you can also reduce the onset and spread of cancer in your Whippet. Feeding a high Omega-3 fatty acid diet instead of a meat-based diet is recommended.

Symptoms of this deadly disease include:

» Bleeding and discharge from any body cavity

» Persistent lameness or unsoundness

» Sores that are recurrent and that do not heal

» Breathing difficulties

» Weight loss

» Eating and swallowing problems

» Lack of appetite

» A feeling of malaise and discomfort in your Whippet

» Bad breath and bad body odour

» Problems with urinating and defecating

» Lumps and bumps that grow larger

h) Skin Disorders

Alopecia

This is also known as bald thigh syndrome. Its cause is hormonal, and it has been found that Whippets being treated with steroids or cortisones may suffer from it. It becomes more apparent when a Whippet's pigmentation fades. Symptoms include a thinner coat on the outer thigh due to the skin being paler. You'll need to consult with your veterinarian for a proper diagnosis and treatment.

A 12% frequency of Canine Pattern Baldness or Progressive

Alopecia was reported in 2000 by Whippet Health Foundations 'Whippet Health Survey'

Acral Lick Granuloma

Your Whippet may well suffer from this condition. A dog will keep attacking a specific part of the body which is usually the legs or paws. Your Whippet may keep licking the area excessively. What happens is that he gradually licks away all of the hair down to the skin, leaving behind a large, and painful wound. New capillaries bead on the surface of the wound, and your Whippet will keep licking and biting this area. Your veterinarian will usually prescribe cortisteroids for this syndrome.

Demodectic Mange

This can be a serious disease if left untreated, but is not contagious between dogs nor does it spread to humans. The demodex mite which causes the problem lives in the hair follicle. Many dogs carry small numbers of these from puppy-hood. The immune system plays a large part in restriction, growth and multiplication of the mite. If there is an immunodeficiency then the parasite is able to multiply resulting in the development of lesions, reddened skin, hair loss and scaly skin. This mange is most common in young adults as well as puppies and generally appears on the front legs and face but can occur elsewhere.

Diagnosis is by skin scrapings and generally large numbers of the mite will be present. Severe generalized occurrences can be difficult to treat and can require regular medication.

An 8% frequency of Demodectic Mange(demodicosis)was reported in 2000 by Whippet Health Foundations 'Whippet Health Survey'

i) Eye Disorders

Cataracts

This condition is typically inherited, though some cataracts are the result of another disease such as Diabetes Mellitus or Progressive Retinal Atrophy. A cataract is the darkening or clouding of the lens in the dog's eye resulting from an accumulation of proteins. There are three classifications to describe the age of onset for cataracts. Congenital (present from birth), juvenile (develop at a young age), or senile (develop later in life). There are also different levels of cataracts based on how much of the lens it covers.

Cataracts are one of the most common eye problems in dogs. If your dog develops cataracts you will notice a change in eye colour, normally to a light blue, white, or grey. You may also notice inflammation inside or around the eye. Other symptoms include squinting, rubbing the eye, bumping into objects, and other signs of vision loss. Cataracts that are caused by genetic factors cannot be prevented but those caused by other diseases can be prevented by managing the primary condition.

To diagnose your Whippet with cataracts, your veterinarian will need to perform a physical exam and he may refer you to a veterinary ophthalmologist. The vet will test your dog's ability to navigate around objects and will check for foreign objects or damage to the eye. Unfortunately, surgery is the only way to permanently remove cataracts but it is not necessary in all cases. Some cataracts are mild and do not cause significant vision problems for the dog. Even if your dog's cataracts do not seem to be impeding his vision, you should still have them checked out by your veterinarian to make sure there are not further complications.

2.35% of Whippets examined between 2000 and 2005 by veterinary opthalmologists (reported by The American College of Veterinary Opthalmologists AVCO 2007) were found to be suffering Cataracts

Progressive Retinal Atrophy

Also simply referred to as PRA, progressive retinal atrophy is an inherited condition that leads to blindness in dogs. This condition was first recognized in the Gordon Setter, but has since been identified in over 100 breeds including the Whippet. Progressive retinal atrophy affects the retina. This is the part of the eye that converts light into signals that travel through the optic nerve to the brain, where those signals are interpreted as vision. In dogs, the retina contains photoreceptors which help the dog to see in the dark.

There are several different forms of PRA which are differentiated by the age of onset and the rate of progression. In dogs with PRA, the retinas either exhibit arrested development, also called retinal dysplasia, or early photoreceptor degeneration. Dogs with retinal dysplasia usual develop symptoms within 2 months of birth and they may completely lose their sight within a year. Dogs having retinal degeneration are usually affected between one year and eight years after birth and the symptoms progress more slowly.

The symptoms of PRA vary from one case to another. This disease does not cause the dog pain and there is usually no change in the outward appearance of the eye. You may notice a change in your dog's behaviour related to a loss of vision such as reluctance to go down stairs or difficulty seeing in the dark. As the atrophy progresses you may notice a dilation of the pupils and an increased reflection of light from the eye. In some cases, the lens of the eye may become cloudy or opaque.

PRA is diagnosed through an ophthalmic examination as well as other tests. There is no treatment for PRA, unfortunately, but most dogs adapt well to a loss of vision. Because the disease progresses slowly in many cases, the dog has time to adapt to changes in vision before becoming completely blind. There is no way to prevent PRA if the dog is genetically predisposed. In this respect, breeders should engage in responsible breeding practices to avoid passing on this hereditary condition.

Glaucoma

Glaucoma occurs due to the fluid pressure in the eyeball increasing. In severe acute cases if not treated as an emergency, within 24 hours this can lead to blindness.

Signs of the condition are a swollen eyeball that clouds over and even the surrounding area will be painful to touch. Usually glaucoma occurs after an injury as well as a lens cataract or dislocation. Again the condition should be treated with immediate effect and may require urgent surgery or medication.

Sudden Acquired Retinal Degeneration Syndrome (SARDS)

Although it is known that diabetes can result in blindness and cataracts, and kidney failure can lead to detachment of the retina and blindness, sudden blindness related to SARDS has no obvious cause.

SARDS in particularly known to affect mid to old age dogs, with females showing a greater predisposition with up to 70% of all cases.

The symptoms of the disease include an obvious difficulty with vision and navigation. The dog will cautiously move about its surrounding and occasionally bump into furniture or other household objects. The condition has also been associated with increased thirst and appetite with consequent increased urination and weight gain. It was initially thought SARDS was connected to Cushing's disease, but studies have concluded that only a few patients with the SARDS condition also had Cushing's disease.

Although it will no doubt be distressing for dog owners who witness the sudden onset of blindness, dogs usually accept and cope well with the condition. In a survey of dog owners with SARDS although just over half felt that the quality of the dogs life had decreased, very few

felt that this would justify euthanasia.

Unfortunately there is no current cure and as the cause is unknown there is no way of preventing a progression. But again the disease is not life threatening and in most cases the dogs can still live a good quality of life.

j) Immune Mediated Diseases

Immune mediated diseases are also known as autoimmune diseases which generally describe a number of conditions that result in the body (immune system) actually attacking and destroying its own cells.

The immune system works to protect the body from foreign bodies such as viruses and bacteria. Without the immune system, these invaders will attack the body and make us or in this case our dogs ill. If the immune system malfunctions, it starts to detect its own bodily cells as foreign and effectively destroys them.

This failure by the immune system usually affects a specific part of the body, so as you can imagine there could be many diseases. The following are typical cases that have been known to affect Whippets.

Steroid responsive meningitis

Steroid-responsive meningitis-arteritis refers to an inflammation affecting the meninges and arteries, which as the name suggests, positively responds to steroid medication. Incidentally The meninges are three membranes, dura mater, arachnoid mater and pia mater, which surround the spinal chord and brain. It can affect any dog breed and this has included the Whippet. It also affects the gastrointestinal system as well as blood vessels in the major organs such as the liver, kidney and heart. It commonly affects young dogs in particular and the onset can be acute or chronic. Symptoms can include:

A general stiff gait, stimulus sensitivity, stiffness and pain in the neck, an increased temperature up to 108°F, paralysis and other neurological difficulties.

The cause is not known, but it is thought the condition could be immune mediated related to an abnormality in the production of the antibody (Immunoglobulin A), in the mouth and mucous membranes.

It is important that this is checked out without delay by your veterinarian. As well as their physical and neurological exam, laboratory blood and urine tests etc. are likely to be necessary. Positive diagnosis is likely to necessitate initial hospitalization including various therapies both physical and medicinal such as steroids and pain killers. Treatment can last quite a few months and must be continued otherwise the condition is likely to revert back. Regular check-ups will also be necessary to ensure there is no relapse.

Systemic lupus

This immune mediated disease can affect and in turn damage many bodily organs. Red blood cells can be destroyed, resulting in anaemia. Blood platelets can be destroyed causing problems with blood clotting. The kidneys can be damaged.

The condition is quite rare, but is considered to be under diagnosed. Typical symptoms include:

Fever, appetite loss, lethargy, swollen/painful joints, lameness, muscular wasting and pain, skin lesions, reddening, ulceration, scaling, hair loss, swollen lymph nodes etc.

The cause of the condition if unknown. Once again a veterinary diagnosis and treatment should take place without delay.

Haemolytic anaemia

Auto Immune haemolytic anaemia (AIHA) involves antibody production that in turn attacks and destroys red blood cells in the liver and spleen. The disease commonly affects bitches and young adults generally. Once again, the occurrence can affect any breed.

An affected dog will become weak and lethargic and consequently a lack of interest in exercise. There is a lack of appetite, increased thirst and vomiting. Heart and breathing rates are increased. Again suspected cases should seek veterinary attention without delay, where diagnosis/laboratory testing and treatment will be needed.

Thrombocytopenia

This condition has a rarer occurrence rate than AIHA. The condition affects blood clotting as platelets are reduced. Signs and symptoms include; nose bleeds, easy and excessive bruising, gum haemorrhage's, blood in the urine and faeces. There is a serious risk of excessive bleeding from any wound and obviously surgical operations. Again suspected cases should seek veterinary attention without delay where diagnosis/laboratory testing and treatment will be needed.

Addison's disease

Also known as hypoadrenocorticism, Addison's disease is a disease that stems from reduced corticosteroid secretion from the dog's adrenal gland. Addison's disease typically affects younger to middle-aged female dogs, though it can affect dogs of any age and sex. Unfortunately, the symptoms for this disease are fairly vague which often makes it difficult to make a diagnosis.

The adrenal gland is located near your dog's kidney and it secretes several substances that play a role in regulating various bodily functions. Two of the most important substances secreted by the adrenal gland are glucocorticoids and mineralocorticoids. Addison's disease is the opposite of Cushing's disease which is characterized by overproduction rather than underproduction of these two substances. Glucocorticoids play a role in the metabolism of protein, sugar and fat. Cortisol is an example of a glucocorticoid. Aldosterone is a type of mineralocorticoid and these substances influence your dog's electrolyte balance.

When your dog's adrenal glands are not functioning properly, the glucocorticoids and mineralocorticoids in your dog's body will not be available in the right levels. This can cause symptoms like lethargy, loss of appetite, vomiting and muscle weakness. Symptoms often come and go which makes it even more

difficult to make a diagnosis. There are several reasons why the adrenal gland might stop producing glucocorticoids and mineralocorticoids. The most common cause is immune mediated destruction of the adrenal gland. Other causes may include infection, tumours, or amyloidosis of the gland.

Addison's disease is diagnosed through a blood test called the ACTH stimulation test in which the dog is given an injection of ACTH, an adrenal stimulation hormone. If the dog doesn't have Addison's disease the dog's body will respond to the hormone by increasing blood cortisol levels. If the dog does have Addison's disease the body will not respond with an increase in cortisol. Fortunately, treatment for Addison's disease is fairly straightforward. It simply involves replacing the glucocorticoids and the mineralocorticoids in the dog's body through medication.

Hypothyroidism

This condition is caused by a deficiency in thyroid hormones. The thyroid is an essential gland in the body which produces a variety of different hormones that play a role in your dog's metabolism. Reduced production of T3 and T4 hormones (liothyronine and levothyroxine) results in hypothyroidism. This condition is most common in small and medium-sized breeds; with certain breeds having a greater predisposition than others. This condition most commonly affects dogs between 4 and 10 years of age, and spayed/ neutered dogs are more at-risk of hypothyroidism than intact dogs.

Some of the most common symptoms of hypothyroidism include lethargy, weakness, mental dullness, unexplained weight gain, hair loss, poor hair growth, scaling, recurring skin infections, intolerance to cold and seizures. Hypothyroidism can be caused by several different things including iodine deficiency, cancer, and heredity. It can also be an after-effect of certain medical treatments like surgery. Extensive testing may be required to diagnose this condition and to determine its cause, and therefore the course of treatment.

Treatment for hypothyroidism typically involves medication and some form of dietary modification. Medical treatments involve synthetic hormone supplements or other medications. Dietary modifications recommended for hypothyroidism include a low-fat diet, especially during the initial phase of therapy. Most dogs respond to treatment for this condition within a few weeks.

In 2007 tests at the Michigan State University established a 2.9% occurrence in Whippets and also established an all dog breed average of 7.5%

Lupoid onychoclystrophy

The immune-mediated skin disease symmetrical lupoid onychodystrophy affects the claws of dogs resulting in claws separating from the claw bed. The area around the paw pad and claws becomes sore, red and tender resulting in lameness.

Treatment is usually with immunosuppressive drugs, but there seems to be a strong connection with the disease and an omega-3 and 6 fatty acid deficiency.

Polyarthritis

Immune-mediated polyarthritis is an inflammatory condition affecting the joints such as the knee and shoulder. Antibodies attack the cartilage joint tissue.

Typical arthritis symptoms occur such as; leg stiffness, reduced motion range, lameness, Joints that swell, crack and become painful. Joints can become unstable and lead to partial or complete dislocation. There are a number of different types so symptoms and consequent diagnosis and treatment will vary.

You can find more information on these conditions at the following link: *http://whippet-health.co.uk/#/immune-disease/4531648503*

k) Whippet Allergies

Dog allergies can be problematic and any dog can be prone to or become allergic to anything from the dust in the home to grains in his diet.

Wheat Allergies

Wheat and grain allergy can cause so many health problems that grain free dog food is actually becoming quite a common product and many pet stores have at least one available variety, if not multiple types. What is wheat allergy though, and what problems can it cause Whippet dogs and their puppies? Wheat related health problems in dogs are actually split into three different reactions; wheat allergy, gluten allergy and gluten intolerance.

Each has a slightly different reaction on the body, all with equal detriment.

In short, wheat in a dog's diet can lead to a number of different allergy related symptoms of varying severity.

Take a look:

Be Aware!

» Itchy skin

» Open sores

» Ear infections

» Breathing problems

» Hives

» Itching of the mouth or throat

» Itchy and watery eyes

» Itchiness

» Dry skin

» Lack of coat condition and dandruff

» Loose bowel movements

» Nasal congestion

» Rash

» Skin swelling

» Vomiting

Gluten sensitivity is a reaction specific to gluten, found within wheat, symptoms include:

Be Aware!

» Changes in behavior

» Pain

» Muscle cramps

» Weight loss

» Fatigue

The biology behind allergic reactions, in very simple terms, is that allergy attacks the immune system of the dog. When the dog is eating a diet high in something that he is allergic to, the body has to constantly fight the introduction of the substance in the body. This leaves the dog's immune system weakened and less able to cope with other infections and illnesses. Although wheat is one of the major factors in dog food allergy, there are many more. Ingredients in dog food range vastly dependent on the brand. Additionally they can include bright colours (to appeal to you, the dog owner) unnatural flavours and shocking chemical preservatives.

Take a look at your favourite dog food for a moment, or spend some time in the aisles of the pet store, the composition of most dog food is pretty terrifying. Long chemical names and a huge list of them are worrying to say the least.

l) Additional Disease Predispositions

Other inherited and predispositions to diseases have been noted as follows.

Hip Dysplasia: This is generally an inherited condition that causes degeneration in the joints and arthritis of the hips. In the case of Whippets the number of reported cases has been minimal. The OFA breed statistics reported in 2010 only 1.4% cases.

Patella Luxation and Elbow Dysplasia were again screened by the OFA in 2010 but too few cases were available to provide any significant frequency.

A 19% frequency of *Retained Testicles (*Cryptorchidism) was reported in 2000 by Whippet Health Foundations 'Whippet Health Survey'

5.19% of Whippets examined between 2000 and 2005 by veterinary opthalmologists (reported by The American College of Veterinary Opthalmologists AVCO 2007) were found to be suffering *Vitreous Degeneration*

A 3% frequency of *Allergic Dermatitis* was reported again in 2000 by Whippet Health Foundations 'Whippet Health Survey'

Deafness was reported in 2000 by Whippet Health Foundations 'Whippet Health Survey' at a 1% frequency. In a separate evaluation BAER(Brainstem Auditory Evoked Response) tests carried out in 2004 established a 2.4% frequency.

Persistent Pupillary Membranes were found at a frequency of 1.21% of the Whippets tested between 2000 to 2005 by veterinary opthalmologists (reported by The American College of Veterinary Opthalmologists AVCO 2007)

According to Sargan DR, Withers D, Pettitt L, et. Al, in their publication, 'Mapping the mutation causing lens luxation in several terrier breeds. J Hered. 2007; *Primary Lens Luxation* was reported with a risk factor of 4.57 times that of other dog breeds. In serious cases this can progress to secondary glaucoma and possibly blindness.

In addition to the preceding a number of isolated cases such as Malignant Lymphoma, Lung Lobe Torsion etc. have occurred but again with no great frequency. Once again, although the preceding may seem depressing and daunting, it is hoped that the cases and frequency percentages of Whippets tested illustrate that the majority of diseases have occurred relatively rarely. There are many genetic tests available and it is hoped that the more serious and frequent diseases are regularly screened for and affected dogs are removed from any breeding program.

m) Additional medical concerns

Surgery and Anaesthetics

Surgery may be necessary as a result of an accident or as a result of a disease or cancer, that necessitates a surgical procedure. I wanted to include the following information regarding anaesthetics and possible concerns that can affect Sighthounds such as the Whippet.

If your Whippet is undergoing surgery, he will always need to have a general aesthetic. Although it may be odd to be concerned about aesthetic use, there have been concerns raised as to risks involved possibly including Whippets. The following quote is worth reading and do not be afraid to question your vet regarding your concerns. You need to be confident that your veterinarian knows about the Whippet breed, and the possible risk associated with anaesthetics. It is unlikely, but some veterinarians may not be aware of the fact that anaesthetics stay longer in Whippets. A Whippet has very little body fur, and because of this, the drug tends to stay in the body for much longer than in other breeds.

Although there are many baseless concerns regarding breeds and anaesthetics, many veterinarians like Dr. Bruno Pypendop, Dr. Med Vet, Dr.Vet Sci, DACVAA, professor and service chief of anaesthesiology at the School of Veterinary Medicine at the University of California, reports that some breeds can be at risk with anaesthesia.

"The only well-documented, breed-specific aesthetic drug concern is with the use of thiobarbiturates in Greyhounds.," says Dr. Pydendop via The Whole Dog Journal. *"But that sensitivity- which is believed to affect all lithe-bodied breeds created for chasing prey at high speeds, such as Whippets and Borzoi- is a moot point since that class of sedatives is not available in the United States anymore."* Pypendop goes on to add that sighthounds have been found to have prolonged recoveries from other drugs too, and their low stores of body fat leave them susceptible to hypothermia, or lowered body temperature, while anesthetized.

whole-dog-journal.com/topics/ dog_health_care.html

" Even if your dog is a good old "all American" canine, considering what breeds might be in his background might be useful when it comes to calculating anaesthesia risks.

Pre-Breeding Health Testing Recommendations

The Whippet Health Foundation (WHF) recommends the following pre-breeding screenings for all Whippets. These are accepted by the American Whippet Club and shown on the Whippet Health Foundation website.

All the health tests have been accepted by the Canine Health Information Centre (CHIC) for Whippets to get their CHIC certification.

» Whippets need to be registered in the WHF open database.

» Whippets may have a CHIC number. This is an option for owners.

» CHIC does not accept test or certification results directly from the Whippet Health Foundation database.

» All thyroid, hip, echocardiogram, BAER needs to be automatically viewable on the Whippet's individual page within the Whippet Health Foundation database.

Requirements

» The Whippet must be registered in the Whippet Health Foundation database CERF, every year.

» Echocardiogram needs to be done by a board certified cardiologist every year.

» BAER needs to be done once.

Recommended

» Thyroid testing by an approved lab every alternate year.

» Myostatin Deficiency test (once)

» OFA Hips or PennHIP evaluation (once)

Whippet Health Foundation: For more information on Whippet disease research, visit: *whippethealth.org*

3.) Preventing Illness — Vaccinations

Though you may not be able to prevent your Whippet from developing certain inherited conditions if he already has a genetic predisposition, there are certain diseases you can prevent with vaccinations. During the first few weeks of life, your Whippet puppy relies on the antibodies he receives from his mother's milk to fend off infection and illness. Once his own immune system develops however, you will be able to administer vaccines to prevent certain diseases like canine distemper, parvovirus, and rabies.

Vaccinations for dogs can be divided into two categories: core vaccines, and non-core vaccines. Core vaccines are those that every dog should receive while non-core vaccines are administered based on your dog's level of risk. Depending on where you live and how often your Whippet comes into contact with other dogs, you may not need to administer any non-core vaccines. According to the AVMA, recommended core vaccines for dogs include: distemper, canine adenovirus, canine parvovirus, and rabies. Non-core vaccines include: coronavirus, leptospirosis, Bordetella bronchiseptica, canine para-influenza, and Borrelia burgdorferi. You will need to speak to your veterinarian about non-core vaccines to determine which ones your Whippet does and doesn't need.

The rabies vaccine can be very stressful for dogs but, unfortunately,

Recommended Vaccination Schedule

Vaccinne	Doses	Age	Booster
Rabies	1	12 weeks	Annually
Distemper	3	6 to 16 weeks	3 Years
Parvovirus	3	6 to 16 weeks	3 Years
Adenovirus	3	6 to 16 weeks	3 Years
Para-influenza	3	6 weeks, 12 to 14 weeks	3 Years
Bordatella	1	6 weeks	Annually
Lyme Disease	2	9, 13 to 14 weeks	Annually
Leptospirosis	2	12 and 16 weeks	Annually
Canine Influenza	2	6 to 8; 8 to 12 weeks	Annually

it is necessary in the United States due to the prevalence of rabies in wild animals. Rabies has been eradicated in the U.K. so dogs living in this area will not need rabies vaccines. It is important to note, however, that some states require an annual rabies vaccine, so be sure to check with your local council regarding requirements in your area. In any case, do not administer a rabies vaccine less than one month before or after a combination vaccine.

Your veterinarian will be able to provide you with specific vaccination recommendations for your Whippet but, for reference, you will find a general vaccination schedule for dogs on the previous page.

Whippet Vaccination Schedule

Vaccinations for puppies in particular should be regarded as vital, but many people continue this into adulthood. All puppy vaccines have substances called antigens. These stimulate a response in your puppy's immune system, protecting your Whippet against any possible future exposure to a specific disease.

Many dog owners and veterinarians alike believe that too many vaccinations or puppy shots are harmful and possibly dangerous to dogs because they can overload the immune system. Instead many owners are spacing out their vaccinations, deliberately giving only one or two at a time. Consult with your veterinarian as to your Whippet's vaccination schedule. Keep in mind that the Whippet, similar to the Greyhound takes longer to eliminate toxins from the body. Vaccines should only be given by your veterinarian. Vaccination records should be kept by you and follow up schedules should be noted. The vaccination shots are usually administered over a 15-day cycle.

Allergies To Vaccines

Serious allergic reactions to vaccines are quite rare. Your vet will obviously only give your puppy vaccines that are necessary for the pup and for the location that you are in. He will also give you all the advice you need about the vaccines and any possible side effects including possible allergic reactions.

Your veterinarian will be able to provide you with specific vaccination recommendations for your Whippet but, for reference, you will find a general vaccination schedule for dogs on the previous page:

Also please have a look at the recommended Vaccine Schedule By Dr. Jean Dodds, DVM
For the latest vaccination table and update with news, please visit:

http://www.itsfortheanimals.com/ DODDS-CHG-VACC-PROTOCOLS. HTM

Please note: Titre testing is commonly practised to establish whether a dog that has been immunized, is in need of a booster for a specific vaccine. This is carried out by a simple laboratory blood test. If sufficient antibodies are present, then there is no need to vaccinate with that specific vaccine. Once again, please note that regular, unnecessary vaccinating, can have an adverse affect on yourdogs health. It would also constitute a waste of money.

4.) Pet Insurance –– Do You Need It

Many new dog owners wonder whether pet insurance is a good option or whether it is a waste of money. The truth of the matter is that it is different in different cases. Pet insurance does for your pet what health insurance does for you; it helps to mitigate your out-of-pocket costs by providing coverage for certain services. While health insurance for humans covers all kinds of health care including preventive care, disease treatment, and accident coverage, pet insurance is a little more limited. Some pet insurance plans only cover accidents while others cover illnesses. Some plans cover certain preventive care options like spay/neuter surgery or vaccinations, but generally only during a puppy's first year.

The costs for pet insurance plans vary from one company to

another and from one plan to another. To give you a general idea of what a health insurance plan might cost you, consider the chart on the next page

Pet insurance works in a very different way than health insurance when it comes to payment. With a health insurance plan you might be asked to pay a co-payment to your doctor when you visit his office but the health plan will forward the remaining payment directly to the provider. With a pet insurance plan you will be required to pay for the treatment up-front and then submit a claim to receive reimbursement for costs up to 90%. The actual amount a pet insurance plan will cover varies from one plan to another and it may depend on the deductible you select as well.

Just as you would with a health insurance plan, having a pet insurance plan requires you to pay a monthly premium. As long as you remain current with those payments, however, you are eligible to receive benefits from the plan. Again keep in mind however, that most pet insurance plans have some kind of deductible in place. A deductible is a set amount that you must pay out-of-pocket before the plan will offer reimbursement for covered services. In many cases, pet insurance plans are useful only for large expenses like cancer treatments that you normally might not be able to cover at a moment's notice. It is not, however, generally cost-effective for things like annual vet exams and vaccinations.

Estimated Cost for Pet Insurance Plans

Pet Wellness Plan	Injury Plan (Emergency)	Medical Plan (Economical)	Major Medical Plan
$18 to $34 per month (£11.70 to £22.10)	$10 per month(£6.50 p/m)	$19 to $27 per month (£12.35 to £17.55)	$25 to $35 per month (£16.25 to £22.75)
Wellness exams, Vaccinations, dental cleaning	Injuries only (such as Poisoning and broken bones)	Basic coverage for accidents, emergencies and illness	Double benefits of Medical Plan
3 levels (Max, plus basic)	Max yearly benefit limit $14,000 (£9,100)	Max yearly benefit limit $7,000 (£4,500)	Max yearly benefit limit $14,000 (£9,100)

**This information is taken from Veterinary Pet Insurance, a division of Nationwide Insurance. Prices are subject to change and are only intended to give a general idea of pricing and coverage options for pet insurance plans.

CHAPTER TWELVE:

SHOWING YOUR WHIPPET DOG

Showing your Whippet can be a wonderful experience for both you and your pet. In training your dog, you will develop a closer relationship with him, and your dog may enjoy the experience as well.

Whippets make excellent show dogs in terms of how patient and well behaved they are. This becomes really important when you consider a lot of waiting around and having to stand on a show bench for long periods of time. However, don't feel too bad as he is bound to enjoy all of the pampering and attention.

1.) Showing Whippet Dogs

It is almost impossible to own a Whippet without wanting to compete in races, dog shows, and other contests. Proud Whippet owners have always flaunted these handsome dogs for over a century. Whippets have proven to be wonderful competitors. With their sleek silhouette and elegant conformation, the Whippet stands out among all dogs at a dog show.

As long as your Whippet is at least six months old, and AKC or UK KC registered, and is not spayed or neutered, has no disqualifying faults, it can be shown. Winning at your fist show is very difficult. There is much to learn about the show world, and you'll need to be very prepared before you start showing your Whippet.

Whippets are one of the easiest breeds to show. They have won Best in Show at some of the most prestigious shows in the world. You will need to attend many dog shows before both you and your Whippet give a polished performance. There are also professional dog handlers that could show your Whippet for you.

To get more information on showing, you'll need to contact your local kennel club and see if they have any handling classes or when the next show is. These are informal and casual events where all dog owners learn. These include puppies, handlers, and even judges.

Losses and wins at these matches should be taken lightly. Even at a serious show, dog handlers and owners should try not to get too serious. The results are the judge's decision.

When competing at a real AKC show, every time the judge chooses your Whippet as the best male or female Whippet, it does not mean he or she is a Champion. Your dog wins up to 5 points. This depends on how many other dogs it defeats.

How To Become an AKC Champion

Your Whippet must win 15 points including 2 majors. This means defeating enough dogs to win 3 to 5 points at a time. As a competitor, you're allowed to enter any class that your Whippet is eligible for: Puppy, Novice. American Bred, Bred by Exhibitor, or Open. The Best of Breed class is for dogs that are already Champions.

The American Kennel Club, also known as the AKC is the United States registry for all purebred dog pedigrees. Whippet owners and breeders will record their pup's ancestry with the pup's sire and dam breeding information, as well as other important information like the pups date of birth, its sex, its breed, and name and address of the breeder. This is done for showing purposes, and also to protect puppy owners from being misled into buying a non-pedigreed dog. A dog's pedigree papers will display your pup's breeding information, and is compiled by your pup's breeder. If your Whippet has purebred Champions as his sire or dam or in his background, then his breeding papers will indicate this, and he'll be much more valuable in terms of cost.

Official Standards For The Whippet

This short excerpt is included to give a brief idea of what the Kennel club standards include and therefore what a judge would look for. The idea here is to prompt you as to what breed standards stipulate for the ideal dog. This may not be of interest to you and it is not to say you have to study breed standards. So by all means skip this part.

While everyone wants a Whippet to be well-bred, and to look like a show dog, you will need to understand what to look out for when choosing a Whippet. As noted previously, the Whippet is a medium-sized dog that is slender, athletic, kind and sensitive, resembling the larger greyhound, in miniature. With a short coat that is sleek, its legs long and slender, the Whippet's body is supple, athletic and curvaceous. The Whippet's ears are semi-pricked when focusing on something. His eyes should be large and kind.

Good looks and the correct conformation according to the AKC and KC official standards also need sound body structure. Soundness refers to a dog's ability to move without being lame or showing signs of a limp. Whippets can run hard and long, and after racing or vigorous exercise should not be lame.

Unsound Whippets may have feet that turn outwards instead of forward. They also may have legs that interfere with each other and impede correct movement. You can look out for this by getting someone to trot your Whippet forward to see if there's an inefficient stride. Soundness is important, and should never be ignored. It is vital to the dogs health and wellbeing as well as showing and racing.

Again the following is included for anyone with a particular interest in the breed standards as formulated and laid down by the respective breed club organizations. They include both the American Kennel Club (AKC) and The Kennel Club (KC), referred to here as KC UK. Also included are the breed standards for the Long Haired Whippet laid down by the International Longhaired Whippet Club (ILWC).

To be fair it is not vital that you know this information in order to obtain a Whippet from a breeder. Nor is it vital for you to know these specifics in order to enjoy being guardian to a Whippet.

According to AKC Breed Standards, the Whippet needs to have the following:

This is an excerpt from The AKC, to give you a taste of what breed standards include:

A medium size sighthound giving the appearance of elegance and fitness, denoting great speed, power and balance without coarseness. A true sporting hound that covers a maximum of distance with a minimum of lost motion. Should convey an impression of beautifully balanced muscular power and strength, combined with great elegance and grace of outline. Symmetry of outline, muscular development and powerful gait are the main considerations; the dog being built for speed and work, all forms of exaggeration should be avoided.

Size, Proportion, Substance: Ideal height for dogs, 19 to 22 inches; for bitches, 18 to 21 inches, measured at the highest point of the withers. More than one-half inch above or below the stated limits will disqualify. (Other information not included here is available in the full breed standard)

Head: Keen intelligent alert expression.

Eyes: large, round to oval in shape. Small and/or almond shaped eyes are undesirable and are to be faulted. Eyes to be dark brown to nearly black in colour. (Other information not included here is available in the full breed standard)

Ears: Rose ears, small, fine in texture; in repose, thrown back and folded along neck. Fold should be maintained when at attention. Erect ears should be severely penalized.

Skull: Long and lean, fairly wide between the ears, scarcely perceptible stop.

Muzzle: Should be long and powerful, denoting great strength of bite, without coarseness. Lack of under-jaw should be strictly penalized.

Nose: Nose leather to be entirely and uniformly pigmented. Colour to be black, dark blue or dark brown, both so dark so as to appear nearly black.

Teeth: Teeth of upper jaw should fit closely over teeth of lower jaw creating a scissors bite. Teeth should be white and strong. Undershot shall disqualify. Overshot one-quarter inch or more shall disqualify.

Neck, Topline, Body: Neck long, clean and muscular, well arched with no suggestion of throatiness, widening gracefully into the top of the shoulder. A short thick neck, or

214

a ewe neck, should be penalized. The back is broad, firm and well muscled, having length over the loin. The backline runs smoothly from the withers with a graceful natural arch, not too accentuated, beginning over the loin and carrying through over the croup; (Other information not included here is available in the full breed standard)

Tail: The tail long and tapering, reaching to at least the inside of the hock when measured down along the hind leg. When the dog is in motion, the tail is carried low with only a gentle upward curve; tail should not be carried higher than top of back.

Forequarters: Shoulder blade long, well laid back, with flat muscles, allowing for moderate space between shoulder blades at peak of withers. Upper arm of equal length, placed so that the elbow falls directly under the withers. (Other information not included here is available in the full breed standard)

Forelegs: Straight, giving appearance of strength and substance of bone. Pasterns strong, slightly bent and flexible. Bowed legs, tied-in elbows, legs lacking substance, legs set far under the body so as to create an exaggerated fore chest, weak or upright pasterns should be strictly penalized. (Other information not included here is available in the full breed standard)

Hindquarters: Long and powerful. The thighs are broad and muscular, stifles well bent; muscles are long and flat and carry well down toward the hock. The hocks are well let down and close to the ground. Sickle or cow hocks should be strict-ly penalized.

Coat: Short, close, smooth and firm in texture. Any other coat shall be a disqualification. Old scars and injuries, the result of work or accident, should not be allowed to prejudice the dog's chance in the show ring.

Colour: Colour immaterial.

Gait: Low, free moving and smooth, with reach in the forequarters and strong drive in the hindquarters. (Other information not included here is available in the full breed standard)

Temperament: Amiable, friendly, gentle, but capable of great intensity during sporting pursuits.

Disqualifications: More than one-half inch above or below stated height limits. Blue eye(s), any portion of blue in the eye(s), eyes not of the same colour. Undershot. Overshot one-quarter inch or more. Any coat other than short, close, smooth and firm in texture.

These were last Approved October 2007 and were Effective from January , 2008

The full standard can be accessed at the following link:

http://images.akc.org/pdf/breeds/standards/Whippet.pdf?_ga=1.56250987.1739120670.1454152497

If the above link does not work please visit AKC at

http://www.akc.org/dog-breeds/whippet/

You should then see the latest link to the most current breed standards.

Also if any of the words used are not familiar to you the AKC has produced a Glossary at the following link:

www.akc.org/about/glossary/

Official UK KC Breed Standard For The Whippet

The written breed standard for UK KC is not included here. The standards do differ slightly between the AKC and UK KC, but there are more similarities than not.

Again, if you would like to read the current breed standard for the Whippet, please click on the following link:

http://www.thekennelclub.org.uk/services/public/breed/standard.aspx?id=1030

If the link is not working at the time you view please visit

thekennelclub.org.uk and type in the search box [Whippet Breed Standard]

The Longhaired Whippet Breed Standard

Apologies to anyone who wishes to know more about the specific Long Haired Whippet, as this has not been covered in the book. However the breed is popular breed amongst sighthound lovers. There is an excellent site that at the time of publication was available at the following link

internationallonghairedwhippetclub.org

The website is packed with lots of information and resources relating to the breed.

As above, the breed standards are not included, but you can access these at the following link:

http://internationallonghairedwhippetclub.org/longhaired_whippet_breed_standard.html

2.) What to Know Before You Show

If you plan to show your Whippet dog, there are a few things you need to know before you register. The exact rules and requirements will vary from one show to another, so pay attention to specific requirements.

Before you attempt to show your Whippet, make sure your dog meets the following requirements:

Required!

» Your dog needs to be fully house-trained, and able to hold his bladder for several hours.

» Your Whippet needs to be properly socialized, and able to get along well with both humans and other dogs.

» Your dog should have basic obedience training, and he should respond consistently to your commands and look to you for leadership.

» Your Whippet should be even-tempered, not aggressive or hyperactive in public settings.

» Your dog needs to meet the specific eligibility requirements of whatever show you are participating in. There may be certain requirements for age, for example.

» Your Whippet needs to be completely up to date on his vaccinations so there is no risk of him contracting or spreading disease among other dogs at the show.

In addition to considering these requirements, you also need to make sure that you yourself are prepared for the show.

The list below will help you to know what to bring with you on the day of the show:

» Your dog's registration information

» A dog crate and exercise pen

» Food and water bowls for your dog

» Your dog's food and treats

» Paper towels or rags for cleanup

» Toys to keep your dog occupied

3.) Preparing Your Dog for Show

Your preparations for the dog show will vary according to the type of show in which you have entered. If you enter an obedience show for example, perfecting your dog's appearance may be less important than it would for a conformation show. Before you even enter your dog into a show you should consider attending a few dog shows yourself to get a feel for it. Walk around the tent where the dogs are being prepared for show and pay close attention during the judging to learn what the judges are looking for in any given show. The more you learn before you show your own dog, the better off you will be. One of the most important things you need to do in preparation for a conformation show is to have your Whippet properly groomed so that his coat is in good condition.

Follow the steps below to groom your Whippet in preparation for show:

1. The night before the show, give your Whippet a thorough brushing then trim his nails and clean his ears as well

2. Give your dog a bath and dry his coat thoroughly before brushing him again.

3. Once your dog is clean, you need to keep him that way. Have him sleep in a crate that night and keep him on the leash during his morning walk.

4. The day of the show, brush your Whippet's coat again.

5. When you arrive at the show, keep your dog in his crate or in a fenced exercise pen so he doesn't get dirty.

When it comes time for judging, just remember that the main reason you are doing this is to have fun with your dog. Do not get too upset if your Whippet does not win. Just take notes of ways you can improve for the next show and enjoy the experience you and your dog had together that day.

CHAPTER THIRTEEN:

BREEDING WHIPPET DOGS

Breeding dogs is not something that you should do on a whim and certainly not something you should do for money. If you think that breeding your dog will be a good way to make a little extra cash you are probably wrong. You will be lucky to come out even, by the time you cover expenses to care for a pregnant female and a litter of puppies. You should only breed your Whippet if you thoroughly prepare yourself through in-depth research. You also need to be sure that you are able to provide the level of care required. You will learn the basics about breeding Whippets in this chapter.

PLEASE NOTE: The following is intended as a brief introduction of what to expect. Like many things, there are many pitfalls and problems that can be avoided with careful preparation. I would also recommend reading the following book to get an idea, and if you have not been put off, then properly research and prepare. I mention this at the end but a detailed book on the subject that you will find many forum members recommend is 'Book of the Bitch'. But for now, hopefully the following will be useful to you.

1.) Basic Breeding Information

I am all in favour of breeding at least one litter of pups in order to keep the generation going of your beloved pet. If you do not wish to breed with your dog, or only intend to breed one litter, you may wish to consider the benefits to your dogs health of spaying or neutering.

There is much debate about when is the ideal time to spay or neuter a dog. Traditionally between 6 months and a year was considered ideal. According to 'Blue Cross' they advocate spaying or neutering before the age of 6 months, but for larger dogs this should be after the first heat. More information is available at the following https://www.bluecross.org.uk/pet-advice/neutering. However, according to the ASPCA, they suggest dogs can be spayed before 6 months of age. Spaying a female dog before her first heat is considered to significantly reduce your dog's risk for developing mammary cancer as well as ovarian and uterine cancers. To find out more, have a look at the following site; https://www.aspca.org/pet-care/general-pet-care/spayneuter-your-pet

If you are considering the option of breeding your Whippet, you will find it useful to know some facts about dog breeding in general. For example, the oestrus cycle (also known as "heat") for dogs occurs twice a year; about every 6 months; though some small-breed dogs have three cycles per year. This cycle typically lasts for 14 to 21 days with the length varying from one dog to another. It can take a few years for an adult dog's cycle to become regular. Heat does not occur in any particular season, it is simply a matter of the dog's age and when she reaches breeding age.

If you plan to breed your Whippet, it will be important for you to recognize the signs of oestrus. The first sign that your dog is going into heat will be the swelling of the external vulva. In some cases, your dog may excrete a bloody discharge early on but this typically does not develop until the 5th to 7th day of the cycle. As your dog's cycle progresses, the discharge will become lighter in colour and more watery. By the 10th day of her cycle, the discharge will be pinkish in colour.

In addition to swelling of the vulva and a bloody discharge, many female Whippets in heat will start to urinate more often than usual. You may also notice an increased appetite. Sometimes the dog will develop marking behaviour, spraying urine on various objects in the home to mark her territory and to attract male dogs. A male dog can smell a female in heat from great distances, so it is very important that you keep your female Whippet indoors when she is in heat. When you take her outside, supervise her closely and never take her to a dog park or anywhere that intact male dogs may be present.

Ovulation typically occurs at the time of your dog's cycle when the vaginal discharge becomes watery. During ovulation is when your Whippet will be most fertile. If you intend to breed her, this is when you should introduce her to the male dog. Your Whippet may not be receptive to the advances of a male dog until this point in her cycle. However, she is capable of becoming pregnant at any point during oestrus because sperm can survive for up to 5 days in the female's reproductive tract. If your female Whippet accidentally mates with the wrong dog you can take her to the veterinarian for a mismating injection. Be aware, however, that there are risks associated with this injection, so discuss it carefully with your vet.

The number of puppies your Whippet carries may vary. The average litter size is about 6 puppies, but up to 10 is not unusual and for a first litter there may only be 1 or 2. In most cases, new mothers will have smaller litters at first and then may carry more puppies until about her fourth litter when the number tapers off again.

Once your Whippet becomes pregnant, she will enter into a gestation period lasting about 63 days (9 weeks). You will not be able to detect your dog's pregnancy until the pregnancy has advanced about 3 weeks. Do not attempt to feel for the foetuses on your own because you could hurt your dog or the developing foetuses. An experienced veterinarian will be able to palpate your dog's uterus around day 28 to 32 of her pregnancy to confirm that she is indeed pregnant. It is safe to perform an ultrasound on a pregnant dog after 25 days, and by six weeks, pregnancy can be confirmed using x-rays.

2.) The Breeding Process

Again, it is debatable as to the best age for a dogs first litter. It is generally considered to breed after the first or second season. The bitch should by this point be fully sexually mature You will start to recognize the signs of heat in your dog and will be able to take precautions against accidental pregnancies. An intact male dog can smell a female in heat from distances up to 3 miles (4.83 km). So do not think that just because your neighbours do not have a dog that your female will be safe. The whole season process takes approximately 3 weeks until your female is safe. Usually by the 18th day of oestrus, the female is still likely to attract the attention of males, but she is unlikely to 'stand' for them. In this respect, she should be safe from any unwanted pregnancies.

Once your dogs are of proper breeding age, you can start to think about breeding. You will need to keep a record of your female dog's oestrus cycle so you will know when she is most fertile; around days 11 to 15 of the cycle. During this time is when your female dog will be most receptive to breeding. So, that is when you should introduce her to the male dog. Mating behaviour usually involves the male dog mounting the female from behind. The male will ejaculate his sperm into the female's reproductive tract where it will fertilize the eggs. Sometimes the two dogs become what is known as 'tied'. Effectively the male is unable to release his penis from the female vagina. So do not become distressed or try to release him in anyway. This is a perfectly natural occurrence and he will release himself in a short length of time. If the eggs are fertilized, conception occurs and the female becomes pregnant. She then enters into the gestation period which, as previously noted, lasts about 59 to 63 days.

It is also important to remember the health of the bitch prior to breeding. Obviously never consider mating her if she has some illness at the time. Even if it is a temporary skin disease that she could pass onto the pups. Ensure that any disease is clear before you breed. You should also ensure that she is neither overweight, nor underweight. Obviously you will restrict her diet if she looks too fat and feed her up if too thin.

The stud dog

The choice of a stud dog will depend on your intentions for breeding in the first place. If you are merely wishing to keep the lineage of your beloved pet, you will no doubt choose a healthy dog with a good pedigree. If you are much more serious about showing, then the pedigree and therefore stud dog, will be very specific towards a dog with a top show pedigree. As far as where to look for a suitable stud dog, I can only refer you back to the resources previously listed. If you are a member of a specific Whippet club, you will no doubt have first hand recommendations there. You can of course always check with the KC or AKC for their recommendation of top breeders. Once you find a suitable stud dog, it is likely that you will have to arrange to travel to or board your dog with them in order to facilitate a successful mating. This is obviously something you need to plan, so keeping records of the oestrus cycle and therefore the optimum time to mate, is vital.

Stages of Pregnancy

Again, you must keep track of when you breed your female dog so you will know when to expect her to whelp the puppies (give birth). Once again, by the third week of pregnancy, around day 21, your veterinarian will be able to confirm whether the dog is pregnant or not. He may also be able to give you an estimate as to her litter size. Treat your pregnant female as you normally would until the fourth or fifth week of pregnancy, then you should start to increase her feeding rations proportionally with her weight gain. This has been covered in the chapter on feeding, so please refer back to that. You only need to increase your dog's diet slightly to account for her increased nutritional needs. Having said that, your dog will know how much she needs to eat, so you may be able to let her feed freely rather than rationing her food. Her feed intake is giving nutrition to her growing pups as well as herself. So in this respect, you do not need to worry about any overfeeding leading to obesity, and you certainly do not want to underfeed her. Your pregnant dog's diet should be high in protein and animal fat with plenty of calcium.

It is also around this time that your Whippet will start to look visibly pregnant. Your dog's belly will grow larger, tighter, and harder and her nipples will become especially swollen during the last week of pregnancy.

Maintaining everyday care

During her pregnancy you should carry on her normal routine of regular feeds and exercise. As she gets heavier she is unlikely to be inclined to race about as normal. However, you should ensure that she is not placed into any excitable situations, which may cause her to chase after something, or play energetically with another dog. But you should make sure that she does still have daily moderate exercise. It is also a good idea to keep up with grooming her. If she has a noticeable discharge from the vulva, then it is important that you wash the area on a daily basis, with warm water. This will of course keep the area clean, but also avoid discharge deposits around the house.

It is also a good idea to weigh the mother once per week on the same day, to keep an accurate record. You will no doubt notice her getting bigger anyway, but weighing her confirms that the pregnancy and pup growth is normal. At approximately the fifth to sixth week of pregnancy, you should notice her breast get firmer.

3.) Raising Whippet Puppies

Whelping box

By the eighth week of your dog's pregnancy, in other words approximately a week before she gives birth, you will need to provide her with a whelping box. You can easily and cheaply construct a whelping box out of ply board with either metal brackets to hold the box together or four pieces of 2 inch by 2 inch timber for each corner. The height of the box should be about 15 inches high, with a front cutaway section about 10 inches high to allow the bitch easy access, but ensuring that pups cannot easily crawl out of the box. If you are not DIY inclined, you can buy relatively cheap cardboard disposable boxes. Simply do a Google search for [whelping box], and you will be presented with a number of possibilities. Whatever box you use, it should be a comfortable place lined with clean, old blankets and towels where she can give birth and care for the puppies. Remember that you may need to change the bedding from time to time if it becomes soiled, so have spare replacement blankets/towels to hand. It is best to place this box in a quiet area where your dog will not be disturbed. If you put it somewhere that is too bright or noisy, she will just find somewhere else to whelp. She should be allowed to spend time in the box and therefore accept this as the best place to give birth. You should also make sure this room is warm and draft free.

Whelping: Other supplies

Ideally, as well as the whelping box, you should prepare yourself with important supplies to have on hand when the time comes. Hopefully you have a spare room or at the very least a corner set up especially as a nursery. I would recommend getting hold of a large cardboard box to place the various items that you may need. The following list will equip you with essential supplies for the whelping as follows:

1. A heat source; this can be a heat lamp, heat pad etc. (as an emergency provision hot water bottles have been known to come in very handy) This is of course to keep the mother and pups warm.

2. Clean towels intended to clean up anything the mother does not.

3. A couple of rolls of paper towelling will also be handy as an extra back up for cleaning.

4. Newspapers will be handy if you need to change the floor covering which could get wet.

5. If you have to cut the umbilical cord, a pair of blunt end scissors, surgical or white thread to tie off the end, cotton wool and antiseptic solution to dab an open wound and clean it. It will be a good idea to have a separate, sterile container to put these items in, to minimize infection. A container with surgical spirit/antiseptic solution, is also a good idea to keep items such as the scissors or a rectal thermometer to check temperatures.

6. You may also wish to weigh the puppies, so a pair of suitable scales will be necessary.

Final stages of pregnancy and giving birth

During the last week of your Whippet's pregnancy you should start checking her internal temperature regularly. Using a rectal thermometer, the normal body temperature for a dog should read between 100°F and 102°F (37.7°C to 38.8°C). However, your female dog's body temperature will drop about 24 hours before contractions begin. Your dog's body temperature may drop as low as 98°F (36.6°C), so when you notice a drop in your dog's temperature you can be sure that it won't be long before the puppies arrive. Your dog will also start spending more time in the whelping box at this time. You can check on her occasionally, but do not disturb her too much or she might go elsewhere to whelp. There are other signs that her giving birth is imminent, these include; general restlessness, making nests, moving blankets about or tearing up paper you may have lying around, she may refuse food etc. It may be nothing immediately to worry about, but you can be sure she will soon go into labour.

If she goes into labour during the day, if you can, stay with her as much as possible. This is particularly important if this is her first pregnancy, as she may be anxious and need your reassurance.

When your Whippet goes into labour, you will notice obvious signs of discomfort. She may start pacing restlessly and panting, switching from one position to another without seeming to get comfortable. The early stages of labour can last for several hours with contractions occurring about 10 minutes apart. This usually occurs in waves of 3 to 5 contractions followed by a period of rest. If your Whippet has two hours of contractions without any puppies being born, take her to the vet immediately. Without a veterinary diagnosis, it is difficult to ascertain what the problem may be, but as with human pregnancies, she may need a caesarean section.

Once your Whippet starts whelping, the puppies will generally arrive every thirty minutes; following ten to thirty minutes of forceful straining from the female.

When a puppy is born, the mother will clean the puppy and bite off the umbilical cord. Not only does the licking, clean the puppy, but it helps to stimulate its breathing as well. You need to let the mother do this without you attempting to handle the puppies unless something goes wrong. If this does not happen use a clean towel to clean the puppy and make sure there is no membrane covering the puppies muzzle.

Sometimes the mother may appear to be struggling to give birth to one of the pups. Its head or its back legs may be stuck out and not going anywhere. It may be necessary for you to help her by wrapping a clean towel around the pup and gently pulling. CAUTION: Only pull when the mother is obviously pushing. Some people advise against helping the mother in this way. But if you get a pup that is being delivered legs first, there is a possibility that the umbilical cord could be wrapped around the pup and potentially strangling it.

If a puppy is not breathing

If the puppy appears to not be breathing, you will need to administer emergency first aid. Wrap the pup in a clean towel and hold his body firmly, upside down in the palms of your hand, as if you were praying, his head should be facing the ground. Now shake him back and forth but not too vigorously, in an attempt to stimulate him into action. If he fails to breath, rub his ribs. Next attempt the Heimlich manoeuvre as follows: Again turn the pup upside down, holding him with his back pressed to your chest. Clasp your hands on his abdomen, just below the ribs. Now give 5 thrusts, reasonably hard and sharp to the abdomen. Now look inside the mouth or if there is some mucous or object expelled, if so remove this.

PLEASE NOTE: If after a few minutes of trying a couple of procedures, I would always advise calling an emergency vet. Whilst you are waiting continue as follows.

If you still have no luck, artificial respiration will probably be your last resort. In this case, it is similar to CPR that you would administer to a human and the following would be the same for an adult dog. You will need to blow air into the pups nose and mouth. Some people prefer to use a plastic food bag with one corner cut off that you place over the pups nose/mouth, so that you are not getting his full muzzle/hair etc. in your mouth.

The procedure should be as follows:

1. Lay the pup on his right side
2. Place your hand or fingers on his ribs at the point the elbow meets the chest/ribs (this is approximately where his heart is). Some breeders will simply hold the pup firmly and simply compress the ribs. Be very careful doing this, as although this is an emergency, you do not want to break the rib cage.
3. Give about 20 compressions per minute. You do this in short bursts. So 60 divided by 20 gives is 3.
4. You should be able to check his pulse in the place where the elbow meets the chest or around his wrist above his front paw. You can also check the femoral artery as

noted in the chapter on first aid. CPR is also discussed there.
5. Repeat once more, and if there is still no pulse/breathing, give mouth to mouth resuscitation.
6. So as above, either place a plastic bag with the corner removed over the pups mouth or simply cup your own mouth over the pups nose and mouth (You should make sure that you make a seal so that no air escapes, and gently blow but similar to how you would breathe out after taking a deep breath. You should now give 3 compressions and then breath air into the pup.
7. Continue this sequence until hopefully the pups starts to breathe. Don't just give up after a few minutes, at least continue until an emergency vet arrives.

Hopefully you will never have to experience this, but it is best to be aware of what to do just in case.

After the mother has given birth

After all of the puppies have been whelped, again the female will expel the rest of the placenta and then allow the puppies to nurse (feed). The bitch may attempt to eat the placenta, which is normal. It is advisable at this stage to get a veterinary check up to confirm that the bitch is healthy and to confirm all of the placentas have been expelled and not likely to cause an internal infection.

It is very important that the puppies start nursing (feeding) within 1 hour of delivery because this is when they will get the colostrum. If there is obviously a pup that has not made its way to the mothers breast soon after it is born then place it on a teat or close by. The colostrum is the first milk produced by the mother and it is loaded not only with vitamins and minerals. It also contains antibodies that will protect the puppies against illness and infection while their own immune systems are developing. After whelping, your female dog will be very hungry, so give her as much food as she will eat. As previously said, do not be alarmed if she consumes the expelled placenta as well. Please remember to count the placenta, as it is possible one or two could remain in the mother and cause an infection if not expelled. In this case she would need veterinary attention. Again do not just leave the placentas left, and if it is practical to do so, remove any remaining along with soiled newspapers.

Whippet puppies are born with their eyes and ears closed. They will also have very little fur, so they are completely dependent on their mother for warmth and care. If you suspect that the pups are not warm enough or are likely to chill over-night, consider getting hold of a heat lamp. This can be sighted above the whelping area. Care must be taken not to overheat either them or the mother. So it is perhaps best to place this at one end or a corner, therefore leaving a part of the whelping area cooler.

Growing puppies

The puppies will spend most of their day nursing and sleeping until their eyes start to open around 3 weeks of age. Between the third and sixth week after birth is when the puppies will start to become more active, playing with each other and exploring the whelping box area. The puppies will also start to grow very quickly as long as you feed the mother enough so she can produce enough milk.

Around six weeks after birth is when you should start weaning the puppies if the mother has not started already. Start to offer the puppies small amounts of puppy food soaked in water or broth to soften it. The puppies may sample a bit of the food even as they are still nursing. But they should be fully transitioned onto solid food by eight weeks of age. If you do not plan to keep the puppies yourself, it is at this time that you should start introducing the puppies to potential buyers. You should never sell a puppy that has not been fully weaned and you should carefully vet potential buyers to make sure that the puppies go to a good home.

Puppies are very impressionable during the first few months of life so you need to make sure they get as many experiences (socialization) as possible. If your puppies are not exposed to new things at a young age they will grow up to be fearful and nervous adults. Give the puppies plenty of toys to play with as their teeth start to grow in around week ten, and start playing with them yourself so they get used to being handled by humans.

This is only a very brief if not relatively detailed introduction to the breeding process. For further reading and much more information, I would highly recommend 'Book of the Bitch' by J.M. Evans & Kay White.

CHAPTER FOURTEEN:

CANINE PSYCHOLOGY – THE WHIPPET MIND

This area of the book is going to talk about true understanding of the Whippet dog. From carefully reading his body language, to keeping his super intelligent mind busy, you will learn it here.

For too many years, we have either misunderstood our dogs or followed completely inaccurate advice on what our canine friends are thinking. We look to experts that state their knowledge confidently and employ self-proclaimed dog "whisperers" like they have some kind of magic eye.

Thankfully though, we can now obtain a far better understanding of our dogs, simply by exploring all of the research done over the last few years.

As a science in itself, canine understanding has surpassed all previous knowledge and continues to do so. In short we have learned more about the mental and emotional capacity of our dogs in the last ten to twenty years, than we learned in the two hundred previous.

We are lucky enough to be able to study our dogs and know exactly what that eye flick or yawn means, because kind and careful science has worked it out. This huge amount of new knowledge leaves far less need for employment of a dog whisperer or interpreter to tell you how your dog feels.

It makes it possible, with just a small amount of learning from recent research, to understand your dog's basic behaviour and needs without the need for any translation.

Knowledge and mutual understanding, between you and your dog, is exactly what this area of the book aims to provide you with.

1.) Whippet Body Language

This first section is the place where you can learn what your dog's body language is saying. It can be easy to misinterpret some behaviours and acts that our dogs carry out naturally. However, when you have read this part of the book, you will read your dog's behaviour in a very different way.

So what is your dog saying with his face, body, posture and tail? Read on to find out;

Eyes

The eyes of this breed will tell you a lot about what he is thinking. To be fair, you will probably know when your dog is anxious and fearful, they simply have a worried stare. A relaxed dog on the other hand, will have a slightly squinty eyed, less startled look, showing that he is happy.

A dog will not usually hold eye contact with you happily, until he has been with you for a long time and feels completely secure to do so.

Some dogs never feel happy to hold eye contact.

Some dogs may stare, and some people believe that this focus is the dog's equivalent of a hug.

A new dog or insecure dog will interpret human eye contact as a worrying event. This can be a learned response or just a natural one but it's quite common. It's usually best not to establish eye contact in this way when you are not absolutely certain that the dog feels secure.

If you stare at a dog that feels insecure, for any amount of time, you will probably see him displaying specific acts that show his unease. He may lick his lips, yawn, look away or raise a paw, this is the dog stating that he is not so keen on your attention being delivered that way.

When is Eye Contact Good

The only exception to eye contact being a worrying affair, is during training sessions, where you are teaching a dog to focus carefully upon you for reward.

This is something you will notice in your training sessions, and is a part of training which naturally builds a dog's confidence.

Half Moon Eyes

If there is any tension or stiffness in his stance and the whites of either of his eyes are showing, then the dog is likely to be uneasy. The white of an eye showing in a 'half-moon" shape is a good early indication that a dog is worried or concerned about something.

Extreme tension, directed focus and an unflinching stare means that the dog is very uneasy. At this point the tension must be broken by taking away any focus from the dog and therefore, diffusing any anxiety that he may feel.

In a lot of cases it is merely part of their learning experience, which is why socialization is so important. The more they are exposed to worrying situations, the more they realize there is nothing to fear, and they no longer react with anxiety.

Body Position and Stance

As a general rule if a dog's body language seems to be leaning back, from the ears to the tail then the dog is relaxed. If everything gives the impression of leaning forwards, from pricked ears (obviously with a Whippet this isn't so obvious with his floppy ears, but you should still see ear movement, that appears to move forward, and most do prick their ears upward), to taut body language, then the dog is generally quite aroused.

Hackles, which is the name given to the hair along the dog's back, can bristle if the animal is either worried or anxious. A common misconception is the belief that hackles mean the dog is feeling aggressive but this really is not the case.

The hair will bristle and stand quite high right along the back with aggression. But it can also be a sign that the dog is insecure or unsure in a social situation.

The Tail

The tail of the Whippet dog tells us a lot about what the animal is thinking. The higher the tail is held the more aroused a dog is.

The tail that is held very low or tucked beneath the dog betrays insecurity; whilst a high tail displays confidence towards an interaction.

You can look at hundreds of Whippet photos and commonly see that their tail is tucked beneath their legs. Notice also, they are usually photos that are either show stances or the dog made to pose for the camera. Again, take a look at natural shots taken as the Whippet is out and about, and see the contrast. The tail will be high and the Whippet looks relaxed and confident.

2.) Whippet Calming Signals

Calming signals are often missed by people even when displayed by their own dogs who have been with them for years. This is because the calming signal is often a very subtle form of communication.

A dog displays calming signals to other dogs and people as a form of specific communication. They also act to calm his own anxiety if he feels worried or insecure.

I recently watched a dog that was tied up outside a store, calming herself with basic signals; although no-one was paying her any attention at all. This particular dog was licking her lips repeatedly as a way to calm her own anxiety.

Dogs do this along with yawning and flicking their eyes to one side very briefly if they feel anxious. These three actions are the main calming signals that dogs display on a regular basis.

A well socialized dog will recognize the briefest calming signal from another. In this case they usually respond with kindness by acting in a way that diffuses the anxiety of the worried dog.

A dog that has not learned to read the language of other canines, perhaps because of a lack of early socialization, will probably ignore polite calming signals and dive in to greet the insecure dog. This can increase the anxiety of the situation and in some cases, lead to dog fights.

Alongside the three already mentioned, other common calming signals include;

> » A very slight paw lift
>
> » Turning away
>
> » Whining
>
> » Dipping the head

» Seeming to focus on something away in the distance

» Sneezing

» Shaking the body as if shaking off water

All of the previous are generally mild signals that a Whippet dog will display during interaction, particularly if the dog is feeling a bit worried, yet not quite stressed.

Strong Calming Signals

The dog that displays strong calming signals may yawn or pant heavily; try to escape the situation or even take a confrontational stance in order to defend himself.

This type of behaviour will come after mild calming signals, and before the dog is severely stressed.

The dog will need to be removed from the situation, or the trigger of the behaviour will need to be taken away, before the dog is able to calm down. It is important not to just expect the dog to get used to the scary trigger, or this can result in fearful aggression.

How many adults or children have you seen trying to make friends with a scared dog by looming over the poor animal and trying to be reassuring Even when the poor, increasingly anxious dog is backing off or growling When really the dog would be far happier if he was just ignored and allowed to get used to the strange human in his own time. This type of scenario is what most often leads to a bitten child or even adult.

3.) Appeasement Behaviour

Another type of behaviour that a dog may display, particularly the younger of the breed, is appeasement behaviour. This type of action involves the dog trying to diffuse any tension in an interaction, in a very puppy like way.

Appeasement behaviour is a very natural act which is usually the dog communicating that he wants to be friends; wants no trouble, or is sorry that he was out of line.

Common appeasement behaviour types are:

» Jumping up

» Urination on greeting

» Rolling over

» Tucking the tail under

» Muzzle licking, as a puppy does to its mother

Early and continuous socialization is usually the best way to avoid this; or at least make the more mature under-socialized dog more confident.

How Dogs Greet Each Other

Well-mannered greeting between dogs is actually quite different to the way that people greet each other. Dogs that respectfully greet each other, can almost seem to be ignoring the presence of the other animal.

The body will curve around, which is a sign of good manners. A respectful dog will never approach another head on, as this is a sign of disrespect. Sadly it is also how socially awkward dogs approach everyone and everything. It is also the way that people approach each other, and the way that they approach dogs.

4.) Dealing with Social Fear

We can take action to modify fear behaviour, and eventually change it into relaxed behaviour.

In some cases dog trainers have wrongly advised that to get a dog feeling happy, in a scary situation, they must flood the dog's senses with a stimulus until the dog eventually learns to cope.

About Flooding

Flooding was once considered a viable method of helping a dog to recover from fear.

The idea was that the exposure to the stimulus becomes so intense that the dog will eventually pass the point of fear into relaxation, and the fear will be 'fixed'.

It has since been learned that this is not the case. The behaviour which was formerly identified as improvement, was actually complete mental shutdown; which is worse for the dog than the fear itself.

About Masking

Masking is the act of putting the dog into the situation, yet threatening him or hurting him if he reacts to it. This is often seen in dominance based dog training. The dog is forced to wear an inhumane collar, or threatened with violence, and pushed into a scary or stress filled situation.

An improvement may be seen at the time, because the collar/handler threatens the already stressed dog into mental shutdown. But the behaviour has not been truly modified, just temporarily disabled. The dog still feels the same, and often even worse, about the trigger when treated this way.

How the Experts Modify Social Fear

The act of modifying social fear, is to gently change the dog's impression of the frightening encounter, stimulus or scary environment. This is a case of rewarding relaxed behaviour when the dog is in the presence of something which worries him.

Whether the act of reward is carried out when the dog is ten paces from it, or fifty paces away from the stimulus, depends on how close a dog can be to the source of his fear whilst staying relaxed. Similarly, progress will be dictated by the dog's ability to stay relaxed, as he gets closer to the stimulus.

In everyday life, this is a case of building the dog's confidence gently, and at a pace which he can handle. With this approach we can gradually get closer to the worrying stimulus by rewarding relaxation as you go. If the dog's behaviour begins to change, then he has been taken too close too soon.

We can use treats, special toys, praise and attention to help a dog stay relaxed.

The Overall Approach

The first thing we do is really observe the dog. See exactly what sets his behaviour off; because only by knowing this can we start to improve things. The thing that sets the behaviour off is called a trigger.

The first behaviour that a dog will show when he becomes aware of something worrying is calming signals. In extreme cases, the dog may react with fear or terror and want to run away.

Remember that common calming signals include:

>> Licking lips

>> Yawning

>> Glancing away

This is the point of necessary action, because calming signals

mean that the dog is uncomfortable in some way. In this case, they mean that he is becoming anxious, because of the presence of the trigger.

So, it is important to move as far away as the dog needs to be from the thing that worries him; in order for relaxation to re-occur and be rewarded. Again, once the dog shows signs of relaxation and self control, you must praise and reward the behaviour. Gradually get them closer to the fearful trigger, and attempt to stay there longer each time.

It can take a long time; but is the only way to change a dog's emotional response and social fear permanently, and in a positive way.

5.) Whippet Training -- How Does He Learn

Your dog's behaviour is part genetic influence, yet mostly environmental conditioning. Again, from the moment he is conceived, the dog's behaviour is being shaped. This is the first step of environmental conditioning, and this learning never stops. Although it has a huge surge in the period between birth and adulthood.

How exactly does a dog learn

Canine training and therefore his learning, is a process of receiving rewards. If a dog finds that something he does is rewarded, then he will repeat it. If the dog finds that the same behaviour provides no reward at all then the behaviour will not be repeated. Any dog merely wishes to please their guardian, so logically they will refrain from behaviour that displeases you.

Where this becomes complicated, is the examination of reward.

The most obvious type of reward are the classic ones; food, treats, toys, games and verbal praise. All of these, timed carefully will teach a dog to repeat a behaviour, but so will other things too. These are the responses that happen by accident, but teach the dog anyway.

Inadvertent rewards are slightly different. They are things that you may not think classically reward your dog.

The following are examples of inadvertent rewards that can easily teach any dog bad habits:

> The mailman retreating when the dog barks (relieving anxiety about an intruder)

> Pushing a dog off when he jumps up (interaction)

> Shouting at a dog as he barks (interaction)

> Passing the dog a morsel from your plate when he asks (food)

Inadvertent rewarding experiences, such as the ones above, are the biggest part of canine learning. Unless we know what to look for we have no idea that our dogs are being rewarded by their environment.

This leaves us confused as to why our dogs are developing problematic habits.

When your dog learns something from a response within his or her environment, the response is called a 'reinforcer' because it makes a behaviour stronger.

Reinforcement may seem quite confusing at first, yet it is well worth taking some time to understand. When you can understand the details of reinforcement, then you will have a flawless knowledge on exactly how your dog learns from his or her environment.

Environmental Learning in Dogs

As a whole story, the dog learns from his environment in four separate ways. Everything that happens to the dog that he learns from, will be one of these four ways. Whether planned or unplanned, set-up or accidental, your Whippet will learn from them just the same.

By understanding the following, you will understand exactly how your dog learns new things.

1) Positive Reinforcementm Something good starts.

Positive reinforcement describes an act that adds something. When the dog is behaving in a certain way and is rewarded, this will strengthen the behaviour. For instance if you give the dog food as he sits, then he is more likely to sit again.

The dog that is fed treats in a training session to reinforce a specific behaviour is being trained with positive reinforcement.

2) Negative Reinforcement Something bad stops.

Negative reinforcement is the act of something being taken away, or stopping, when the dog changes his behaviour.

For instance the dog that is pulling on the leash whilst wearing a pinch collar learns that when he stops pulling, the pinching stops too.

3) Positive Punishment Something bad starts.

Positive punishment describes something being added to a behaviour in order to teach the dog not to carry out the behaviour again.

For instance, if a dog barks and I quickly squirt him with water so that he stops, I have used positive punishment.

4) Negative Punishment Something good stops.

Negative punishment describes the act of taking something away when a behaviour is carried out. This is used to show the dog that if he behaves a certain way, something that he likes will be lost.

So if a dog is being played with and nips your hand. You then take away the act of playing with him; the dog should quickly learn not to nip or the game will end. It is important to note here why it is necessary to phase out food rewards gradually. If you suddenly stop giving treats when

he has been used to it for so long, then he is likely to feel confused and that he is perhaps being punished.

Which Is The Best Method For Training A Whippet

Each of these learning methods will work if carried out to perfection. Yet some methods are kinder than others. In this book we will not be using positive punishment (something bad starts) nor will we use negative reinforcement (something bad stops).

We avoid these training methods, purely because we want our dogs to be happy. Happy dogs should not be subject to 'bad things" happening in their training sessions.

Positive reinforcement (something good starts), and negative punishment (something good stops), can be combined perfectly to teach your Whippet dog everything that he needs to know about the world.

These methods can be used to carefully modify unhelpful behaviours, and to teach useful behaviour in every aspect of your life with your dog.

A Note on Positive Punishment

There is another reason why we will not be using positive punishment in this book. The method can have an opposite effect on a behaviour to the one which is planned.

By its very nature, positive punishment requires the dog to carry out a particular behaviour in order for it to be punished. Each time a behaviour is carried out it is practiced, and every time a behaviour is practiced it is strengthened.

Therefore by punishing a dog each time he does something, we are allowing him to do it; therefore to learn it, and this increases the likelihood of a repeated act.

For instance if the dog barks at passers-by and we add a squirt of water to his face every time he barks, we are actually doing nothing to change the behaviour itself. We are simply allowing the same train of thought which the dog always has, leading up to a frenzied torrent of barking, to remain the same.

Thus we are actually expecting the dog to either change his own behaviour or foresee ours before deciding how to respond to a passer-by. It's a big expectation for any dog, who are by nature well-known to live in the moment.

Which is exactly why positive punishment is a poor method when trying to train a Whippet or any dog at all.

6.) How Attention Works

One of the most common ways that we add positive reinforcement to a behaviour is with attention. Dogs adore attention from the people they love. The reason that attention will shape a dog's behaviour, is because it is positive reinforcement in action.

Negative attention works in exactly the same way as positive attention. Which means that whether you tell a dog that he is good, or shout at him for being bad; when he carries out an act, you are still giving him attention that he craves. Positive reinforcement merely makes the act stronger.

Any dog with a behaviour problem such as jumping up or barking, that is constantly corrected with attention, is being rewarded for the behaviour. In other words, the fact that you respond to the dog, albeit in a negative way, the dog is still getting the attention it craves.

Because attention is so easy to give to our dogs, attention seeking behaviour can become a real problem.

When the dog looks at you and barks. When he steals things and chews them up whilst you are trying to take them off him. And when he jumps up constantly, he is displaying attention seeking behaviour.

I once had a situation with two West Highland White Terriers that would guard whoever was on the sofa. So whichever dog it was, would growl at the other dog, warning it off. If I touched the dog sat next to me, the growling and snarling got worse. This wasn't aggression that was in anyway directed at me, but purely directed at the other dog. However, as soon as I learned to ignore this, and particularly as soon as I stood up, the dog had lost its focus and reinforcement. They would literally look around at each other, wondering what they were going to do next.

This type of behaviour works if it brings attention, therefore a cycle is established.

Take a look:

> » We chase the dog around the park calling his name. He has our full attention and a great game too.

> » When we tell a dog that is barking, to be quiet, we are actually rewarding the dog for the bark. (telling it to be quiet is giving it attention)
>
> » Pushing a dog away when he jumps up is a rewarding process. We are giving him physical and emotional attention.
>
> » We may have been previously ignoring the dog, and so he picks up something he shouldn't have, and we give him attention.

Dogs generally do what we teach them to do by our responses. How does the dog feel though

Take a look at my example here;

A particular dog is becoming a nuisance when jumping up. He recently knocked someone over and his whole family are covered in bruises. The dog has always jumped up; he learned it as a puppy. Back then it was encouraged, because he was much smaller, and the act was far less intrusive. He knows his guardian is not happy with him jumping up because they seem to be angry when he does it.

Yet it used to make them happy, so the dog tries harder and harder to bring back that happy reaction. Also, his guardian is touching him and speaking to him (albeit in a frustrated way); and the dog likes that, because he loves this person. Now

unless something in the owner's response changes, the dog will continue to provoke that exact response by jumping up.

This type of innate learning causes most of what the dog has learned so far in his life. As dog caretakers we must take responsibility for the way the dogs in our homes act. For our dogs take their guidance from us, and us alone.

To raise a nicely mannered puppy, it's a really good idea to monitor your own delivery of attention. Remember that attention causes repeat behaviour; and lack of attention will give the dog no reason to repeat his act.

If you follow this rule and make a habit of it, then you will be carefully shaping many of your dog's behaviours with little effort at all.

Extinction – Stop That Behaviour for Good!

So what can we do about behaviour that has already been learned And how can we apply the rule of reinforcement to that

Well, if attention causes a behaviour to be repeated, and lack of attention gives the dog no reason to repeat his behaviour (my previous Westie example), a simple shift of attention will make a great deal of difference.

First of all though let's take a look at extinction.

Extinction is the name given to anything that goes away and does not come back. In behaviour terms, this means the act that ceases to be repeated, such as jumping up or begging at the table.

If a behaviour goes un-rewarded for long enough, the dog will display something called an extinction burst where the act gets momentarily worse. Shortly after that, the act will go away altogether, a result known as extinction.

At this point it is therefore vital for the dog owner not to give in, for success is closer than it has ever been!

The reason that extinction is often not reached, is because the dog owner often gives in and responds to the extinction burst, thinking that ignoring the behaviour is not working. When the increase in behaviour is actually showing that not only is it working, but that the approach is almost complete.

When working towards extinction, the other thing to introduce is more attention to the behaviour you want. This will take focus from the unwanted behaviour and make him keener to produce good behaviour.

We will be looking at examples in the chapter on behaviour.

Chapter Fifteen

Whippet Behaviour Problems.

In this area of the book I wanted to talk about potential behaviour problems that the Whippet may develop. Like people, dogs have their own specific personalities. The behaviour that the Whippet displays is partly based on his nature, and mostly a result of the nurturing effect that life has had on him so far. Most canine problems can be halted before they get too severe, or even modified into manageable acts. It's important to have an understanding of behaviour before trying to make any changes.

1.) Dealing with Common Behaviour Problems

Once again it is not fair to generalize, as two dogs of the same breed could be either high maintenance or no trouble at all. Generally however, if your dog doesn't get enough exercise or attention he is likely to develop problem behaviours which may require professional training to correct. What you need to understand before you try to tackle any behaviour problem, is that many behaviours that you might consider problematic are actually natural behaviours for your dog.

For example, chewing is a very natural way for puppies to learn about their world. They also do it to ease the pain of teething. When your puppy fulfils his need to chew by gnawing on an expensive pair of shoes, is when the behaviour becomes a problem. The best way to deal with problem behaviours is not to teach your puppy to avoid the behaviour altogether but to channel that behaviour toward a more appropriate outlet. Below you will find tips for dealing with some of the most common behaviour problems in dogs:

Chewing – The best way to keep your Whippet from chewing on things he shouldn't be chewing on is to make sure that he has plenty of toys available. Many dogs chew on things out of boredom, so ensuring that your Whippet gets enough exercise and play time, will also help to keep him from chewing on things around the house. If chewing does become a problem all you need to do is replace the item your dog is chewing on with one of his toys (swapping). Ideally you would have taken care of such items in your initial puppy proofing stage. However, we can't always be sure which he will chew and which he will ignore. You are therefore better off keeping every potential chewable item that you wish to keep intact, out of his reach.

If after this you still find your Whippet has found something you had forgotten about and is chewing on it, tell him "No" in a firm tone and take the object away. Immediately replace the object with your dog's favourite toy, then praise him when he starts chewing on it. Eventually your Whippet will learn what he is and is not allowed to chew on around the house.

Digging – Just like chewing, digging is a behaviour that dogs often exhibit when they are bored. While digging is a natural behaviour for dogs, it becomes problematic when your Whippet chooses to do it in the middle of your favourite flower bed, or under your fence. A simple way to deal with this problem is to provide your Whippet with a small section of the yard where he is allowed to dig. Bury a few toys or treats in the area to encourage your Whippet to dig there. If you find your Whippet digging in the yard, tell him "No" in a firm voice and lead him away from the area and into his special digging zone. Reward and praise him when he starts to dig there instead. If this becomes particularly problematic, you may simply have to fence off any such areas.

Jumping Up – Obviously the medium to small size of the Whippet is unlikely to affect anyone but the smallest child. However, jumping up can develop into an annoyance that we should curb. We have already covered this to an extent elsewhere, but go into a bit more depth here. What many dog owners do not realize is that they actually teach their dogs to jump up on people when they come in the door or when the dog gets excited. When your Whippet is a cute and cuddly puppy it can be tempting to reward him with pets and cuddles when he crawls into your lap or jumps up at your legs. When your Whippet grows up, he expects you to react in the same way to this behaviour because you have reinforced it. In order to curb this problem behaviour you simply need to teach your Whippet that jumping up will not get him what he wants; your attention. You therefore ignore the behaviour. Quite often as your Whippet jumps up many people instinctively hold out their hands to stop the dog. Again, this is affirming the jumping up with physical contact. The best approach is to get into the habit of turning your back, the moment he jumps up. He may try again, but will soon realise, the only way you acknowledge him is when he greets you without jumping up.

The Whippet is a very affectionate breed with family, but he can be a little wary around strangers unless properly socialized. For this reason, jumping up is not a behavioural problem that is particularly common with the Whippet but it is still possible. To teach your Whippet not to jump up on people, you may need to enlist the help of a friend or two. Have your friends stand outside the front door to your house and ring the doorbell. This should get your Whippet excited. After ringing the doorbell, have your friend enter the house. When your Whippet jumps up, your friend should place their hands behind their back and ignore the dog for a few seconds before turning around and leaving again.

After a few repetitions of this, have your friend give your Whippet the "Sit" command. If he complies, allow your friend to calmly pet the dog for a few seconds before leaving again. Repeat this sequence several times until your Whippet remains calm when the doorbell rings. It may take quite a few repetitions to recondition your dog against jumping up, but with consistency you can make it happen.

Whining – Similar to jumping up on you, your Whippet's whining has one goal; to get your attention. When your Whippet whines at you, stand up calmly and leave the room; go into another room and close the door. Wait for a few seconds until your Whippet stops whining, then return to the room and pet him calmly. Repeat this sequence every time your dog whines at you, and he will eventually learn that whining does not earn him your attention.

Barking – In most cases Whippets are not an overly vocal breed, but some dogs tend to bark more than others; especially when they get excited. The easiest way to teach your dog to stop barking is actually to teach him to bark on command first. Again, you will need to have a friend stand outside your front door and to ring the doorbell. Get your Whippet's attention and give him the "Speak" command. As soon as you give the command, have your friend ring the doorbell to get your dog to bark. When he does, praise him excitedly and reward him. After a few repetitions, your dog should start barking on command before the doorbell rings.

Once your dog learns to bark on command you can then teach him a "Hush" command. Give your Whippet the "Speak" command and let him bark a few times before telling him "Hush". When he stops barking, praise him and offer him a treat. Repeat this sequence several times until your Whippet gets the hang of it. Whippets are an intelligent breed that will be eager to please, so this shouldn't take too many repetitions.

So to recap, first teach the dog to bark and add a command ("Speak/Bark") to it. Next, start to reinforce the short pauses between barks and add a command ("Hush/Quiet") to THEM. The dog will learn that the pauses are rewarded too; therefore he is rewarded for being quiet as well as to bark. But he must learn to bark on command first of all, before being taught to be quiet on command. As with any of your previous training, it is important to mark the behaviour so that there is no confusion and your dog knows exactly what is expected.

Again the command word can be 'quiet' or 'be quiet'. Remember to be quick with this next bit of making him quiet. You want him to know at what point he receives a treat for being quiet. What you will hopefully get to, is the stage where you are no longer rewarding the barking, but you ARE rewarding the 'quiet'. In this way he shouldn't be so keen to bark, particularly if he knows there is no treat to follow. Of course, it is unlikely that you will stop the natural impulse for him to bark, but at least now, you should be able to quickly stop him.

The second option is better for a dog who doesn't bark very much. Once again the clicker is a great tool, but what you need to do this time, is show the dog his reward and encourage him to offer behaviours that will earn him the reward. In a way this is teasing the dog, by showing him the treat, but refusing to give it.

He will go through his repertoire in order to try and get the treat from you. Eventually he should make a sound, it may not be a bark it may not even be a growl, just a squeak. The most important thing to do is reward any sound. That sound can then be shaped into a bark by then gently withholding a reward bit by bit until the dog barks. Again, it is kind of teasing the dog, but is only necessary in these initial stages. A lot of people use this when they want to give them a treat for no apparent reason, but you wish the dog to "ask" for it. So they say something like, 'say please', whilst they are offering the treat. Obviously you only give the treat when they bark.

It may seem odd to teach your dog to bark when you wish them to stop. The point of this is that YOU are in control, telling him to either bark or stop barking. What you are doing is 'tricking' the dog into stopping with his barking, by your command/reward approach. Of course once he has mastered the 'stop barking' command, you are unlikely to need the 'start barking' command. So again, I am not suggesting that you will ever stop a dog from barking, particularly a dog with a high predisposition to bark. What you will have with this training approach however, is more control and the ability to stop him sooner.

2.) Will He Chase The Cat

The answer to this question really has many variables. An adult Whippet that has never encountered cats may well give chase. As you have already read, Sighthounds are notorious for chasing small pray. After all this was their original function. A puppy that is brought home and introduced to a bold and confident cat immediately, will probably not. The elderly dog that lived with a cat in his previous home may not chase either.

Cats can generally stand their ground with all but the most determined and tenacious dogs. They use the needles on their feet very well. Most dogs that chase cats, do so often because the cat is already running away. As you already know, dogs in general, and Whippets specifically, loves games involving a chase.

If you live with a cat, (or really any small animal, rabbit, hamster etc.), and are bringing home a new dog it is important to carry out careful introductions. The best idea is to give the cat somewhere high to sit and observe the dog below. It is not a good idea to introduce a dog and cat without giving the cat an escape route. In the case of the other small animal, it is best to keep them safely in their cage/enclosure at first.

It may take some time for your cat to get used to the new dog. Or they may get on really well straightaway. Cross species relationships are usually quite successful if the two animals are introduced carefully, and have been well socialized.

3.) Teething

If you live with a Whippet puppy you must be prepared for teething time.

As his adult teeth begin to come through at a few months old your puppy will be desperate to chew things.

The baby teeth will probably either be swallowed or lost as the new teeth come through from underneath. It's unusual to find a puppy tooth but you might.

It is a great idea to provide the teething puppy with his own toys for this difficult time. Pet stores have a vast array of puppy teething toys, and it's worth buying your dog at least two or three of different materials.

In addition, you can give your puppy a plastic bottle with frozen water in or some suitably sized ice cubes made with stock and frozen. This will soothe the hot gums, whilst the teeth are coming through.

Carrots too are great teething chews, along with being a healthy snack that might just save your best shoes.

It's important to note here that even with teething toys, your puppy may still find electrical cables an attractive alternative. As mentioned in the puppy proofing section, never allow your puppy access to any electrical cabling. If you cannot sufficiently hide these, then unplug and preferably tie these up out of harms reach. You do not need me to point out the obvious, that a chewed live cable, could result in a fatality.

4.) Bite Inhibition

Bite inhibition is one of the reasons that a dog must stay with his or her mother for at least the first seven to eight weeks of life. What is bite inhibition though, and how does it affect your life with the Whippet dog?

In the litter, and when interacting with his mother, the puppy first learns to inhibit his own bite. When suckling from his mother she will correct the young puppy if his teeth are used too freely.

Similarly later on, at three weeks old and beyond, the puppy can expect to be corrected by his siblings

if he nips too hard during friendly interaction and play.

From the aforementioned interactions, the puppy learns that he can touch his immediate canine family with his teeth but must not nip too hard, for this will get him into trouble.

When you bring the puppy home it is important to continue this learning. For the first few days you can allow your puppy to put his teeth onto your hands in a controlled manner. If the puppy bites too hard though, it is important to correct the behaviour with a sharp sound "NO" and stern stare, as his mother and siblings would do. Again, never attempt to hit or even tap his nose, as this can have an adverse affect.

After that first few days you can begin to teach the puppy that his own toys and chews are a far more suitable plaything than human skin. Redirect any nipping behaviour onto a toy and your puppy will get the idea quite quickly.

The reason that bite inhibition learning must be a two stage process is that the dog is eventually taught not to bite people. Before though, he must learn that for some reason, if he ever feels that he has to bite in order to survive then he must do the least damage possible.

5) A Note on Growling

It is important to know your own dog, where growling is concerned.

Take a look at the scenario within which the growl occurs. Observe your dog's body language and the signs that show how he must be feeling, before deciding why your dog may be growling.

Generally in the dog world, growling is an early warning system that something is not right. The growl from an aggressive dog can be delivered seconds before a bite.

If a dog growls at your approach or attention, then it is a request to be left alone. You should adhere to that, for the dog has very few methods of communicating his wishes.

Dog growling during play and tug games is actually common. So if your Whippet growls when he is playing, it is probably him expressing himself rather than a display of aggression. Although it can sound pretty fierce, play based growling is usually nothing to worry about.

6) Resource Guarding

Resource guarding is something that any dog can develop, but it is usually as a result of a learning experience. A dog that has been truly hungry for instance is likely to develop resource guarding of food which may settle when the dog feels secure, or it may not.

a) Fear Guarding

When a dog is scared of losing a resource he may be reactive to anyone who approaches the resource. He may growl or even bite. To then approach the dog and focus on the resource, is doing nothing more than intensifying the fear. Therefore, the dog is likely to be more aggressive, not less.

When resource guarding is based on fear, confrontation is the last thing that will end the behaviour.

Fear aggression is actually the one within which a dog is most likely to bite.

Take a second to imagine how you would feel if you were really worried about losing something. Then I came along and threatened you in order to take it away. Now imagine if you think your survival depended on that resource. Would you fight me for it? I suspect that you would.

This is exactly how a dog feels when he is resource guarding through fear.

Now imagine for a moment how you would feel if I approached and offered more of the resource that you were scared of losing. Imagine if I offered an abundance and simultaneously paid no attention to your resource at all. How would you feel then? I suspect that if I flooded your general area with many similar resources, and took none away, you would begin to relax.

This is exactly the approach that we take with a dog that is scared of losing his food, and so guards it. We put a few different food bowls down which are a good distance apart, then we add food into each of them in order to make up the dog's entire meal.

It is important to begin by keeping a distance until eventually the dog is aware that each time a bowl is approached, something nice is going into it.

b) Swapping

If you are raising a Whippet puppy, then it is a good idea to teach swapping very early on. Every dog should know how to swap, because this is a good and fair way to take something away from the dog, that he shouldn't have.

When you play with toys then swap regularly, retrieving with balls is a really good way to practice this. You can show the dog that you are happy to throw the next ball just as soon as he has handed over the one he just fetched back.

c) Stealing

The dog that steals things and refuses to give them back will benefit from learning to swap too. The important thing to remember with this, is that the behaviour is likely to stem from attention seeking, maybe even boredom.

Therefore if your dog is stealing things to get your attention, you may be better off ignoring the behaviour as it will eventually become extinct. If you go for this approach, remember to keep all valuables out of the dogs

reach, otherwise you may have no choice but give in to an extinction burst.

Attention seeking behaviour that results in stealing, is the only behaviour where the dog shouldn't be given something else.

The attention seeker is best completely ignored when he is guarding a resource, because this can cause the behaviour to be repeated.

d) I AM His Resource – This Dog Guards Me

This can happen around other people and/or dogs. It is therefore important, in everyday life, that the dog is well socialized and taught relaxed behaviour around other people and dogs.

Any overly aggressive behaviour in this circumstance really needs to be carefully monitored.

It is usually associated with under socialization and resource guarding. It is unlikely, but if serious aggression occurs, then this is best viewed by a local and qualified professional dog behaviourist.

7) The Dog Hates the Car

This can happen with any dog breed, so again is not necessarily breed specific.

Hyperactive behaviour in the car can be as a result of general fear, or specific sight enhancement.

The cars going by so quickly or a general flooding of the senses can over stimulate a dog, leaving them quite anxious. Even the puppy that has been socialized in the car can possibly develop this distracted behaviour later on.

There are some things to try when travelling with your dog which may help:

> » Herbal sickness remedies; if your dog is being or feeling sick, then remedies may help in the short term to make him feel better when travelling.

> » Rescue remedy; this Bach flower remedy may just take the edge off the anxiety when travelling; enough that your dog can relax.

> » A crate and blanket; putting your dog in a crate and covering it with a blanket may prevent the behavior developing. With this approach, the dog never gets to see the movement from the car window.

You can also try teaching the dog to stop barking on command as previously discussed but the stimulation beyond the car windows may simply be too much for the dog to cope with, and this approach may not work.

8) My Dog Won't Come Back

As previously mentioned in the chapter on training even the very best behaved pet will suffer if he isn't given the opportunity for a daily walk/run. A bored dog will become depressed, destructive or even aggressive. It is thought that some dog owners refrain from giving their dogs the off lead runs they need for fear that the dog won't come back when called. It is great that an owner cares for the dogs safety, but is not really helping the dog receive vital exercise.

Please again refer back to Chapter Six, Training your Whippet dog and specifically the section of obedience training, *"Come"*. Following the instructions and guidance there, should solve this problem.

9) Fears and Phobias

Whether they have lived in a safe home since puppy-hood, or were raised in a different environment, any dog can develop fear behaviours. Fireworks, thunder, travel, other animals and people are some examples of why your dog can become afraid.

A dog that is fearful has a very distinct body language. He will tuck his tail below his hind quarters and cower. He may try to leave the situation and look away from the frightening stimulus. It is vital that a scared dog is never cornered.

A scared or worried dog will often display calming signals. We have covered these in a previous chapter, and again, these are signals that dogs use in order to diffuse a worrying situation. Some calming signals as previously mentioned include yawning; a stressed dog will yawn frequently.

The yawning response is often mistaken for tiredness by an uninformed human. However, once you know what to look for, it is easily recognizable. Licking his lips; a calming signal and stress response, can take the form of a single nose lick or more. Sniffing the ground is a "leave me alone, I am invisible" plea.

Your job as the owner of a fearful dog is to neither ignore nor encourage the fear. Be aware of the situations in which your dog feels threatened and gently build him up, so that he can cope better with them. Introduce new and worrying situations gradually, and amalgamate them with rewards such as playing with a toy or receiving a treat for relaxed behaviour.

A very important point is to never over sympathize with your dog as this can reinforce the fear. If he gets too much attention when he is afraid, he will either repeat the behaviour for the attention, or even worse think that the stimulus is a threat which you too recognize. If he sees that the stimulus doesn't concern you, then your dog will learn that it shouldn't concern him either.

A scared dog should never be cornered or forced to accept attention. If he is, then he will become more scared, growl and possibly even snap. It is better to help him relax around people without them paying him any attention, than to push him into a negative reaction.

If the fear has an environmental cause, for instance fireworks, then it is worth trying a natural remedy to appease your dog's fear. Rescue remedy which can be bought in most chemists/drug stores, is suitable for short-term treatment of a worried dog. Your vet may also be able to suggest something to get your dog through difficult times such as on bonfire night or New Year's Eve, when there are a lot of fireworks.

10) Dogs and children

Most dogs that have been brought up with children, manage really well in a family environment. It's worth remembering that if an adult dog has never encountered children, he may find them worrying. They do, after all, move differently to adults and sound different.

If you have a dog that is worried about children, it is really important that you make your pet feel safe and secure when there are children around. And for both the dog and child's sake never take any risks. You can get children to give the dog treats, otherwise completely ignore him. He ideally needs to get used to them in his own time.

Never under any circumstance, leave a dog with a young child. There are too many cases of dogs attacking children. Dogs can be unpredictable, and children do not have the awareness that an adult has in being able to read signals that the dog needs to be left alone. Sometimes children see dogs as a toy to play with. Dogs can soon tire of a child's constant attention. It is best to teach the child that they have to respect the dog and not unnecessarily tease or harass the dog.

11) Rolling in Poop

What can you do to stop your Whippet rolling in faeces and coming home stinking of poop

The only real option you have in this circumstance is to increase your control and watch your dog carefully.

The act of rolling in poop is an innate behaviour which means it is part of their genetic nature. The good news is that although the behaviour is natural, even the worst habits can be changed.

Your job is to ensure you have the most possible control over your dog on walks and can recall him back easily. Then it's simply a case of watching him carefully whenever he is near an area where he may roll. You then simply call him back when he shows any interest in the smelly stuff.

The more recall practice and training that you carry out, the easier it will be to call your dog back when he spots something smelly.

Obviously if the worse happens, then your only option is to give him a bath and thoroughly dry him.

I have only ever had one dog roll in anything, and it was in fact the carcass of a dead fox. The Lurcher in question, took great delight in rolling in the remains. I don't know whether it was an instinctive celebration of the death of an enemy, or something else. Most of the time, of all the dogs I have ever walked, they all seem to seek out other dogs faeces and simply scent mark the pile by urinating on it.

12) Separation Anxiety

Separation anxiety is when a dog fears being alone to the point of becoming severely stressed or distressed.

It is currently thought to be for one of an unknown number of reasons. There are two types of separation anxiety, amid other undefined reasons for the disorder. These are fear of unexpected noises or over attachment to the owner.

There is no evidence of this if dogs are left with other dogs and therefore finding any relief from additional canine company. This type of anxiety seems to be linked specifically with the absence of human presence from the home. As every dog is an individual, so is their experience when suffering from separation anxiety.

Some suffer greatly and become destructive to themselves and their surroundings. Others simply become sad and depressed when left alone. They leave no trace of the stress, thus leaving owners unaware that anxiety occurred at all during the dog's alone time.

The actual anxiety becomes a phobia and can become so severe that the dog develops serious stress related behaviours causing poor health, self-harm and obsessive worrying about being left alone. Dogs associate this with the behaviour of their owners, and become stressed very early, in regular routines that lead to alone time.

To prevent separation anxiety in your own dog you have a number of options. The best one, if you are leaving your dog regularly, is to employ a willing neighbour or relative to periodically check in on your dog. Alternatively a doggy day caretaker or similar canine professional. This usually takes the form of a canine crèche area or similar and is wonderful for meeting the dog's mental and physical needs alongside ensuring the dog is not alone regularly for long periods of time.

A dog walker is the minimum provision that a full time, at home dog, should have when everyone is out at work all day.

The other possibility here is having two dogs. Companionship can make all the difference, whereby the dogs keep each other company and entertained. However, this doesn't always work and some dogs can still become overwhelmed with separation anxiety, resulting in the aforementioned negative behaviours.

If separation anxiety becomes a real problem, a local dog behaviourist may be the answer. They can observe your dog and create a modification program to try and alleviate his stressed reaction to being alone. This can work really well when carried out carefully.

13) Chasing Behaviour

Again, please do not forget that Whippets will chase, if given the chance. You do need to be generally aware of certain consequences of chasing behaviour that could affect any dog.

Chasing wildlife, livestock or similar animals, can be a problem with most dog breeds. Just as other animals are easy targets, so are cars, pedestrians and bikes.

Chasing behaviour can also be a really dangerous game with potential fatal consequences. In the UK for example, a farmer is legally entitled to shoot a dog chasing wildlife.

If the behaviour is displayed at a dangerous level, you may need to find help locally from a dog trainer/behaviourist. Otherwise you can teach your dog that looking towards you, when he sees something he would normally chase after, is his most rewarding option. Of course this is dependent on you being vigilant and second guessing a potential chase.

You may initially need to provide extra motivation (favourite treat etc.) to break your dog's attention away from whatever he is planning to chase.

The steps that we take to reform chasing behaviour are similar to those which we use for social fear.

It is a gradual process of teaching the dog to stay relaxed with the trigger at a distance. You also need to Teach the dog to focus on you because you are extremely interesting. Eventually you build the dog's capacity to be near the trigger whilst he also stays relaxed and controlled.

It's important to focus on your dog's behaviour carefully, and reinforce every time he looks towards you instead of at the trigger. If you can master this art alone, then your control over the behaviour of your Whippet dog will improve dramatically.

It is important too that you don't allow him to do any chasing at all if you can help it. If you have to put him on the leash in risky areas then do that rather than allow your dog to enjoy the chase. Again, anticipation is the key here.

Any dog that gets the chance to chase squirrels, rabbits or other animals, is strengthening the desire to chase them and repeated practices of chase behaviour can easily become obsession.

14) Aggression

The Whippet as a dog breed, although relatively friendly, can potentially deal with worrying situations with an aggressive response. Aggressive behaviour is worrying to us as owners. There are many types of aggression but most of them are caused by fear for one reason or another.

A dog's body language will usually change greatly before he becomes aggressive.

The process from fear to bite will go something like this:

» The dog will focus on the stimulant (the thing that he's worried about) Calming signals will follow, the dog may glance away, yawn or try to leave the situation. If the calming signals do not take away the stimulant, the dog will then change his posture, shift his bodyweight, his hackles may raise and he may growl.

» If growling doesn't work the dog will show his teeth. If flashing the teeth doesn't work he may snap at the air between him and the stimulant.

> » The next thing that may occur is that the dog may freeze. This is a very brief act and can be missed if you're not looking for it. The freeze is the dog making a decision to either fight or flee the threat. If he can't leave the situation or the stimulant is not removed, the dog is at severe risk of biting. This is because he feels he has no choice, and to be fair, he has given a lot of warning.

Some dogs, as an exception to the above, have learned to cope so well with their fears that they don't even show that they're scared or uncomfortable before the aggression manifests.

This is because the reaction of aggression has been used by the dog for so long that he relies on it as a default reaction to fear. This dog will bypass everything and go straight to aggression. Any dog that does this, needs to be seen by a qualified behaviourist.

a) Aggression to Dogs

Dog to dog aggression can be based in lack of socialization. In other words they are unsure of and therefore potentially fearful of other dogs. The dog simply does not know how to behave around other canines so he becomes scared, and in turn uses attack as a form of defence. Often a dog will seem to be aggressive towards others when really he

is not thinking of fighting at all; he just doesn't know what else to do.

b) Aggression to People

Aggression towards people is often fear of the person that the aggression is aimed towards. It could also be general fear of the situation which the dog is dealing with at the time. An example is a dog in kennels that shows his teeth through the bars because he's scared and confused.

I have only touched on the basics of aggression here, there is so much information that the subject could fill an entire book.

The main thing to remember though is to observe your dog and if you feel he may be uncomfortable or unhappy in this situation watch out for the process described above and proceed as described.

15) A Local Dog Trainer

If you are having serious problems with the behaviour of your dog it is vital to consult an expert.

When looking for a local trainer please ensure that they follow the guidelines that I have given here for behaviour modification.

> » Look for a kind trainer or behaviorist that uses careful and dog friendly methods to modify any unhelpful behavior that your dog has learned.

> » Do your research and avoid anyone that wants to hurt, dominate or force train a dog. It will not work and will eventually make the behavior worse.

> » Dog training and behavior is an unmodified profession therefore there are, surprisingly, a lot of self-proclaimed experts out there with no qualifications or scientific knowledge.

16) Some additional thoughts on dog training

As you will have probably gathered having read this far, dog training is a varied subject and one which has many myths. The main misconception that we see regularly, is that of dog and wolf pack logic, in short, dominance. To a certain extent, the following has been covered in the chapter on training. However, please find below additional information and information that is worth repeating.

a) What is the dominance theory

Excessive dominance in dogs is a scientific theory which has been around for many years, and has really taken hold of our dog interactions.

Way back in the 1930s and 1940s Swiss animal behaviourist Rudolph Schenkel created a very specific environment where wolves were pushed together in a group; not of their choosing, and then observed.

There was a lot of friction in the group because wolves live as families and wild wolves do not simply choose a group and move in. Fences added to the friction and aggressive behaviour ensued.

Dominance theory has since been revoked, and proof to the contrary has been developed. Yet people, usually uneducated dog trainers, still state that dominance within the pack, is the cause of all unhelpful dog behaviours. This type of trainer states that we must establish dominance over our family dogs in order for them to behave nicely. It is true, as you have read about certain behaviour issues, that our dogs wish to please us and will do anything for our attention. So if we are dominant and are harsh towards a dog they will realize something is wrong and wish to correct this with passive, compliant behaviour.

b) How Do Dominant Dog Trainers Work

Establishing dominance as advised by dog trainers that practice the theory, involves the act of taking control of the dog's behaviour. This is the same approach that the leader of a wolf pack would take towards an unruly member of the group. It is often stated as 'being an alpha'.

This would involve physical manipulation, ignoring the dog on greeting and going through doors first. It would also involve forcing, rather than training a dog to behave in a certain way.

There is another good reason for stepping away from the dominance theory. Dogs are not wolves. Although dogs descend from and are therefore genetically related to wolves, the existing genes carry a very small percentage of the inherent wolf. For over twenty thousand years, dogs and wolves have evolved separately.

Their behaviour has evolved away from each other. Therefore by practicing this theory we are treating dogs like wolves. They are not, and in addition, we are assuming that captive wolves behave the same way as those living naturally in the wild.

Luckily the dog behaviour world is evolving too. We are making changes based upon the study of actual dog behaviour. So, with our increasing knowledge, this type of 'dominance theory' thinking should eventually become obsolete.

c) What is the alternative

The other form of dog training I have previously mentioned is 'positive reinforcement training', and this is undoubtedly, the one which I favour. It is based upon careful understanding and study of dogs as the species they are. Whippets are so gentle and sensitive that any kind of dominance training is unlikely to be necessary anyway.

So if you are looking for further help from a dog trainer, it is vitally important that you check credentials and methods, as not all dog trainers know the truth about dogs.

CHAPTER SIXTEEN:

CARING FOR YOUR SENIOR WHIPPET

When you first bring home your Whippet puppy, it's difficult to imagine that in only 12 or 14 years later, you will have to say goodbye.

1) The Senior Whippet

All dog breeds approach old age in the same way, but at different times, depending on their breed and size. Smaller dog breeds tend to live longer. Some dog breeds are still jumping agility courses at 13 years of age. Again, depending on the size, many other purebred dogs may only live to 8 or 9 years of age. Keep in mind that good health begins during puppy-hood and lasts a lifetime.

Your Whippet has most likely been your best friend for life. You've both shared so many experiences. Your Whippet will depend on you throughout his life. You've made a commitment to take care of him from puppy-hood to the end. Keep in mind that your Whippet will change as he ages. His body and natural exuberance may sometimes allow you to forget his age. Then one day you'll look into your Whippet's eyes and notice his silvery face, and stiffened gait. He'll most likely sleep longer, and may be less eager to play. As your Whippet nears his ten or twelve year mark, he may start slowing down on his walks. Getting your Whippet to live comfortably during his senior years need not be a challenge, but needs to be well-prepared for.

a) Caring for your Senior Whippet

Most Whippets will show signs of slowing down by greying of the coat and usually around the eyes and face. They will have a flaky coat, loss of hair, slowness of gait and enjoying the family couch more than usual. Activities like running, jumping, eating and retrieving will become more difficult for him. That said, other activities like sleeping, barking, and a repetition of habits may increase. Your Whippet will want to spend more time with you, and will go to the front door more often when you are leaving.

As your Whippet ages, he'll need certain therapeutic and medical preventative strategies. Your veterinarian will advise you on special nutritional counselling, veterinary visits and screening sessions for your senior Whippet. A senior-care Whippet program will include all of these.

Veterinarians will determine your Whippet's health by doing blood smears for a complete blood count, which will include the following:

» Serum chemistry profile with electrolytes

» Urinalysis

» Blood pressure check

» Electrocardiogram

» Ocular tonometry (pressure of the eyeball)

» Dental prophylaxis

Extensive screenings for senior Whippets is recommended well before dog owners begin to see the symptoms of aging, such as slower movement and disinterest in play and other activities.

By following this preventative program, you will not only increase your Whippet's chance of a longer life, but you'll also make his life so much more comfortable. There will be so many physical changes like loss of sight through cataracts, arthritis, kidney problems, liver failure, and other possible degenerative diseases. Adding to that you may notice some behavioural changes related to aging. Whippets suffering from hearing and eyesight loss, dental pain or arthritis may often become aggressive because of the constant pain that they have to live with. Whippets that are near deaf or blind may also be startled more easily at the slightest environmental changes. Do your best not to move furniture around in your home, and to keep things as they are, as this can be unsettling for them. Senior Whippets suffering from senility may do many unusual things, and will often become impatient.

b) House Soiling Accidents

These are associated with loss of bladder control, kidney problems, loss of mobility, loss of sphincter control, physiological brain changes, and reaction to new medications. Your older Whippet will need more support than ever, especially doing his toilet business.

Avoid feeding your senior Whippet too many unhealthy treats. Obesity is a common problem in older dogs as they naturally become less active. Additional weight will put extra stress on his joints and his body's vital organs. Some breeders suggest supplementing meals with high fibre foods that are also low in calories. You can also ask your veterinarian for a special prescription diet that best suits the needs of your senior Whippet.

c) Every Day Tips

» Never punish or use harsh tones against your senior Whippet for anything at all.

» Protect your Whippet, and foresee his reactions to any environmental changes.

» Pay special attention to his immediate needs such as going to the toilet, pain levels and eating habits.

» Visit your veterinarian often and work together on providing your senior Whippet with the best of care.

» Keep your Whippet company. Your Whippet does not understand why he's losing his sight or hearing. The world may seem to be a strange place to him right now. Comfort him frequently, and try to leave a family member with him when you go out. Your Whippet will appreciate the companionship.

» Older Whippets may not be able to wait until morning to go outdoors. Provide him with alternatives such as puppy pads or spread out newspaper, to relieve himself on during the night/early hours.

Be consistent with your schedule and do not change the way things are in your home. Doors that have always remained open should stay that way. Leave his favourite couch in the same place.

d) Keeping a Diary

You may wish to keep a diary to note the day-to-day record of how your Whippet is feeling and whether he is eating, drinking and walking. As a dog owner you are able to observe all your Whippet's activities, and record how your Whippet feels and behaves.

e) Check list of questions about your aging Whippets condition

» Is your Whippet still happy to see you and how does he respond? Is it with his usual wag or does he seem to be less responsive than normal?

» Record his respiratory rate each evening when your Whippet is resting peacefully. Record the breaths taken per minute.

» Does he still come to you when called? What is his reaction to your being there? Record the levels of anxiety and pain. When he wags his tail or walks to you.

» Can your Whippet still walk? Does he still get up and come to you? How far can he walk until he tires?

» How much pain does your Whippet seem to have? Does he have many episodes of pain? Does he yelp when handled or display signs of aggression when handled?

» Does your Whippet eat if presented with his favorite foods? Does your Whippet pick at his food or refuse to try some?

» Does your Whippet still drink fluids? How much fluid per day/week. Dog owners can measure fluid intake per day.

» Is your Whippet defecating, and how often does this occur? Are all his feces normal?

» Is any disease/illness worsening or improving?

> » Weigh your Whippet every day or every week. If he is losing weight, how much weight is your Whippet losing each week or month? Weight is an important indicator of health.

f) Is There An Emergency Health Deterioration Stage

Your Whippet could suffer from an acute situation that is related to their condition. These chronic or acute episodes of disease related deterioration require immediate veterinary treatment. Some internal cancers will present themselves with haemorrhaging and states of severe shock and collapse. Congestive heart failure results in distressed breathing and pulmonary edema. Whippets with renal failure, for example, will start vomiting blood and go into shock.

g) Symptoms of Pain in Your Senior or Terminally Ill Whippet

It is always devastating when medical treatment does not work. But it's also important to think about the potential suffering of your Whippet and how he was before the illness or injury. So as to determine whether your Whippet is in pain or not, veterinarians and most importantly Whippet owners need to have a way to determine a Whippets' pain and pain threshold.

Typical symptoms are as follows:

> » Whimpering, whining and yelping when touched.

> » Your Whippet yelps when he tries to get from point A to point B.

> » Your Whippet is often depressed, and does not want to interact with other animals or people in the household.

> » Sleeplessness, listlessness and hiding under the bed or in dark places.

> » Your Whippet is squinting which is typical for head and eye pain in animals. Some dogs will squint both eyes when experiencing head pain.

> » Your Whippet has an elevated heart rate.

> » Your Whippet injures himself by attacking or injuring the pain inflicted area.

> » Chattering of the teeth is suggestive of mouth pain and dental pain, but is also indicative of shock, overall trauma and pain throughout the body.

> » Your Whippet is drooling excessively. This is suggestive of pain and trauma.

2) Time To Say Goodbye!

If you are lucky, those 12 to 14 years or so, are what you get; a number of years that feel so very short. Nonetheless, mercifully, although we are aware of the unfair discrepancy between our dogs' lifespan and ours, we always somehow manage to push aside this fact; that is, until we are facing the very end with our dogs.

The heart-breaking decision to "put down" or euthanize your dog is an issue frequently faced by pet parents and veterinarians. You will never be prepared for this day. Putting your Whippet to sleep is an extremely difficult and upsetting decision that you will need to make with your veterinarian. As a Whippet owner, you will usually be making this decision when your Whippet goes through one or more life-threatening symptoms that will force you to seek veterinary help immediately.

If the prognosis indicates that the end is near and that your Whippet is in great pain, euthanasia may be the right choice. It is a difficult and heart-breaking decision for any dog lover. But if the dog is suffering then it is cruel to prolong their agony.

3) What is Euthanasia

Just the thought of euthanasia or putting our Whippet to sleep is enough to make anyone cringe. There are varying opinions about this final decision. What are the rights and wrongs? Are we actually helping our dogs or being selfish? Do we have the right to end a life?

Euthanasia refers to the planned and painless death of a dog that is suffering from a painful condition, or who is old and cannot walk, cannot see or unable to control his bodily functions. It is usually done with an overdose of an aesthetic.

The process of euthanasia takes a matter of seconds. Once the injection takes place it quickly enters the blood stream and the dog goes to sleep. The overdose suppresses the heart and brain function, in turn causing an instant loss of consciousness and therefore, pain. The animal dies peacefully while asleep.

The difficult decision to euthanize your senior or sick Whippet is never an easy one, and one that may take a while for you to come to terms with. This time is usually stressful for you and your family. If this is a first time in dealing with the death of a loved one, you'll need your family by you.

4) What happens afterwards

I know many vets who will give the owner of their beloved pet, the option to take them away and bury them in a quiet area of their garden. This may well be a favourite spot that their Whippet frequented. You are generally advised to dig a hole deep enough to avoid the problem of foxes or similar predators, digging the body up.

If your Whippet is buried in a pet cemetery, or in your yard, it's also a good idea to plant a special tree or stone over the site. A few dog owners prefer to leave their deceased dogs at the veterinary clinic. Today, many pet parents opt for individual cremation. Your veterinarian can help to arrange the cremation service, and will also be able to advise you on where to find a suitable pet cemetery.

Most dog owners have given a considerable amount of thought as to what makes a fitting tribute to honour our dogs. There's no better way to do this than by commissioning a great portrait of your Whippet. This simple act will keep your memories alive and bring you happiness when time has healed your pain. After spending nearly a decade together sharing life's most special moments, you'll be able to recall your Whippet's most happy, crazy and sometimes most peaceful moments with a portrait. Professional studio photos are also a great alternative to this. After some time you may miss not having your friend around. You may perhaps wish to give a loving home to another Whippet.

Obviously you are not attempting to replace your friend, but have such love for the breed that this seems a natural thing to consider. Many dog owners breed one litter of pups for this very reason. In that way they keep the generation of their beloved dogs intact.

Adopting a Whippet from a rescue is another excellent option. Perhaps you may want to adopt a different breed so that you'll not make comparisons. Most dog owners will usually choose the same breed because they understand and love the temperament. Perhaps the best thing that you can do for yourself as well as your departed Whippet will be to adopt another Whippet.

" If there are no dogs in heaven, then when I die I want to go where they went."
-Will Rogers

CHAPTER SEVENTEEN:

WEBSITES, MISCELLANEOUS RESOURCES & CONCLUSION

In reading this book you have received a wealth of information about the Whippet breed and its care. As you prepare to become a Whippet owner yourself you will need to stock up on supplies including food, toys, a crate, and other accessories. To help you find high-quality supplies for your Whippet, check out some of the relevant websites in this chapter. You will find links to relevant websites for Whippet food, Whippet toys, Whippet crates and dog beds, and other Whippet accessories.

1.) Food For Whippet Dogs

Providing your Whippet with a healthy diet is the key to maintaining good health. In this section you will find a collection of relevant websites for Whippet food.

United States Links:

"High Endurance Adult Dog Food." Nutro Natural Choice.

http:// www.nutro.com

http://www.nutro.com/natural-dog-food/nutro/dry/high-endurance-3020-chicken-meal-whole-brown-rice-oatmeal-recipe.aspx

"Active Care Healthy Joint Formula." Breeder's Choice.

http://www.goactivedog.com/

"Pedigree Active Targeted Nutrition with Chicken, Rice and Vegetables."

Pedigree. http:// www.pedigree. com

http://www.pedigree.com/really-good-food/active-nutrition-for-dogs. aspx

"Which Dog Food is Right for My Dog?" SelectSmart.com.

http:// www.selectsmart.com
http://www.selectsmart.com/ dogfood/

United Kingdom Links:

"Active – Chicken and Rice." Burns Natural Food for Pets.

http:// burnspet.co.uk

http://burnspet.co.uk/products/ burns-for-dogs/dog-food-for-active-dogs.html

"Taste of the Wild Dog Food." Taste of the Wild.

http://www.tasteofthewildpet-food.com/

"Field & Trial – For Working and Active Dogs." Skinner's.

http:// www.skinnerspetfoods. co.uk

http://www.skinnerspetfoods. co.uk/our-range/working-dogs/

"VetSpec Active Nutritional Supplement." VetSpec for Dogs.

http:// www.vetspec.co.uk

http://www.vetspec.co.uk/prod-ucts/vetspec-active/

"Active and Working Dog Food." PetPlanet.co.uk.

http:// www.petplanet.co.uk

http://www.petplanet.co.uk/dept. asp?dept_id=6&NavSource=TN

2.) Crates And Beds For Whippet Dogs

Your Whippet's crate is the place where he can retreat if he wants a nap or to take a break. In this section you will find a collection of relevant websites for dog crates and beds.

United States Links:

"Crates, Carriers & Pens." Drs. Foster and Smith.

http:// www.drsfostersmith.com

http://www.drsfostersmith.com/ dog-supplies/dog-cages-crates-car-riers-pens/ps/c/3307/10627

"Dog Beds." Cabela's.

http:// www.cabelas.com/

"Crates." PetSupplies.com.

http:// www.petsupplies.com

http:// www.petsupplies.com/ dog-supplies/ crates/ 9113/

"Crates, Gates and Containment." PetsMart.

http:// www.petsmart.com

http:// www.petsmart.com/ dog/ crates-gates-containment/ cat-36-catid-100013

United Kingdom Links:

"Orvis Dog Beds." Orvis United Kingdom.

http:// www.orvis.co.uk

http:// www.orvis.co.uk/ dog-beds# close

"Dog Crates." PetPlanet. co.uk.

http:// www.petplanet.co.uk

http:// www.petplanet.co.uk/ cat-egory.asp? dept_id = 771

"Dog Crates and Kennels." Amazon.co.uk.

http:// www.amazon.co.uk
Please search Amazon for dog crates and kennels

"Dog Crates." RSPCA.org.uk.

http:// www.rspca.org.uk

http:// www.rspca.org.uk/ advice-andwelfare/ pets/ dogs/ environment/ crates

"Dog Beds and Bedding." Pet-Supermarket.co.uk.

http:// www.pet-supermarket. co.uk

http:// www.pet-supermarket. co.uk/ Category/ Dog_Supplies-Dog_Beds_Bedding

3.) Toys and Accessories for Whippets

Having the right toys and accessories for your Whippet is very important. In this section you will find a collection of relevant websites for Whippet toys and accessories.

United States Links:

"Interactive Dog Toys." Petco.

http:// www.petco.com

http:// www.petco.com/ N_22_101/ Dog-Toys.aspx

"Dog Toys." Chewy.com.

http:// www.chewy.com

http:// www.chewy.com/ dog/ toys-315

"Bowls & Feeders." PetSmart.

https:// www.petsmart.com

https:// www.petsmart.com/ dog/ bowls-feeders/ cat-36-catid-100010

"Dog Toys." Drs. Foster and Smith.

http:// www.drsfostersmith.com

http:// www.drsfostersmith.com/ dog-supplies/ dog-toys/ ps/ c/ 3307/ 3

United Kingdom Links:

"Dog Toys." PetPlanet.co.uk.

http:// www.petplanet.co.uk

http:// www.petplanet.co.uk/ dept.asp? dept_id = 16

"Dog Feeding and Watering Supplies." Amazon.co.uk.

http:// www.amazon.co.uk

Please search Amazon for dog feeding and watering

"Dog Toys." VetUK.

http:// www.vetuk.co.uk

http:// www.vetuk.co.uk/ dog-toys-c-439

"Toys." Battersea Dogs & Cats Home.

http:// www.battersea.org.uk
Please search for toys on their site

"Dog Bowls & Feeders." Pet-Supermarket.co.uk.

http:// www.pet-supermarket. co.uk

http:// www.pet-supermarket. co.uk/ Category/ Dog_Supplies-Dog_Bowls_Feeders

4.) General Dog Care Information

The key to being the best Whippet owner you can be is to learn everything there is to know about dog ownership. In this section you will find a collection of relevant websites about various aspects of dog ownership.

United States Links:

"Dog Care." ASPCA.org.

https:// www.aspca.org

https:// www.aspca.org/ petcare/ dog-care

"Pet Care Center: Dog." PetMD.

http:// www.petmd.com

http:// www.petmd.com/ dog/ petcare

"Dog Care and Behaviour Tips." The Humane Society of the United States.

http:// www.humanesociety.org

http:// www.humanesociety. org/ animals/ dogs/ tips/? referrer = https:// www.google.com/ "Dog Diet and Nutrition." WebMD.

Pets WebMD

http:// pets.webmd.com http:// pets.webmd.com/ dogs/ guide/ diet-nutrition

United Kingdom Links:

"Dogs – Dog Welfare." RSPCA.org.uk.

http:// www.rspca.org.uk

http:// www.rspca.org.uk/ advice-andwelfare/ pets/ dogs

"General Advice About Caring for Your New Puppy or Dog." The Kennel Club.

http:// www.thekennelclub.org.uk

http:// www.thekennelclub.org. uk/ getting-a-dog-or-puppy/ general-advice-about-caring-for-your-new-puppy-or-dog/

"Caring for the Older Dog." Blue Cross for Pets.

http:// www.bluecross.org.uk

http:// www.bluecross.org.uk/ pet-advice/ caring-older-dog

"Caring for Dogs and Puppies." Battersea Dogs & Cats Home.

http:// www.battersea.org.uk

http:// www.battersea.org. uk/ WEBShopItem? pid = 01tb-

0000003JjxKAAS

"Dog Food Nutrition." Dog Breed Information Center.

http:// www.healthstory.co.uk

http:// www.healthstory.co.uk/ dogbreedinfo/ nutrition.htm

Miscellaneous Resources

Whippet Racing Organizations UK

WhippetClubRacingAssociation

http://www.wcra.btck.co.uk/

National Pedigree Whippet Racing Association

http://www.npwra.btck.co.uk/

Kings Park Whippet & Dog Racing Club

http://www.whippetracing.org.uk/

Stockton on Tees Whippet Racing Club

http://www.stocktonwrc.co.uk/

Heart Of EnglandPedigree Whippet Racing Club

http://www.heartofenglandpwrc. co.uk/

The British Whippet Racing Association

http://www.thebwra.co.uk/

Whippet Racing Supplies

http://www.whippetracing.org/information/whippetracingsupplies.htm

British Sighthound Field Association

http://lurecoursing.org.uk/

Whippet Racing Organizations U.S.A.

Whippet Racing Association

http://www.whippetracing.org/

The North American Whippet Racing Association

http://www.nawra.com/

National Oval Track Racing Association

http://www.nawra.com/

Continental Whippet Alliance

http://www.continentalwhippetalliance.com/

The Whippet Forum

http://www.thewhippetforum.com/

Midwest Whippet Racing Association

http://midwestwhippetracing.org/Midwest_Whippet_Racing_Association,_Inc/about_us.html

Other organisations

UK Kennel Club Registration

The UK Kennel Club alone registers over 250,000 dogs each year. These dogs are purebreds and crossbreeds. The Kennel Club registration system is open to all dogs, and they have developed different registers to suit all dogs and their owners including crossbreeds. Breeders will generally register your puppy on your behalf, if not contact the following.

For more information on KC registrations, visit:
http://www.thekennelclub.org.uk/registration/

Whippet Clubs and Associations

The Midland Whippet Club (MWC)

This club was formed in 1948, and is the third specialist Whippet Club, but the first regional club for Whippet fans. The Midlands Whippet Club became a venue for Whippet shows in 1958, and to this day hold three Whippet shows a year. For more information, visit:

http://www.midlandwhippetclub.co.uk/

The National Whippet Association (NWA)

This club was formed in 1936. Thanks to Mrs. Conway-Evans who kept the Whippet breed alive during the war. In 1945 the NWA held an open bench show with 16 classes. They had 271 entries. This historical club was the second Whippet Club formed in the UK, after the Whippet Club.

Today there are 11 breed clubs covering all regions and holding shows, seminars and social gatherings for Whippet lovers. The Whippet continues to be a popular breed thanks to the dedication of all the club members throughout the years. For more information, visit:

http://nationalwhippetassociation.webeden.co.uk/

The National Kennel Club (NKC)

This club was formed in 1964, and has operated to help dog owners of every breed register their purebred dogs. It has always been fair and impartial to all breeders, pet parents, and all the various breeds that they represent. The advantage of this club is that all breeds, even the rare breeds can be shown with equal status together with the most popular breeds. The NKC licenses its entire dog shows, events show judges and all dog-related events. For more information, visit:

http://nationalkennelclub.com/ Breed-Standards/Whippet.htm

The Whippet Club

The Whippet Club is the only breed club in the UK to cater for all working Whippet disciplines. It was formed in 1899, and is the world's first Whippet club. For more information, visit:

http://www.thewhippetclub.com/
or

https://www.facebook.com/ TheWhippetClub

Other Whippet Clubs:

http://northerncountieswhippetclub.webs.com/

http://newhippetsociety.webs.com/

http://whippetclubofwales.webeden.co.uk/

Resources; Further Reading and Information

Whippet News

To order Whippet News Monthly magazine, visit:
http://whippetnews.co.uk/

AKC Gazette:

http://www.akc.org/pubs/gazette/

ASFA Field Advisory News:

http://asfa.org/

For online Whippet news, visit:

http://ewhippetzine.com/

http://www.dogforum.co.uk/ topic/78116-whippet-news/

Dog World:

http://www.dogworld.co.uk/

Sighthound Review:

http://sighthoundreview.com/

Whippet World:

http://whippetworld.net/

Animal Protection Organizations To Support

Humane Society International (HSI):

http://hsi.org/

(SPCA)

http://spcai.org/

(ASPCA)

https://www.aspca.org/

International Whippet Rescue:

http://whippet.rescueshelter.com/international

International Animal Rescue:

http://www.internationalanimalrescue.org/

International Fund For Animal Rescue (IFAW) :

http://www.ifaw.org/

Soi Dog Rescue:

http://www.soidog.org/en/about-soi-dog/

Other Links

The British Association of Homeopathic Veterinary Surgeons:

http://www.bahvs.com/

Houndz In The Hood:

http://www.houndzinthehood.com/chart-whippet.html

International Association of Animal Massage & Bodywork: ALSO Association of Water canine Therapy:

http://www.iaamb.org/preferred-educational-providers.php

Tellington TTouch UK:

http://ttouchtteam.co.uk/

PETA:

http://www.peta.org/international/

Ark Naturals

https://arknaturals.com/

Doggie doors are also a great way to promote healthy Toilet habits. These are a great way for your dog to come and go as he pleases. Be aware that other pets and animals could enter back into your house. You would also not want to leave

these open whilst you are away from the house, in case of intruders having easy access to your property. The following are a few examples, but again research as many possibilities as you can.

https://www.petdoors.com/

http://store.intl.petsafe.net/en-gb/doors/large-dog

Whippet Training

http://www.whippetsavvy.com/tag/positive-reinforcement/

http://www.thewhippet.net/whippet-training.html

http://www.thewhippetclub.com/obedience/

For general obedience training videos, please search YouTube.

Conclusion

Hopefully you have read this far and have found the contents useful, informative and inspiring. There is a lot to consider when buying any dog, and consequently to appreciate their needs. Hopefully this book reflects that. For the most part, dogs that are properly looked after with love, care and respect, will repay you with unconditional love and devotion, many times over. The intention of the book was not to overwhelm you the reader and put you off committing to being the guardian of this fantastic Whippet breed. The intention was simply to give you as broad an appreciation as possible, so that you are fully prepared and equipped to properly look after and appreciate your new friend. As you will realize, having read the various chapters, keeping a dog happy does not necessarily come without its problems. However, with correct awareness and training, many potential problems can be avoided. The health and welfare of your new Whippet should go without saying, so please do everything you can to provide healthy food and a safe warm environment. In essence, it doesn't take a lot to keep your dog happy and healthy. At the very least you should be providing the following:

(i) A warm safe habitat. (ii) Healthy food and fresh water, daily. (iii) Routine health procedures such as worming, flea treatment and veterinary check-ups. (iv) Basic training and regular daily exercise. (v) As much love and attention as you can provide.

Please remember that physical health can be counteracted by lack of mental stimulation. Whilst you can groom a dog all day long, thus pampering and giving him attention, if he doesn't get a free run, then he won't be truly happy. Secondly it is vital to embrace scientific finding on the way your dog learns. In summary; Dominance dog training is a myth that bypasses scientific findings on actual dog behaviour. A dog learns from his environment and the attention, response that his own behaviour provokes. This is positive reinforcement in action. Punishment after a behaviour will not make the behaviour go away, because each time a behaviour is carried out it is forming a habit. It is possible to mask an unhelpful behaviour but it makes the dog feel bad and actually makes the behaviour worse. True behaviour modification takes time and is carried out with kindness. The only true form of punishment to use is taking away attention when a behaviour is problematic. This is called negative punishment and finally, our dogs do talk to us and we need to respect this by learning a little of their language. Thank you for reading and allowing me to explain a little of what I know about your dog's mind and needs.

INDEX